Y0-BKB-448

THE
AMERICAN POLITICAL SCENE

THE AMERICAN POLITICAL SCENE

by

A. N. Holcombe   Edward B. Logan
J. T. Salter   Harold R. Bruce
James K. Pollock   Harwood L. Childs

Edited by
Edward B. Logan

1 9 3 6

Harper & Brothers Publishers
New York and London

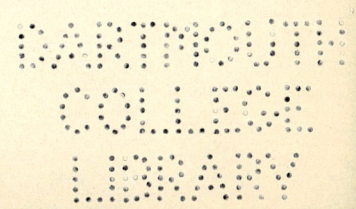

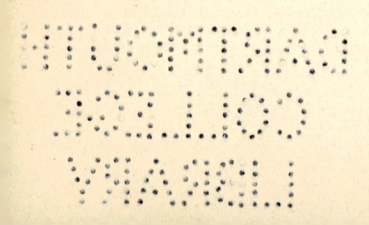

THE AMERICAN POLITICAL SCENE
Copyright, 1936, by Harper & Brothers
Printed in the United States of America

FIRST EDITION

H–L

All rights in this book are reserved.
No part of the book may be reproduced in any
manner whatsoever without written permission.
For information address
Harper & Brothers

Contents

	Page
PREFACE	vii

Chapter

I. PRESENT-DAY CHARACTERISTICS OF AMERICAN POLITICAL PARTIES   1
A. N. Holcombe, *Harvard University*

II. PARTY ORGANIZATION IN THE UNITED STATES   53
Edward B. Logan, *University of Pennsylvania*

III. THE POLITICIAN AND THE VOTER   89
J. T. Salter, *University of Wisconsin*

IV. PRESIDENTIAL CAMPAIGNS   127
Harold R. Bruce, *Dartmouth College*

V. THE USE OF MONEY IN ELECTIONS   170
James K. Pollock, *University of Michigan*

VI. PRESSURE GROUPS AND PROPAGANDA   205
Harwood L. Childs, *Princeton University*

Preface

IN WRITING and publishing this book, dealing with some of the underlying forces in American political life, in the midst of a strenuous presidential campaign, the authors run the risk of having it considered as of the nature of campaign material and applicable only to this presidential contest. But such was not the purpose in planning the book nor is such the character of the contents as it has been written.

The purpose of the book is to present an analysis of the most important forces which determine the course of American politics, made by those who have done a great deal of thinking and research with respect thereto. Applicable to this presidential campaign, yes—but applicable to any presidential campaign and applicable to state and local campaigns. Why is this man placed in public office and that one defeated, what efforts are being made to make the voters act in the desired manner, why is this policy adopted, that one rejected? These are questions that are of concern to most of us in this day when government as never before has invaded our lives, furnishing a living to millions, helping people to have homes, reaching out further and further to regulate business, imposing heavy tax burdens, making us ever conscious of its operation.

Studying the formal governmental system is important, but does not tell us why governments act as they do. The results people receive under any form of government depend very largely upon the men who run the government, who hold the public offices, and upon the influence and controls which act upon them as they perform their official duties. It is hoped that herein will be found explanation of some of these influences and controls which operate in selecting our public officials as well as in governing their activities after selection.

In writing the various chapters the authors have not only used their latest research material but have brought in the most recent studies available in the subjects of which they write. Numerous references are given for the reader who wishes to do additional reading pertaining to the various subjects.

EDWARD B. LOGAN

THE
AMERICAN POLITICAL SCENE

Chapter I: Present-day Characteristics of American Political Parties

by ARTHUR N. HOLCOMBE
Professor of Government, Harvard University

THE most striking characteristic of the two great parties in American politics is their longevity. The Democrats have now been operating under their present name and with a continuous organization for more than a century; the Republicans, for more than eighty years. The present is the twenty-first consecutive campaign which the presidential candidates of the major parties have waged against each other. The issues which originally divided Republicans from Democrats have long ceased to hold the attention of the voters. Even the campaign orators now show little interest in them. But the parties continue on their way.

Another striking characteristic of the major parties is their ability to divide the bulk of the nation's voters between them and to exclude independent political organizations from any but a minor rôle in national politics. In the electoral college, where Presidents are officially chosen, the general rule is that all the votes are divided between the candidates of the two great parties. The latest exception was the election of 1924, when an independent candidate, the elder LaFollette, carried one state, his own state of Wisconsin. In 1912 the Progressive party carried half a dozen states, but the circumstances were peculiar. The "Bull Moose" candidate, Theodore Roosevelt, had been the most popular contender for the regular Republican nomination, and preferred to split the party rather than submit to what his followers believed to be intolerable injustice at the national convention. Though he carried more states than the regular candidate, the Republican party, after the smoke of battle cleared away, was found substantially intact. It is necessary to go back to the election of 1892 to find a durable independent party making serious inroads into the electoral college vote. The Populists carried several Far-western states, but were ruined by their success. In the next campaign the Democrats took over their leading issue, and they accepted the Democratic candidate for the Presidency. Though the Populists maintained an independent organization through several campaigns, they never again won a place in the electoral college. Altogether, among the twenty campaigns in which Republicans and Democrats have jointly participated heretofore, there have been only five in which the candidates of minor parties obtained electoral votes.

The record of the popular voting in presidential elections points to the same characteristic of the American party system. At every election minor parties solicit the support of the voters for their candidates. In 1932 there were five candidates of minor parties who carried on more or less active campaigns. Their combined popular vote, however, was less than three per cent of the total. In a majority of the twenty campaigns which the two great parties have waged over the Presidency, the minor parties have polled less than five per cent of the total popular vote. With the exceptions of 1856, 1860, 1892, 1912 and 1924, the Republicans and Democrats have succeeded in polling at least ninety per cent of the popular vote. Their general predominance in the political scene is indisputable.

A third outstanding characteristic of the major parties is their ability to maintain through the years a not-too-unequal division of the bulk of the voters. Neither party has ever gained for its presidential candidate the support of more than sixty per cent of the total popular vote. The record was made by Harding in 1920 and has been closely approached only by Hoover in 1928 and by Roosevelt in 1932. Ordinarily, the winning candidate has received less than fifty-five per cent of the total vote. In seven of the twenty campaigns he has received less than fifty per cent. On the other hand, the losing candidate has usually made a respectable showing. No Republican candidate since 1856, if the split in the party during the "Bull Moose" campaign of 1912 be disregarded, has polled less than forty per cent of the total vote. The Democrats have fared worse in several of their campaigns. Neither Judge Parker in 1904, nor any of the candidates in the three campaigns following the World War, was able to poll as much as forty per cent of the total popular vote. But these apparently crushing defeats have not destroyed the character of the bipartisan system in national politics.

A survey of the record of elections since the present major parties began to dominate the political scene in 1856 shows three clearly defined periods in the relations between the parties. The first was the period of Republican supremacy, which began with the election of Lincoln in 1860 and ended with the loss of control over the House of Representatives in the election of 1874. During this period of fourteen years the Radical Republicans controlled all the political branches of the federal government and were able to give effect to their policies. A period of twenty-two years followed in which the two great parties were so evenly matched in strength that neither of them could control for long both the Presidency and the Congress. Except for two years in the Harrison administration and for the same length of time in the second Cleveland administration, effective party government was impossible. Then, following the exciting free-silver campaign of 1896, came another period of Republican supremacy in Washington. For fourteen years the Conservative Republicans were in the saddle. The split in the party and the bolt of the Progressives in 1912 cleared the way for the Wilson administration, but this interlude of Democratic ascendency was ended by the return to "normalcy" in 1920 and the resumption of control by the Conservative Republicans. This period of Republican supremacy continued until the collapse of the Hoover administration under the strains and stresses of the great depression.

It is evident that on the whole the Republicans have been the stronger party. They have controlled the Presidency and the Congress together for forty-two of the eighty-two years since the foundation of the party in 1854. During the same period the Democrats have controlled the political branches of the federal government for fourteen years, two under Buchanan, two during the second Cleveland administration, six under Woodrow Wilson, and the past four. During twenty-six of these eighty-two years neither party has held full control of the political power in Washington. Periods of Republican supremacy have alternated with shorter periods of partisan deadlock or Democratic ascendency.

It might be expected that such alternations of power would continue in accordance with the normal changes in the moods and temper of the voters. The Radical Republicans lost control of the federal government in the first election following the panic of 1873. The Conservative Republicans came into power at the congressional and presidential elections following the panic of 1893. The Democratic victory in 1912 might seem to break the rule that political crises are closely associated with economic crises. But the Democratic victory in 1912 was not brought about by a shift of voters from the Republican to the Democratic party. The Conservative Republicans lost control of the federal government when they lost control of their party through their dissensions with the Progressives. They regained control of the government when they regained control of their party. The latest revolution of the business cycle caught the Republicans unprepared. Will they recover their former authority after an interlude of Democratic ascendency? Or does the present setting of the political scene presage a permanent change in the relations between the two great parties, or even, perhaps, a new realignment of the parties?

On the face of the latest election returns there is little to indicate that the future of the major parties will be greatly different from their past. Yet there are signs of impending changes in their relationship to each other and to the country.

The most significant is the increasing volatility of the electorate. The voters have shown themselves more disposed to change sides in recent campaigns than in those of earlier years. From 1860 to 1908 the Republicans never polled more than fifty-six per cent of the popular vote, nor less than forty-three per cent. But in 1912 a majority of them temporarily left their party and, though most of these dissatisfied Republicans drifted back during the Wilson administration, their adherence has been much less firm than in the years from Lincoln to the elder Roosevelt. The LaFollette campaign in 1924 revealed the growing instability of the Republican party, and the desertions to the Democrats since 1930 have surpassed those of any previous crisis in the party's history. The Democrats also have shown distressing symptoms of increasing instability. Cox in 1920, still more Davis in 1924, and Smith in 1928, proved unable to hold the party lines. The triumph of 1932 demonstrated the party's power of recuperation, but enhanced the general impression of partisan instability. Certainly, party ties rested more lightly on the voters than they did a half-century earlier. The habit of party regularity was plainly declining. In the present campaign the signs of the times point more strongly than for many years toward fundamental changes in the alignment of the major parties.

Why, young men and women inquire of their elders and of one another with growing frequency, should a new voter become either a Democrat or a Republican? It is not easy—indeed, it is not possible—to give a convincing answer, if the reply is based upon no better evidence than is afforded by the planks of the party platforms and the declarations of the party candidates. Party platforms have tended to grow longer with the passing years, and less intelligible. Often they seem designed rather to conceal the differences among the members of the party than to expose those between the party as a whole and its opponent. Platforms may speak out boldly on unimportant or incontestable issues, but in dealing with the paramount problems in the minds of the voters they are apt to be verbose, deceptive and obscure. Political critics fill the ears of the public with complaints about the emptiness of the official declarations of party policy. The party leaders do little to render them more explicit and thus to abate the grounds of criticism. To find more satisfactory answers to the riddle of the parties, it is necessary to look below the surface of partisan contention. It is necessary to pursue the verbal controversies to their origins among the underlying forces which influence the setting of the political scene.

Political analysis of the major national parties begins with the record of the popular voting in presidential elections. In 1932 the Democrats carried forty-two of the forty-eight states and elected their candidate with 472 of the 531 electoral votes. The Republicans carried only six states with 59 electoral votes. But in 1928 the Republicans carried forty of the forty-eight states with 444 votes, while the Democrats carried only eight states with 87 votes. Six states went Republican at both elections, four in New England (Maine, New Hampshire, Vermont and Connecticut), together with Pennsylvania and Delaware. Eight states went Democratic at both elections, two in New England (Massachusetts and Rhode Island) and six in the Lower South (South Carolina, Georgia, Alabama, Mississippi, Louisiana and Arkansas). The other thirty-four states supported the Democratic candidate in the election of 1932 and the Republican in 1928. On the face of the returns not much more is indicated than the fickleness of a great many voters. If a longer view, however, be taken of the political scene, there emerges from the election statistics a durable pattern of voting behavior which gives real character to the national political parties.

The firmest figure in the partisan pattern is the Solid South. The ten states extending along the South Atlantic and Gulf coasts from Virginia to Texas, and including Arkansas in the back country, have regularly for many years, cast larger majorities for the Democratic presidential candidates than any group of states in any other section of the country. These ten states, together with Tennessee, formed the Southern Confederacy in 1861. Though most of them were carried by the Republicans one or more times during the period of reconstruction after the Civil War, they never failed to support the Democratic presidential ticket in all the campaigns between 1876 and 1928. In the "Al" Smith campaign of 1928 four of these states, Virginia, North Carolina, Florida and Texas, cast their presidential votes for the Republican candidate. But they returned the Democratic candidates for Congress by the usual majorities, and in 1932 all were back again in the fold. It is an unequaled record of party regularity in American national politics.

The solidarity of the Solid South is not an altogether natural phenomenon. In the early years of the Republic, partisan distinctions were as conspicuous there as in any other portion of the Union. The owners of the great plantations along the coast were generally arrayed against the small farmers in the back country and the pioneers on the frontier. The plantation owners were also far from united among themselves, since the tobacco planters of the Old Dominion had interests somewhat different from those of the sugar and rice planters of the Lower South. The development of cotton as the staple crop of the larger part of the South brought greater unity of interests, but popular leaders like Jefferson and Jackson always made a stronger appeal to the smaller farmers and frontiersmen than to the great planters. Important partisan divisions persisted throughout the Upper and Lower South down to the period of the Civil War. It was the war and the unintelligent, though intelligible, process of reconstruction after the war that created the Solid South.

The growing diversification of interests in the Solid South threatens its traditional solidarity. The states which compose that section have been the states with the largest percentages of Negroes. The density of the Democratic vote has been apparently a direct function of the density of the Negro population. But the migration of Negroes to the cities, especially to those in the North, has disturbed the normal relationship between Negroes and whites. Moreover, in the mountainous regions of western North Carolina and Virginia, as in eastern Tennessee and Kentucky, where the Negro population is sparse, there are large blocks of Republican voters. The poor mountain whites still cherish ancient grievances against the great planters and their followers on the fertile plains. On the plains, also, new divisions of interest have sprung up with the development of cotton manufactures and other urban industries. In one of the states of the Solid South, Florida, the urban population has come to outnumber the farmers and planters and other inhabitants of the open country, though in the rest of that section the rural population still holds sway. It is clear that even in the South "the old order changeth."

A second major figure in the partisan pattern is the Northeast. On the ordinary maps this is the section of the country which contains the six New England states and the three adjoining states on the North Atlantic coast. On the maps of the political analyst it may be identified as that section of the country in which the Democratic party gained more than it lost in the "Al" Smith campaign. Outside of the nine Northeastern states there was only one state in the whole Union, Illinois, in which Smith clearly brought net gains to the Democratic party. In that state Smith's strength lay in Chicago, and in the Northeastern states likewise it was his strength in the great cities which chiefly explains his superiority at the polls over other Democratic presidential candidates. But it was not alone in the great cities of the Northeast that Smith ran well in 1928. Although he carried only Massachusetts and Rhode Island, where the urban population is densest, he cut into the regular Republican majorities even in Maine and Vermont, which are still predominantly rural. Smith's popularity in the Northeast was a definitely sectional phenomenon.

The political character of the Northeast is less easily described than that of the South. New England and New York became strongly Republican when the party was first organized, but Pennsylvania was not carried by the Republican party in a presidential election until 1860, and in that election New Jersey was divided between the Republicans and the Douglas Democrats. While Pennsylvania presently became a strong Republican state, New York soon became a doubtful one and remained doubtful until the Bryan campaign in 1896. New Jersey also remained a doubtful state during most of this period, and at times the Democrats even broke the ranks of the New England states by carrying Connecticut. Beginning in 1896, the Northeast was almost solidly Republican down to 1928. The split in the Republican party in 1912 enabled Woodrow Wilson to carry most of the Northeast by a plurality of the votes, but the only Northeastern state to desert the Republican party at any other presidential election between 1896 and 1928 was New Hampshire in 1916. While the Northeast was the only section of the country in which Smith proved to be a strong candidate in 1928, it was also the section in which Roosevelt encountered the most opposition in 1932. In fact, he lost five of the nine Northeastern states while carrying every other state in the country except Delaware. It is evident that the Northeast, like the Solid South, is different from the rest of the country.

The political character of the Northeast is not only more difficult to describe than that of the South but also more difficult to explain. In the early years of the Republic the Northern and Eastern states contained many small farmers and frontiersmen, and, like the Upper and Lower South, furnished many electoral votes for the parties of Jefferson and Jackson. But the maritime and commercial interests of the seaboard towns, and later the manufacturing interests which sprang up in the vicinity of the numerous waterpower sites, preferred to cooperate in national politics with the great planters of the more prosperous parts of the South, forming the sectional coalitions known as Federalist and Whig. Today the farmers are reduced to a small minority of the voters in the Northeast. In Massachusetts, Rhode Island and New Jersey less than five per cent of the population lives on farms, in Connecticut and New York not much more than five per cent, and in Pennsylvania not over ten per cent. Even in rural states like Vermont less than a third of the inhabitants actually live on farms. Urban interests dominate the political scene and give character to both of the major parties.

The distribution of the urban voters in the Northeast between the two great parties has been complicated by differences of class, race and religion. It is evident that the popularity of "Al" Smith in 1928, not only in New York but also in the other Northeastern states, cannot be explained solely by the general policies to which he was pledged or the particular measures which he advocated. But the strength of the opposition to Roosevelt in 1932 clearly reflected the special economic conditions which distinguish this section from the rest of the country. Except in New York City, the leading business men have been generally affiliated with the Republican party for many years and have sought through its instrumentality to frame the policies and promote the measures which their interests have seemed to require. Even in New York City the commercial and financial leaders have tended to be strongly Republican since the struggle over "free silver" in 1896. The Republican party in this section of the country has reflected more definitely than any other group in national politics the special interests of urban industry and of modern capitalism. It is this specialization of interests which seems chiefly to explain the solidarity of the by no means thoroughly solid Northeast.

The third major figure in the partisan pattern is the West. "West" is a convenient expression which has had many different meanings in American history. Regarded as a geographic area, it began in the western portions of the seaboard states. Pennsylvania was the most typically "western" of the original states. With the westward movement of population the "West" shifted over the Appalachian mountains and across the prairies and plains of the Mississippi valley to the Rocky mountain region, the inter-mountain plateaus, and the Pacific coast. Its progress has left numerous landmarks in local nomenclature.

Western Reserve University is located in Cleveland, Ohio. Northwestern University flourishes in Chicago and Evanston, Illinois. Occidental University is established in Southern California. Traces of the "West" may be found in all sections from the Atlantic to the Pacific.

In American politics the "West" is rather a state of mind than a definite geographical area. It is a state of mind which has reflected the conditions of life in newly settled regions and on the frontier. It has been more hospitable to what have been believed to be liberal and progressive ideas than have the older portions of the country. It has been more sensitive to the vicissitudes of agriculture and of industry. It has been less tenacious of habitual partisan preferences than has been the Northeast or the Solid South. It is more national than the Northeast or the South, being in some measure a mixture of both. Yet it is intensely conscious of its sectional individuality.

However the West may be defined on the map, not all its parts are equally "western." California has become a state with a predominantly urban population, like the great states of the Northeast. In both the other Pacific coast states the city dwellers outnumber those who live in the open country, though by less wide a margin than in California. In Colorado and Utah, also, large cities impart a more urbane character to the politics of those states than would be natural amidst the rusticity which prevails in most of the Mountain states. But while most of the Western states are predominantly rural, they are not equally agrarian. In Arizona the percentage of the population living on farms is as low as in New Hampshire or Delaware, which are classed as urban states, and in Nevada it is not much higher. In the Dakotas, on the other hand, the farm population is as dominant as in Arkansas and Mississippi.

The contemporary political West begins with Wisconsin. It extends across the Mississippi to Minnesota, Iowa, Kansas, Nebraska and the Dakotas. It includes all but one of the Mountain states and all the states on the Pacific coast. It accounts for more than a third of all the states in the Union. This is a section which was solidly Republican in 1920 and in 1928, but it is the section in which the reaction against the Hoover administration was most decisive in 1932. It is the section in which Senators LaFollette and Wheeler, running on the Independent Progressive ticket in 1924, made the greatest inroads into the normal strength of the major parties. It is the section in which, in 1916, the appeal on behalf of Woodrow Wilson to keep the country out of war played the greatest havoc in the Republican ranks. Clearly, this section, as the Northeast and the Solid South, is different from the rest of the country.

Perhaps the most characteristic expression of the political traits of the West in recent years was manifest in the election of 1924. LaFollette's Independent Progressive party developed strength enough to take his own state away from the Republicans and to put the Democrats down into third place in a dozen of the Western states. The Democrats ran behind both the Republicans and the Progressives in every state along the Canadian border from Wisconsin to the Pacific coast, down the coast to California, and back through Nevada, Idaho, Wyoming and South Dakota, to Iowa. In Nebraska the Democrats barely held second place through the influence of the Bryan brothers, and in Kansas, Colorado, Utah and Arizona they were hard pressed by the Progressives. In 1912, also, this was the section of the country in which the Roosevelt Progressives made their best showing, though they actually carried only four of the Western states, Minnesota, South Dakota, Washington and California. Earlier still, the Populists scored their chief victories in this section. But it is not necessary to multiply instances of the hospitable disposition of the West toward independent political movements. It is evident that the leading trait of Western politics, compared with the politics of the Solid South or even of the Northeast, is its partisan instability.

Besides the three major sections in American politics there are three intermediate sections lying between the major sections. The first of these, in political importance, lies between the Northeast and the West, and for lack of a better name may be called the Middle States section. The original Middle States in American politics lay on the Atlantic coast, but the Middle States, politically speaking, have gone westwards steadily, following the political "West." This section now consists of four states, Ohio, Indiana, Illinois and Michigan, which mingle Northeastern conservatism with Western liberalism and progressivism in fairly balanced portions. They are states in which the industrial and urban population predominates, though not to the extent of its predominance in most of the Northeastern states. The percentage of the population actually living on farms is low, though not so low as in most of the Northeastern states. Modern capitalism, as in the Northeast, tends to dominate the political scene. Agrarianism, however, as in the West, has not altogether lost its former sway.

The rôle of these mid-western "Middle States" in national politics is complicated by their position close to the border between North and South. Virginia, Kentucky and other states of the Upper South contributed largely to their original population, as well as did New England and the Middle Atlantic states. The early settlers from these different sections brought their characteristic sectional attitudes with them and gave to the political campaigns in the present mid-western Middle States, particularly the three immediately north of the Ohio River, a uniquely intersectional character. Michigan, which was originally settled chiefly by Northerners, was formerly more definitely Northwestern, like Wisconsin, Iowa and Minnesota. It did not become a typical Middle State until in recent years the growth of automobile manufacturing and other great capitalistic industries created a predominantly urban population and compelled a new adjustment between Western and Northeastern political attitudes. In the other Middle States also the development of urban industry in recent years has tended to strengthen the characteristic Northeastern political attitudes at the expense of those reflecting the character of the Upper South and West.

The partisan record of the Middle States reflects their peculiar situation at the center of equilibrium between Northeast and

West, and also for many years, though not recently, at the center of equilibrium between North and South. Generally Republican in presidential elections, they have been less stable than the Northeast and, at least since the Bryan campaigns, more stable than the West. Solidly Democratic in 1932, they were solidly Republican in the three preceding elections. The defection of Ohio to the Democrats in 1916 was as decisive of the result in that closely contested campaign as the more notorious defection of California. In 1912 the Bull Moose Progressives carried one state in this section, Michigan, with a degree of success attained in no Northeastern state except Pennsylvania. Prior to that election Michigan had been Republican, generally strongly Republican, in every presidential election since the organization of the party. Ohio, Indiana and Illinois, on the other hand, had always been closely contested down to the Bryan campaigns, and often doubtful, if not Democratic.

The second of the intermediate sections is the border between North and South. Five states, Delaware, Maryland, West Virginia, Kentucky and Tennessee, belong in this section. They were originally slave states and possessed important interests in common with the other states of the South. In none of them could the Republican party originally obtain any considerable support. Only one of them, Tennessee, actually joined the Southern Confederacy; the people of West Virginia, indeed, broke their connection with the mother state rather than attempt to leave the Union. In all of them the small farmers were too conscious of their traditional opposition to the great planters to follow willingly in so desperate an enterprise as secession. The "poor whites" in the Appalachian mountain valleys were particularly hostile to the political leadership of the dominant slaveholders of the Lower South. It was from this class of mountain whites that Lincoln picked Andrew Johnson to run with him on the Union ticket in 1864. Around them the Republican party leaders gradually built up, in the border states, a substantial following which survived the abortive effort to found a new Republican party in the South with the support of Negro votes.

At the present time the political character of these border states is very different from what it was in the period of radical Republicanism. Delaware has become predominantly urban and industrial, and seems to be almost as strongly Republican as Pennsylvania. In Maryland, which has also become a predominantly urban state, the influence of the South has persisted more strongly, though the Republicans carried the state twice for McKinley against Bryan, and three times in the 1920's. In West Virginia, Republican influences have strengthened with the economic transformation of the state following the development of the soft-coal industry. Its political orientation tends to turn toward Pittsburgh and the Northeast rather than toward Richmond and the Upper South. Kentucky and Tennessee have remained more agrarian and have been more consistently Democratic. The Republicans, however, carried the former state in 1896 and again in 1924 and 1928, while Tennessee went Republican in 1920 and 1928.

The last of the intermediate sections is the border between South and West. Three states, Missouri, Oklahoma and New Mexico, belong in this section. The first and second of these, though not situated in the South, were originally settled chiefly by farmers and planters from the South and were endowed with the Southern political traits. Missouri, being a grain-growing state with many settlers from Kentucky and Tennessee, naturally tended to follow the Upper South in its politics, while Oklahoma, lying partly within the cotton belt and being settled more largely from the Lower South, tended to follow the Lower South more closely. Further political complications have followed the growth of manufactures in Missouri and the discovery of oil in Oklahoma. Kansas, which was originally a bone of contention between the sections, finally fell under the control of the free-state men and became definitely "western." Many of its early settlers came from strongly Republican New England, and after the Civil War many Union veterans were attracted there by the liberal terms of settlement under the Republican Homestead Act. Since many Kansans mingled with the early settlers in Oklahoma, the northern part of that state, which happened to lie in the wheat-growing region, acquired a distinctly different political character from that of the more southerly portions of the state. New Mexico has always possessed a peculiar political character on account of the large Spanish-speaking population, and remains uniquely Southwestern.

The confusion resulting from the mixture of ancestral political habits and conflicting economic interests is better illustrated in the Southwestern border section than in any other section of the country. Missouri, which was carried by Douglas in 1860, and then became Unionist for two elections, went over to the Liberal Republicans in 1872, and thereafter was Democratic until the end of the century. From 1904 to 1928 it was carried by the Republicans, except in 1912 and 1916 in the two Wilson campaigns. In 1932 it went Democratic, as did most of the rest of the country. Oklahoma has regularly been Democratic except in 1920 and 1928. New Mexico has been more closely contested, the Spanish-speaking population apparently holding the balance of power between settlers from the South and those from the North and West. In short, the political character of the Southwestern border is more mixed than is that of either of the other intermediate sections.

The relations between the sections furnish the key to American national politics. As Frederick J. Turner has wisely observed:[1] "Statesmanship in this nation consists not only in representing the special interests of the leader's own section, but in finding a formula that will bring the different regions together in a common policy." The conditions of the problem which American statesmen—that is, the party leaders—have to solve are revealed by the distribution of electoral votes among the sections. This distribution is shown in the accompanying table:

---

[1] Frederick J. Turner, *The Significance of Sections in American History* (Henry Holt and Company, New York, 1932).

SECTIONALISM IN AMERICAN POLITICS, 1936

Sections	Number of States	Representatives	Electoral Votes
1. The Northeast	9	122	140
2. The North-South border	5	31	41
3. The South	10	93	113
4. The South-West border	3	23	29
5. The West	17	86	120
6. The Middle States	4	80	88
Total	48	435	531

It is evident that no one of the three major sections holds the balance of power between the other two. There are too many votes in the intermediate sections. But any two of the major sections can gain control of the federal government by forming a combination which includes the intermediate section. (If the combination were formed between the South and the West, it would be necessary not only to carry the Southwestern border states but also to pick up an additional state in the border section between the South and the North.) The Northeast section is the only one which can theoretically win a presidential election without help from either of the other major sections, but to do so its candidate would have to carry every one of the Middle States and also the states in the border section between North and South. Thus, the balance of power lies in the intermediate sections.

Under these circumstances, finding a formula that can bring a winning combination of sections together in a common policy can be no easy task. In the earlier years of the Republic the former "Wests" did for a long time hold the balance of power between Northeast and South, but neither the Northeast nor the South was then as nearly solid as it became in later years. At present the West together with the Middle States can theoretically hold the balance between Northeast and South, but these two sections cannot be united as easily as the earlier "Wests." The problem of national statesmanship, as defined by Turner, has always been one which has exercised to the utmost the powers of the great party leaders.

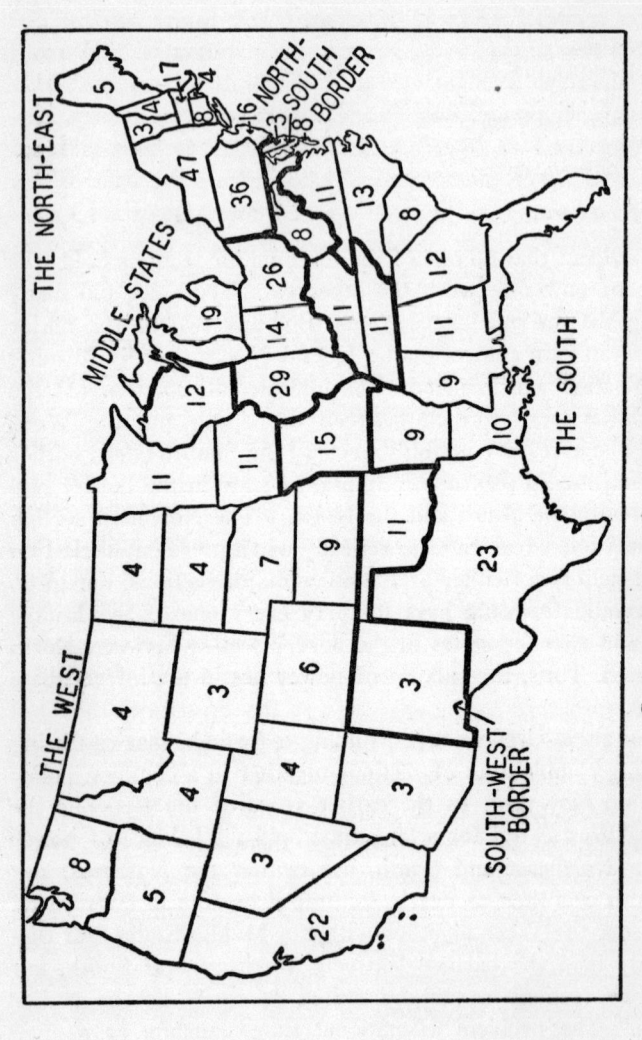

SECTIONALISM IN AMERICAN POLITICS
Electoral Vote of Major and Intermediate Sections in 1936

There have been many different solutions of this basic problem of American politics. The Federalists tried to build a majority by a combination of Northeast and South against the West, but this proved to be an unstable combination and could not maintain its hold on power without the strong hand of Washington. Jefferson, who from the political point of view was a Western, not a Southern, leader,[2] and later Jackson built up victorious sectional combinations by organizing the bulk of the West and attracting to the main body of their supporters a sufficient following in both Northeast and South to gain firm control of the federal government. Clay, Webster and Calhoun tried to form a sectional combination to rival that of the Jacksonian Democrats, but their Whig coalition never possessed the solidarity of the Democrats, and could not be as effective an instrument of national statesmanship. On the whole, down to the Civil War period partisan strategy favored sectional combinations drawing their strength from all three major sections, though relying more heavily upon the West than upon either of the others. It was no accident that the Federalist party, which paid little attention to the West, was one of the less successful of the major parties.

The anti-slavery Republican party was founded upon a combination of Northeast and West against the South. This combination, though strong enough to win the Presidency, did not possess the strength needed to control the Congress under normal conditions. Hence the frantic efforts of the Republican leaders, first to extend their power into the South by means of Negro votes and later to strengthen themselves in the West by the admission of new states and the cultivation of Western interests with appropriate measures. But Populism ruined Republican hopes in the West as the failure of Negro suffrage had ruined them in the South, until the bold attempt of the Democrats under Bryan's leadership to repeat the achievements of

[2] Charles A. Beard, *The Economic Origins of Jeffersonian Democracy* (The Macmillan Company, New York, 1915).

Jefferson and Jackson under less auspicious circumstances solidified the Northeast and Middle West and gave the "sound-money" Republicans under more conservative leadership a less precarious supremacy in national politics than the anti-slavery Republicans had ever had. Woodrow Wilson came into power through the accidental division of his opponents rather than through any special strength of his own, and retained power through the accidental intrusion of European affairs upon the American political scene. Now, at last, Franklin D. Roosevelt leads against the Republican lines a new assault which apparently carries a greater threat to the old order in national politics than any of the earlier campaigns since the present party alignment was first established.

The real character of sectionalism in American politics, and hence of the major political parties also, does not appear from a superficial inspection of the election returns. The politician who knew no more about the political attitudes of the people of the different states than was revealed by the results of the latest presidential elections would be at a loss to explain their apparent fickleness. The shifting of thirty-four states from the Republican to the Democratic side between 1928 and 1932 does not show what really happened. Maine, New Hampshire, Vermont, Connecticut, Pennsylvania and Delaware, which voted Republican at both elections, are not the only states in which Republicanism flourishes. Nor are Massachusetts and Rhode Island, which voted Democratic at both elections, with South Carolina, Georgia, Alabama, Mississippi, Louisiana and Arkansas, as solidly Democratic as the company which they kept would suggest. In uneven contests, like those of 1928 and 1932, tidal waves of popular votes may wash particular states far away from their usual moorings, while others hold out against the tide or drift sluggishly with it. In states where the results are close, pluralities of the popular vote fall in favor of one candidate or the other in the most casual manner; and a state where the margin of victory over defeat is less than ten per cent of the total vote is in a very different category from one in which the victorious candidate receives two or three times as many votes as his defeated rival.

Fruitful analysis of the election returns begins when the states are arranged in accordance with the extent of their deviation from the average. In 1932 Roosevelt polled over fifty-seven per cent of the total popular vote in the forty-eight states, while Hoover polled barely forty per cent. States in which the popular vote for the candidates of the two major parties was distributed in approximately the same way as in the whole country may be described as average states at that particular election. States in which the vote for the Republican and Democratic candidates deviated from the average by a considerable amount—let us say by at least five per cent—may be described as states with a Republican or Democratic deviation. When all the states are assigned to their proper places in accordance with such an arrangement, the pattern of national politics begins to emerge from the obscurity of the ordinary voting statistics.

The pattern for 1932 is interesting. There were ten states with a Democratic deviation in the Solid South. There were four others (Tennessee, Missouri, Oklahoma and New Mexico) in the two border sections. There were six more (Wisconsin, the Dakotas, Nebraska, Nevada and Arizona) in the West. There were seven states with a Republican deviation in the Northeast (all but New York and Rhode Island), one (Ohio) in the Middle States section, and one (Delaware) on the North-South border. The nineteen remaining states fell into the category of the average. A majority of the nineteen lay in the West. Three others (Illinois, Indiana and Michigan) lay in the Middle States section, three (Maryland, West Virginia and Kentucky) in the North-South border section, and two (New York and Rhode Island) in the Northeast. There was no state with a Republican deviation in either the South or the West, and none with a Democratic deviation in either the Northeast or the Middle States. The border between North and South was the only section with one or more states in each of the three categories. The Solid South and the South-West border were the only sections with all their states in one category.

The differences between this pattern and that for 1928 are significant. In 1928 three of the states in the South (Virginia, North Carolina and Florida) were among the average states. Three of the Northeastern states (New York, Rhode Island and Massachusetts) were among the states with a Democratic deviation, and three others (New Hampshire, Connecticut and New Jersey) were among the average states. Only Maine, Vermont and Pennsylvania were among those with a Republican deviation at both elections. In the West no state was among those with a Democratic deviation in 1928, and six appeared among those with a Republican deviation. In the Middle States section there is no difference in the location of three states, while one (Michigan), an average state in 1932, was one of those with a Republican deviation in 1928. In the border between North and South there is no difference, and in the Southwest border there is a general preference for the Republican instead of the Democratic side. Altogether, twenty-six states shifted their position between 1928 and 1932, while twenty-two remained in the same category at both elections.

By constructing a series of such patterns for presidential elections, it is possible to determine what may be called the political climate of the United States. This may be defined as the average deviation of the individual states from the average distribution of popular votes for the whole country over a considerable period of time. If the average distribution of votes between the two major parties at the four elections since the World War be taken as normal, the political climate will measure the extent to which the states depart from this normal. By assigning to each state its proper number of electoral votes, a simple table may be prepared which will serve to illustrate how party leaders make the calculations upon the basis of which the party strategy in presidential campaigns is determined.

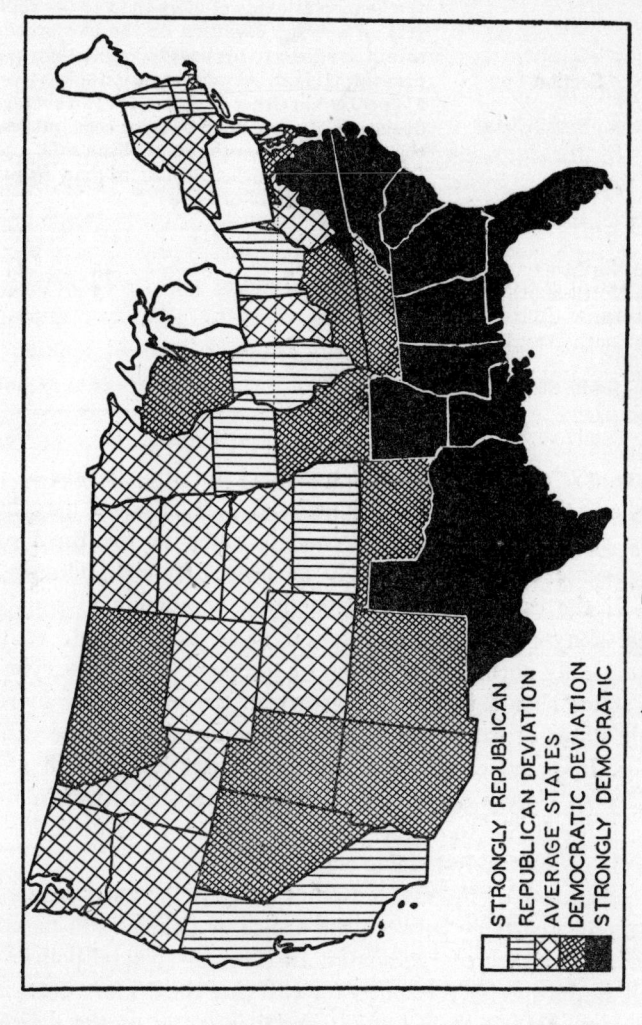

American Political Climate, 1920-1936

Section	Number of electoral votes which may be cast by states which show (I) an average deviation on the Democratic side of more than 10 per cent, (II) an average deviation on the Democratic side of less than 10 per cent but more than 2½ per cent, (III) an average deviation of less than 2½ per cent in either direction, (IV) an average deviation of more than 2½ per cent but less than 10 per cent on the Republican side, and (V) an average deviation of more than 10 per cent on the Republican side				
	I	II	III	IV	V
1. The Northeast	..	..	51	45	44
2. The North-South border	...	30	8	3	..
3. The South	113	..	...	...	..
4. The South-West border	...	29	...	...	..
5. The West	...	26	52	42	..
6. The Middle States	...	..	14	55	19
Total	113	85	125	145	63

Since 266 electoral votes are necessary for the election of a President, the problem of the national party leaders may be clearly stated. It is, to carry enough states in the third or average-state category to supply at least fifty-eight electoral votes, if the candidate be a Republican, or enough to supply at least sixty-eight electoral votes, if he be a Democrat. With a theoretically normal distribution of the popular vote, carrying these states should insure the victory in the presumably more reliable states of categories IV and V, or I and II, as the case may be. In practice, of course, prudent party leaders will not calculate so closely as is suggested above, since a margin of safety is desirable to cover losses from abnormal deviations among the presumably reliable states.

The character of the major parties compels the party leaders to distinguish sharply between the choice of policies and measures and the choice of candidates. In choosing general policies, as well as the specific measures for carrying them into effect, it is necessary to suit them to the special interests of the major sections from which the party ordinarily derives the bulk of its support in the Congress. If clearly defined measures and policies cannot be suited to the partisan sectional interests, then it becomes necessary to effect compromises that will be acceptable to the interests concerned, or else to evade the issues by glittering generalities and equivocation. If this is not done, the campaign will be ineffective in the very sections where the party should be strongest, and the leaders, if successful, will have difficulty in carrying out their program after the election. Hence the vagueness and ambiguity of many planks in the national platforms, and the apparent lack of principle and the insincerity so often denounced by the critics of American party politics. On issues of minor or only local importance the platforms of the two great parties may speak out boldly, but on the major issues there must often be obscurity and confusion. This is a part of the price which the American people pay for the services of national parties in a country where sectionalism prevails.

In choosing their candidates, however, the party leaders have to be mindful of considerations that are very different. If the platforms are properly constructed, the interests of the party in the states with a strong party deviation can be safely left to the local leaders. In fact, in states with a strong party deviation, as in the Solid South from the Democratic point of view, the management of the campaign can be left entirely to the local leaders, and neither platform nor candidates need give much attention to the special interests of these states. After the election, of course, in case of success the local leaders can demand much more consideration from the Congress for their special sectional interests. But in the choice of candidates little regard need be paid to their popularity in the comparatively reliable states. It is to the doubtful states that the appeal of the candidates must be mainly directed.

It is evident from the characters of the major political parties that the tests of availability for presidential candidates must be different. Party leaders on both sides are well aware that the largest blocks of doubtful votes under "normal" conditions are in the Northeast (particularly in New York) and in the West. But the circumstances which shape the character of the Republican party compel its leaders to make their basic appeal to the Northeast and the West. Hence, they must seek to embody in the national platform the formula which will bring those two major sections together in a common policy. Hence, also, the candidate must be selected with an eye particularly on his vote-getting ability in the intermediate section. It is not surprising, therefore, that eight of the eleven men who have been elected to the Presidency on the Republican ticket should have hailed from the Mid-western Middle States. Two of the other three, Theodore Roosevelt and Calvin Coolidge, were originally nominated for the vice-presidency and owed their availability for the subsequent presidential nominations to the accidents which first brought them into the White House. Herbert Hoover is the only real exception to the rule of availability among successful Republican candidates. The unsuccessful candidates (apart from candidates for a second term who failed of reelection), namely, John C. Fremont, James G. Blaine and Charles E. Hughes, were also exceptions to the rule.

Availability for the Democratic presidential nomination has likewise reflected the circumstances which have shaped the character of that party. Unlike the Republicans, the Democrats have sought to build their party upon a combination of all three major sections. Since the Civil War their strategy, except in the Bryan campaigns, has been based upon the hope of adding to the Solid South enough votes in each of the other two major sections to give their candidate the necessary electoral majorities. The nature of the American political climate makes it practically impossible for them to win a close election without carrying doubtful states in the Northeast, the Middle States section and the West. If they lose New York, they must carry, in a close election, every other doubtful state in the whole country. Under the circumstances the Democratic party leaders have logically sought their presidential candidates in New York. It is not surprising that eight of the twelve men who, since the Civil War, have run for the Presidency on the Democratic ticket, have hailed from New York. Pursuing the same strategy, the Democrats have often taken their vice-presidential candidates from the Mid-western Middle States. Once, in 1920, they reversed their tactics and took their presidential candidate from Ohio and their vice-presidential candidate from New York. But they have never sought presidential candidates in the border sections. Those sections, like the Solid South, could safely be left to shift for themselves if the ticket made a strong appeal to New York and the Middle States.

William Jennings Bryan, the only real Westerner among these Democratic candidates, rejected the customary party strategy. He directed his campaigns toward a combination of South and West, regardless of the opposition of the Northeast. But his leadership never brought success. Woodrow Wilson, who in 1916 made the Bryan strategy succeed without perhaps really intending to do so, was originally brought forward as a candidate with a special appeal to New York, though not himself a New Yorker. It is now clear that Wilson's victory in 1916 was the product of an accidental union of South and West, resulting from the intrusion of foreign issues into domestic politics. It did not signify a permanent realignment of the two great parties on the basis of a new combination of the sections. It is equally clear that the nature of the American political climate compels the Democrats either to concentrate upon the capture of New York in presidential elections, or, as Bryan desired, to effect a realignment of parties upon the basis of a new sectional combination.

The nature of the political climate compels the Republicans likewise to carry New York as well as some of the doubtful states in the Middle States section or in the West. This explains the Republican propensity to choose their vice-presidential candidate from New York or to nominate for the vice-presidency a man from some other Northeastern state who can make a strong appeal to New Yorkers. Theoretically the Republicans might elect their candidate without carrying New York by winning the bulk of the doubtful states in other sections of the country. Actually that has not been accomplished since 1876, and was not accomplished even then without carrying some states in the South. The Republicans have lost one election, that of 1916, when they did carry New York, and they cannot hope to win again under the existing circumstances without carrying that state. Thus the power of the Republican party seems to depend upon the preservation of the existing party alignment. The Democrats, on the other hand, might continue to flourish under a different alignment. They might even increase their power if they adopted a partisan strategy designed to appeal more strongly to either New York or the West.

It is such possibilities that lend interest to the study of national politics. But it is clear that the analysis of the election returns must go beyond the voting statistics of the various sections or even of the individual states. It is necessary to analyze the forces within the states which influence the responses to the appeals of the national party leaders. In general, the leading economic interests in any section are associated with the party which is dominant in that section. But when no party can dominate a section, the distribution of sectional interests between the two great parties is more complicated. The political analyst is thus primarily concerned with the identification and measurement of "interests" and with tracing their influence upon the character of the parties. Critics of American politics deplore the importance of the "interests" in the major parties, but it is the influence of the "interests" that gives the parties their individuality and much of their character.

The most important influences, within the states, which affect the calculations of the party leaders are those which result from the division of population between city and country. American politics was originally agrarian politics. The people of the original states lived for the most part in the open country and were chiefly occupied in the cultivation of the soil. In eight of the original states the first census reported no city or town with as many as eight thousand inhabitants. Ninety-six per cent of the entire population of the United States lived in smaller towns or on the land. New York and Philadelphia were the only cities large enough to elect each a Congressman of their own. Boston, Charleston and Baltimore were the only other places that might have dominated a congressional district. At least one hundred of the 105 Congressmen in Washington's time may fairly be assumed to have represented rural rather than urban interests.

The nature of agrarian politics insured a deliberate preference for rural over urban interests. "The inhabitants of the commercial cities," declared Jefferson in a letter to one of his correspondents, "are as different in sentiment and character from the country people as any two distinct nations, and are clamorous against the order of things established by the agricultural interest." Jefferson added that "though by command of newspapers they make a great deal of noise, [they] have little effect on the direction of policy." Jackson's testimony confirms that of Jefferson. "The agricultural interest of our country," he declared in his first annual message to Congress, "is so essentially connected with every other and so superior in importance to them all that it is scarcely necessary to invite to it your particular attention. It is principally as manufactures and commerce tend to increase the value of agricultural productions and to extend their application to the wants and comforts of society that they deserve the fostering care of Government." As late as 1840, when a more careful census of occupations was taken than in any previous enumeration of the population, agriculture was still the leading occupation in every state except Rhode Island. In the country as a whole, persons engaged in agriculture outnumbered those engaged in manufactures almost five to one.

The century which has passed since Jackson lived in the White House has witnessed an astonishing growth of urban industry and of urban population. By 1900 there were 545 cities of eight thousand inhabitants or more in the United States. Yet two-thirds of the people still resided in smaller places or in the open country. The World War marked the final passing of the rural districts as the dwelling-place of a majority of the American people, and the rise of the urban population to the first place. By the most recent census the rural population is estimated at under forty-four per cent of the total. Over twelve per cent of the people now live in cities of more than one million inhabitants; over seventeen per cent, in cities of less than one million but more than one hundred thousand; and nearly eighteen per cent in smaller cities with populations exceeding ten thousand. If all the inhabitants of incorporated places with a population of as much as five thousand are counted as rural, the rural part of the American people is still in a minority.

Time was when such a development was viewed with grave alarm. Jefferson's opinions are well known. Writing in 1787 from Paris to his friend Madison, he predicted that "when we get piled upon one another in large cities, as in Europe, we shall become as corrupt as they." Later, writing from Monticello to another friend, he declared: "I view great cities as pestilential to the morals, the health, and the liberties of man. True, they nourish some of the elegant arts, but the useful ones can thrive elsewhere, and less perfection in the others, with more health, virtue, and freedom, would be my choice." This predilection for life in the country continued to characterize the dominant opinion among the American people throughout the nineteenth century. It continued to demand the use of political power for the purpose of favoring the agricultural interests over those of commerce and manufactures.

The traditional prejudice against the cities and against urban interests in national politics seemed to be sanctioned by the best authorities of the period. In Jackson's time a discerning French writer, Alexis de Tocqueville, made a careful study of American politics and returned to his native land to write a book filled with discriminating praise of American institutions. Though he found much to admire in America, he viewed the growth of cities with unconcealed alarm. Among the principal causes which, he believed, tended to maintain the republican form of government, he listed the absence of a great capital city. Then he added a memorable warning: "The United States have no metropolis; but they already contain several large cities. . . . The lower orders which inhabit these cities constitute a rabble even more formidable than the populace of European towns. ... I look upon the size of certain American cities, and especially on the nature of their population, as a real danger which threatens the future security of the [Republic]; and I venture to predict that [it] will perish from this circumstance, unless the government succeeds in creating an armed force, which, while it remains under the control of the majority of the nation, will be independent of the town population, and able to repress its excesses." A half century later, in Grover Cleveland's time, another discerning foreign observer, James Bryce, made another careful study of American politics, and, like de Tocqueville, recorded his opinions in an immortal book. Bryce also was distrustful of the influence of cities. "The growth of cities," he wrote, "has been among the most significant and least fortunate changes in the character of the population of the United States."

It is not surprising that the spirit of agrarian politics continued to be suspicious of the urban population and hostile to its peculiar interests. As the influence of the urban population in national politics grew, the conflict between rural and urban interests became sharper. American politics ceased to be almost entirely agrarian and sectional; it became increasingly urban and class-conscious. Now, at long last, the urban population actually outnumbers the rural, and the struggle between city and country, and among different classes in the cities, threatens to become as important a factor in national politics as the traditional struggle between sections. Already the states in which the urban population is more numerous than the rural possess a majority of the votes in the electoral college. But the distribution of the urban population among the states is so unequal that the urban states do not yet possess a majority of the votes in the Congress. A revolution in American politics is manifestly in process, but it has not yet been completed.

The ability of the rural population to maintain an influence in national politics greatly disproportionate to its numbers is one of the anomalies of the American political system. It results from the capital fact that a large majority of the urban population is situated in a minority of the states. Though a substantial majority of the whole population of the United States is urban, according to the census of 1930, in only twenty-one of the forty-eight states is a majority of the population urban, and in several of these the urban population exceeds the rural by no more than a slender margin. Hence, a majority of the Senators of the United States are dependent for their election upon bodies of voters which are still predominantly rural in composition. The urban states, however, include a disproportionate number of the more populous states. Therefore, although the Senators from the urban states are outnumbered by the Senators from the rural states, there are more presidential electors from the former than from the latter. Under the latest apportionment the twenty-one urban states have 310 votes in the electoral college, a clear majority of the total. The urban states, by forming a combination among themselves against the rural states, could seize the Presidency and hold it indefinitely, but they could not dominate the Senate.

The disproportionate power of the rural population in national politics is increased by the unequal distribution of urban and rural voters among the congressional districts. If the seats in Congress could be distributed exactly in accordance with the distribution of population between city and country, the urban population would now have 244 seats, while the rural population would have only 191. But so great a portion of the urban population is concentrated in the largest cities where there are no rural voters, and so many other urban voters are scattered over the countryside in small cities where they are outnumbered and politically submerged by the rural population, that the urban population cannot hope to dominate a number of districts corresponding to its numerical importance. The over-representation of the rural population is further magnified by the retention in many states of obsolete districting laws designed to favor the rural population at the expense of the urban. The consequence is that the number of districts dominated by the urban population, though not easy to estimate with accuracy, is certainly much less than a majority of the whole.

In order to understand how the distribution of population between city and country and among different classes in the cities affects the calculations of the party leaders, it is necessary to estimate the voting strength of the states and districts which may be dominated by the urban population as accurately as possible. For this purpose the distinction which the census for 1930 makes between metropolitan and other urban areas is useful. The former term is designed to show the magnitude of each of the principal areas of urban population, regardless of the actual city limits, by including in a single total both the population of the central city itself and that of the suburbs or urbanized areas surrounding it. In some cases the population of two or more cities located in close proximity, together with that of their suburbs, is combined in a single metropolitan area. Ninety-five such areas were reported, each having an aggregate population of one hundred thousand or more and containing one or more central cities of at least fifty thousand inhabitants. Without the District of Columbia, which is not represented in Congress, these metropolitan areas contained approximately fifty-four million inhabitants. The total rural population of the United States, including that of incorporated places with less than 2500 inhabitants, was very nearly the same. There remained about fourteen and a half millions residing in urban areas outside the metropolitan areas.

The voting strength of the urban population, in the Senate and in the electoral college, may be roughly estimated without difficulty. All the states in which the population of the metropolitan areas forms a clear majority of the total may be put down as predominantly urban in politics. The other states in which a majority of the total population are reported as urban may be put down as doubtful, though more probably urban than rural. The remaining states may be put down as predominantly rural. The rural states are not, of course, necessarily agrarian in politics. The population of such states actually living on farms may be outnumbered by the rural population engaged in mining or other non-agricultural pursuits. In fact, such is apparently the case in West Virginia, Arizona and Nevada. The results of such a classification are shown in the accompanying tables. All

NUMBER OF SENATORS

Section	Metropolitan	Other Urban	Rural	Total
1. Northeast	12	2	4	18
2. North-South border	4	0	6	10
3. South	0	2	18	20
4. South-West border	0	2	4	6
5. West	2	10	22	34
6. Middle States	6	2	0	8
Total	24	18	54	96

NUMBER OF ELECTORAL VOTES

Section	Metropolitan	Other Urban	Rural	Total
1. Northeast	128	4	8	140
2. North-South border	11	0	30	41
3. South	0	7	106	113
4. South-West border	0	15	14	29
5. West	22	35	63	120
6. Middle States	74	14	0	88
Total	235	75	221	531

the Northeastern states except Maine, New Hampshire and Vermont, fall in the metropolitan division. All the Middle states except Indiana fall in the same division. Delaware and Maryland in the North-South border section also fall in this division. In the three other sections only California can be classed among the metropolitan states. Most of the other urban states are small Western states. The South is solidly rural except Florida, and the Southern border sections are predominantly rural. The section with the largest number of rural Senators, however, is the West. The extraordinary inequalities between the representation of the sections in the Senate and in the electoral college are brought out strikingly by these tables.

The voting strength of the urban population in the lower branch of the Congress cannot be so easily estimated. It is a fair assumption, however, that all congressional districts which are situated wholly within a metropolitan area, or which contain a metropolitan area of at least a quarter of a million population, are predominantly urban in politics. Other congressional districts, containing a smaller metropolitan area or lying partly within a larger metropolitan area, may often, though not necessarily always, be dominated by the urban population. Congressional districts, which neither lie wholly or partly within a metropolitan area nor contain a metropolitan area of any size within their own limits, will generally, though certainly not always, be subject to domination by the rural population. Upon these assumptions the congressional districts, including states in which Congressmen are elected at large, may be distributed among the urban and rural population as shown in the accompanying table.

NUMBER OF CONGRESSIONAL DISTRICTS

Section	Metropolitan	Other Urban	Rural	Total
1. Northeast	62	35	25	122
2. North-South border	4	9	18	31
3. South	7	10	76	93
4. South-West border	5	2	16	23
5. West	19	14	53	86
6. Middle States	26	17	37	80
Total	123	87	225	435

The congressional representation of the Northeast is predominantly metropolitan. Metropolitan and other urban districts together dominate the Middle States. The other four sections are predominantly rural. It is clear that the distribution of population between city and country is much more fairly reflected in the House of Representatives than in the Senate, where the country population is greatly over-represented. But it is less fairly reflected than in the electoral college, where the operation of the general ticket system of choosing presidential electors compensates for discrimination against cities in laying out congressional districts.

The final step in the analysis of the present partisan alignment is to classify the various types of districts in accordance with the distribution of the popular vote between the major parties. For this purpose it is not enough to divide the districts into Democratic and Republican upon the basis of the results of the latest congressional elections. The elections of 1934 were too one-sided to give a true picture of the distribution of party strength among the different types of districts in the various sections of the country. A less distorted picture is presented by a further division of the Democratic districts into the strongly Democratic, where the Democratic vote was at least twice as great as the Republican, and the comparatively close districts. The results of the 1934 congressional elections are set forth upon this basis in the accompanying tables. The Republicans hold less than one-fifth of the rural districts, nearly one-fourth of the metropolitan districts, and more than one-third of the urban districts. More than a third of the rural districts were strongly Democratic, a third of the metropolitan districts, and less than one-fifth of the other urban districts. The largest blocks of close districts lay in the rural West and Middle States and in the metropolitan Northeast. Altogether, 144 districts were strongly Democratic, 187 were close, and 104 were Republican. A majority of the strongly Democratic districts were located in the South or in the adjacent border sections. Nearly one-fifth were located in the metropolitan Northeast and Middle States. The rest were scattered. Approximately half of the Republican districts were located in the Northeast. The rest were mostly scattered over the Middle States and West. The Republican strength in the border states lies in the mountain districts of eastern Tennessee and Kentucky and in the Ozarks. Close districts were situated in western Virginia and North Carolina and on the South-West border. The Democrats made a poor showing in the Northeastern rural districts except in the mining regions of Pennsylvania. The Democrats were weak also in the rural districts of the Middle States. The distribution of party strength in the rural districts of the West follows a more complex pattern, but in general the Republicans make their best showing on the Pacific Coast.

METROPOLITAN DISTRICTS

Section	Republican	Close	Strongly Democratic	Total
1. Northeast	18	21	23	62
2. North-South border	0	2	2	4
3. South	0	0	7	7
4. South-West border	0	3	2	5
5. West	6	11	2	19
6. Middle States	5	16	5	26
Total	29	53	41	123

OTHER URBAN DISTRICTS

Section	Republican	Close	Strongly Democratic	Total
1. Northeast	19	15	1	35
2. North-South border	2	5	2	9
3. South	0	0	10	10
4. South-West border	0	1	1	2
5. West	3	9	2	14
6. Middle States	7	10	0	17
Total	31	40	16	87

RURAL DISTRICTS

Section	Republican	Close	Strongly Democratic	Total
1. Northeast	14	11	0	25
2. North-South border	2	11	5	18
3. South	0	6	70	76
4. South-West border	1	10	5	16
5. West	15	31	7	53
6. Middle States	12	25	0	37
Total	44	94	87	225

The explanation of the distribution of party strength in the rural districts awaits a further inquiry into the nature of rural interests. The agricultural area of the United States may be divided into an eastern and a western half—the former characterized, broadly speaking, by a sufficient and the latter by an insufficient amount of rainfall for the successful production of crops by ordinary farming methods. The eastern half is further divided by the influence of temperature and topography. The cooler and hillier portions of the East are better suited for pasturage than for the cultivation of staple field crops. Dairying is consequently the most profitable rural industry, and the dairy belt constitutes a major influence in the politics of the region. The warmer and more level portions of the humid East and South seem to have been especially designed by nature for the production of cotton, except for the region close to the South Atlantic and Gulf Coasts, where climatic conditions are less hospitable to cotton but well suited to the production of subtropical fruits, sugar and rice. Between the dairy and the cotton belts lies the great region in which the dominant form of agriculture is the growing of corn and wheat and other grains, although in certain localities tobacco furnishes the major crop.

The western half of the agricultural area of the United States is also subdivided into special regions by the influence of temperature and topography. The plains and intermountain plateaus, where water is not available for irrigation, have furnished the basis for a great livestock industry, chiefly cattle raising but in some localities sheep raising. Where water is available and the land is sufficiently level for irrigation, various crops may be grown, dependent upon the elevation and the temperature, ranging from apples and sugar beets to citrous fruits and long-staple cotton. On the North Pacific Coast there is an area of abundant rainfall and a cool climate where dairying flourishes as in the Northeast and northern Middle West. Lumbering and fishing help to set off this region from the arid portions of the West. California, too, with its Mediterranean climate and agricultural productions joins in giving the Pacific Coast a distinct character of its own. In the mountainous regions the mining industry challenges the supremacy of agriculture and grazing, and further complicates the interests of the rural West.

It is evident that the rural districts possess a great diversity of interests and cannot easily be united in national politics. The regions where the leading money crops are produced in excess of domestic requirements are vitally interested in the development of foreign markets, and will normally support a political party which proposes to use the constitutional powers of the federal government for that purpose. Cotton has been a great export crop for many years, and it is not without reason therefore that the cotton belt constitutes one of the principal special interests in American politics. Tobacco, corn (chiefly in the form of pork and beef), and wheat (in the natural state or in the form of flour) have also been leading exports throughout the years, and it might be supposed, therefore, that the tobacco, corn and wheat belts would also form a leading special interest in national politics. In fact, the tobacco belt has been closely allied with the cotton belt in national politics for many years, but the grain growers have pursued an independent course. Dairy farmers, on the other hand, and also the producers of subtropical fruits, sugar and rice, have not been able to satisfy the demands of the domestic market. This circumstance logically dictates a different attitude toward the use by the federal government of its constitutional powers. It must be expected that the dairy belt of the Northeast and Northern Middle West, therefore, as well as the Pacific Coast, will form a separate special interest. On the Great Plains of the West and in the mountainous areas, the attitudes of the rural interests in national politics are naturally more complex, making of those regions a convenient battleground for parties which appeal primarily to the special rural interests in other sections.

The strength of the parties in the principal agricultural regions may be roughly measured by the distribution of the rural districts in the congressional elections of 1934. The results of these elections are shown, as before, in the accompanying table. The partisan pattern revealed by this classification of congressional districts is much more significant than that presented by the classification of rural districts according to sections. The agricultural regions correspond more closely than do the geographical sections to the diversity of agricultural interests, and the election returns consequently throw a good deal of light upon the puzzle of the parties. It is evident that the Republicans are not only relatively weaker than the Democrats in the rural districts

Rural Districts

Agricultural Regions	Republican	Close	Strongly Democratic	Total
1. The grain-growing regions	13	57	10	80
2. The cotton belt	0	0	61	61
3. The Eastern and Northern dairy belts	24	24	0	48
4. The Western Plains and inter-mountain plateaus	3	11	8	22
5. The rural Pacific Coast	4	2	2	8
6. The Southeastern subtropical coast	0	0	6	6
Total	44	94	87	225

as a whole but also derive the bulk of their agricultural support from the dairy belts. The close districts which appear to lie in the dairy region actually are situated chiefly in the coal-mining areas. The Republicans hold a number of districts in the grain-growing regions, chiefly, in fact, in the corn belt and in the wheat belt, but are relatively stronger in the districts on the Pacific Coast. On the plains and in the mountain area there is some fighting ground where the parties may struggle on fairly equal terms under normal conditions, but in the cotton belt and Southeastern subtropical coast region the Democrats have the field entirely to themselves.

The truth is that the agricultural regions hold the answer to the riddle of the parties. It was in the agricultural regions that the strength of the major parties originally lay, and it is in terms of their respective special interests that their characteristic differences must be largely explained. The largest block of close districts lies in the grain-growing regions, and it is the grain growers who have dominated American politics throughout the greater part of the history of the nation. This they have done, at first by overpowering their opponents, and later by holding the balance of power between the cotton planters and the dairymen. It was the organization of the bulk of the grain growers into a solid party that gave the Jeffersonian Democratic-Republicans their early supremacy in national politics. It was the repetition of this achievement by the Jacksonian Democrats which secured for them their ascendency over the ineffective Whigs. It was the success of the Anti-slavery Republicans in capturing the bulk of the grain growers north of Mason and Dixon's line and the Ohio River that put an end to the ascendency of the Democratic party. The cotton belt and the dairy belt were bound to oppose each other as long as the agricultural interests remained leading factors in national politics, and the corn and wheat belts were bound to hold the balance of power as long as the cotton and dairy belts remained fairly equal contenders in the struggle for supremacy.

It is the growth of cities and of special urban interests that tends to upset the traditional alignment of parties. In the smaller cities, especially in those where commercial interests are more important than manufactures, the politically dominant elements have usually reflected the political complexion of the surrounding rural area. This is still the case in the cotton belt. But in the larger cities, and in most cities where the population has grown as much or more from foreign immigration as from the movement of people in from the surrounding countryside, urban politics has become more complex. This is most strikingly the case in the great cities of the Northeast and Mid-western Middle States. In the smaller cities in these sections Republican ascendency still reflects the ascendency of the Republican party in the adjoining rural areas, but in the great cities a radically different, and peculiarly urban, alignment of parties has come into existence. The character of the parties in these metropolitan districts no longer reflects the traditional divisions among the early farmers and planters. The metropolitan party character seems to be dominantly the result of independent economic and social forces. The investigation of these forces should make possible the completion of this description of the present-day character of the major political parties.

The distinctive characteristic of urban politics is the development of new forms of class-consciousness. There have always been class divisions among the American people, but in the earlier periods of national politics the principal classes were derived from the conditions of agriculture in the different sections of the country and class-consciousness tended to merge into sectional consciousness. To be sure, the great planters of the Upper and Lower South carried their local conflicts with the small farmers and frontiersmen into national politics, and there were localities in the North where tenant farmers and agricultural laborers tended to take opposite sides, in national as well as local politics, from the owners of the great estates. But the predominant agricultural type was the independent small farmer, and so numerous were the members of the independent small-farmer class in most sections of the country that they succeeded in establishing their supremacy in national politics under such leaders as Jefferson and Jackson, without developing an acute sense of class-consciousness. They constituted, in fact, a great middle class which tended to even the temper and moderate the tone of American politics. Merchants and manufacturers as well as great planters had to adjust themselves as best they could to the political combinations effected by the dominant interests in American life. But representatives of northern merchants and manufacturers such as Daniel Webster, and of great planters in the Lower South such as John C. Calhoun, were far less effective national leaders than middle-class politicians like Jackson and Clay.

The growth of great cities brought new types upon the political scene. Captains of industry and great financiers tended to segregate themselves on the right, the proletarian masses on the left. But both within the ranks of the industrial wage earners and among their capitalistic employers the traditional American middle-class point of view tended to persist, despite the advent of crowds of alien immigrants, and the characteristic class-consciousness of modern capitalism has grown much more slowly than have the cities. Even in the present century it was still possible for Theodore Roosevelt, when writing his autobiography, to identify "the interests of the people as a whole" with "the interests of the average men and women of the United

States," and for Woodrow Wilson, when campaigning for the Presidency, to describe "the great problem of government" as that of knowing "what the average man is experiencing and is thinking about." Moreover, consciousness of class among the industrialized masses of the urban population has been complicated by consciousness of grave differences in race and religion. Americanism, by emphasizing the importance of tolerating such differences, has tended also to belittle the significance of the economic and social differences which might otherwise have been more destructive to the middle-class traditions of American politics.

But the influence of the new economic and social forces in the cities upon the character of the major parties cannot be ignored. Naturally, it is in the metropolitan areas of the Northeast and Middle States that this influence has been greatest. In these areas the number of strongly Democratic and close districts is far out of proportion to the Democratic strength in other parts of the North and West, and forms a special interest in the Democratic group of interests second in importance only to the cotton belt. It is not only in New York City that the effect of this influence is manifest, though the large delegation of Tammany Congressmen is one of the striking exhibits in contemporary national politics. Across the Hudson in northern New Jersey, and also in Boston, Chicago, Cleveland and Detroit, similar political developments must be noted. This development, as observed in Chicago, has been carefully studied by Professor Gosnell of the University of Chicago.[3] His analysis of the 1932 election returns in that city leads him to the conclusion that the major party which enjoys the least success over a period of years "tends to attract to it those elements which have the least social prestige and economic security." Noting that the Republican party was the one which had normally held the reins of government in national and state politics for a considerable

[3] Harold F. Gosnell and Norman N. Gill, "An Analysis of the 1932 Presidential Vote in Chicago." in *The American Political Science Review*, vol. xxix, no. 6 (December, 1935). See especially p. 983.

period of time, he added: "The men of wealth, the scions of the older Protestant families, the women with money and leisure, were attracted to the Republican party. On the other hand, the foreign born, those who happened to emigrate recently from Catholic countries, those who had difficulty in getting jobs in this country, naturally gravitated to the Democratic party." These conclusions seem to be generally applicable to the alignment of parties in the great cities of the Northeast and Middle States.

With the continued growth of cities, the ability of the grain growers to hold the balance of power in national politics is increasingly jeopardized. At the same time the importance of the elements in the great cities which might hold the balance between the rising forces on the left and on the right is magnified. This element is neither the capitalist class nor the proletarian masses. As the capitalist economy evolves, it employs decreasing proportions of unskilled factory workers. Other groups have come to the fore. Technicians, engineers, professional men and women, civil servants, skilled and "white collar" workers, provide the ingredients for a new middle class. As proletarian and capitalistic class-consciousness increases, that of the urban middle class will surely increase also. The leaders of the socialistic and communistic minor parties, like the would-be leaders of special capitalistic or Fascist parties, are quick to deny the possibility of an effective class-consciousness for the urban middle class. But nothing would be more consistent, under the new conditions of a city dwellers' world, with both the traditions of American politics and the interests of the urban middle-class itself, than the development of precisely such a class-consciousness.

It is such considerations as these that give rise to the belief that important changes in the alignment of national parties may be approaching. No radical reconstruction of parties may take place in the present campaign, but the way is apparently being cleared for a change in the old partisan pattern. It was foreshadowed by the Smith campaign in 1928. The Democratic party has frequently nominated a New York governor for the Presidency, but Smith was the first who definitely represented the new urban spirit of revolt against the dominant agrarian traditions in national politics. Smith's success would have meant a profound change in the character of the Democratic party, and hence also eventually in that of the Republican party. But Smith failed, and the agrarian elements in the Democratic party remained in control. Yet the urban elements in both major parties are manifestly impatient under the present party alignment.

The agrarian forces in national politics will not easily be dislodged from their strategic positions in the two great parties. The cotton belt and the dairy belt seem unlikely to lose their partisan complexions as long as the grain growers continue to hold an important share in the balance of power. The waning strength of the grain growers has been reinforced by the rising strength of the agrarian interests in the Farther West, that of the cattlemen and wool growers, the sugar-beet producers and the orchardists. Their influential position in national politics seems likely to remain intact, at least for another decade. An exclusively urban movement in national politics could only have the result of driving the various agrarian interests together into a unified agrarian party. Such a party could hold the Senate for a greater number of years than any urban politician likes to contemplate. Whatever realignment of parties proletarian or capitalistic leaders might like to bring about, the urban middle classes are not likely to become willing tools for the execution of their designs. Rather will they probably prefer to maintain a partisan alignment consistent with the preservation of the middle-class spirit in American politics. This does not mean necessarily the preservation of the existing alignment, but it does mean great obstacles in the way of those who wish to transform American politics by building new major parties on the basis of proletarian or capitalistic class-consciousness.[4]

[4] See A. N. Holcombe, *The New Party Politics* (W. W. Norton and Co., New York, 1933), chap. v.

What seems most likely as the next phase in the development of the character of the major political parties is the rise of the middle class in the great cities of the Northeast and Middle States to a more influential position in national politics. Such a position does not imply the definite affiliation of the urban middle class in a body with either of the major parties. It implies merely such a division of that class between the two great parties as will enable a portion of them, by swinging from one side to the other in response to the ebb and flow of the circumstances, to exert a disproportionate effect upon the results of elections. In short, it means sharing the balance of power with the grain growers. The establishment of such a balance of power is a much more promising enterprise than an attempt to organize a new party in the name of the new majority, who live in the cities, for the purpose of dominating the political scene. After all, the success of national party leaders does not depend upon victory in presidential elections. Such victories do sometimes make new national leaders, but the lack of such victories does not necessarily destroy old party leaders. Party leadership ultimately depends upon the ability to hold the leadership in the states, and in the sections which leading states represent. National leadership may often be found in the White House. It will always be found in the Capitol, particularly in the Senate.

The rise of the urban middle class to a more influential position in national politics does not even necessarily involve any radical shift in the existing partisan pattern. This pattern is woven from the materials which are afforded by the existing distribution of interests among the whole body of people. The established major parties are coalitions of sectional and class interests. New parties which might be created by means of a realignment of the established parties would still be coalitions of the same interests. They could only be the product of new combinations of the existing materials. Short of an economic cataclysm, they could not be greatly different from those which now exist. The existing parties are going concerns which possess valuable assets in the guise of great traditions, associated with former leaders who left their mark on American history, campaign slogans, and the inertia of large numbers of voters who have formed the habit of taking a certain side in the party battles. They are going concerns which are strongly fortified by primary laws, ballot laws, patronage laws and other legal privileges. It will not be easy to make radical changes in them, despite the animosity of many critics who denounce their alleged irrationality, and the skepticism of many voters who deplore their lack of principle.

The higher strategy of party leadership is founded upon the calculation of the durable forces which are capable of dominating the behavior of voting majorities in districts, states and sections. These are not exclusively economic. Social, racial and religious forces also must be considered. But in the long run the economic forces seem to be most effective. In other words, there is more rationality in national politics than many of the critics have been willing to admit. There are sound reasons why a cotton planter should be a Democrat and a wool grower a Republican. To be sure, the number and the variety of special interests are so great that it is idle to expect all of them, or even many of them, to be effectively represented by a major political party. Most special interests must utilize special-interest organizations or the ordinary lobby to secure the special representation which they desire.[5] There is always the possibility of partisan raids on either side by directing special appeals to particular interests that are unattached to either major party or that might be detached from the opposing coalition, as the present Roosevelt administration has obviously sought to detach soft-coal miners from a traditional preference in certain localities for Republicanism. Such tactics may change the result in a few pivotal states. Except for these minor operations, ordinary party leaders are likely in general to try to hold the established lines, hoping to get into power, when out, by taking advantage of the cyclical ups and downs of affairs, rather than

---

[5] See A. N. Holcombe, *Government in a Planned Democracy* (W. W. Norton and Co., New York, 1935), chap. ii.

by trying to bring about fundamental changes in the character of the parties. Extraordinary leadership will be required to accomplish any radical partisan realignment.

During a recent presidential campaign a well-known newspaper offered a prize for the best answer to the question, "What is the difference between a Democrat and a Republican?" The winning answer, which happened to be submitted by a woman, was as follows: "A Republican is a person who thinks a Democratic administration bad for business; a Democrat is a person who thinks a Republican administration bad for business." This answer, which at first sight seems frivolous or cynical, contains an essential truth concerning the nature of the major parties. This truth is concealed in the ambiguity of the word "business." It begins to emerge in the light of the answers to the further inquiries, "For whose business may a Democrat think a Republican administration bad?" and, "For whose business may a Republican think a Democratic administration bad?" In short, the character of the parties is determined chiefly by the nature of the special interests which are associated with them.

The latent causes of partisanship, as Madison sagaciously remarked in the celebrated tenth number of *The Federalist*, are sown in the nature of man. "So strong is this propensity of mankind to fall into mutual animosities," he wrote, "that, where no substantial occasion presents itself, the most frivolous and fanciful distinctions have been sufficient to kindle their unfriendly passions and excite their most violent conflicts. But the most common and durable source of factions has been the various and unequal distribution of property. . . . A landed interest, a manufacturing interest, a mercantile interest, a moneyed interest, with many lesser interests, grow up of necessity in civilized nations, and divide them into different classes actuated by different sentiments and views. The regulation of these various and interfering interests forms the principal task of modern legislation, and involves the spirit of party and faction in the necessary and ordinary operations of the government." Since the causes of partisanship cannot be removed, Madison's con-

PRESENT-DAY CHARACTERISTICS

clusion was that the protection of the public interests is best to be sought by controlling its effects. The greater the number and variety of the special interests, he believed, the greater the difficulty of forming a combination among them dangerous to the general welfare. Hence his conviction that a new and more nearly perfect union must be superior to the individual states or any lesser union.

The same course of reasoning leads to the conclusion that the two great parties are superior to the minor parties which would exist if the major parties could be broken down into the special-interest groups of which they are composed. The leaders of minor parties often display an unbalanced devotion to a particular interest and a vexatious disregard for all other interests, which would be ruinous on the part of the rulers of the country. But the leaders of the major parties are compelled to take a broader view. The wider extent and more diversified interests of the major parties are the best guarantee which the people possess that power will be used with moderation. If the practical business of government consists largely in the adjustment of the conflicts of interest arising among the people, politicians, who understand the nature of the people's interests and are responsible for their treatment of them to powerful and durable parties, may well be the most serviceable rulers that the people can reasonably expect to obtain.[6] The American system of bipartisan politics is subject to just criticism at many points, but lack of character in the major parties is not a just ground of criticism.

The vindication of the character of the existing major parties depends ultimately upon the serviceability of the particular combinations of interests by which they are constituted. Woodrow Wilson in his campaign speeches used to claim superiority for the Democratic party, regarded as an instrument of the popular

[6] See A. N. Holcombe, *The Political Parties of Today* (Harper & Brothers, New York, 2nd ed., 1925), p. 384. See also T. V. Smith, *The Promise of American Politics* (The University of Chicago Press, 1936), chap. vi, "Americanism," especially pp. 247 ff.

will, over the Republican combination of interests, for the reason that, resting on an appeal to all three of the major sectional interests, it must come nearer to representing the general interest of the whole body of people than a party which, like the Republican, rests upon an appeal to only two of the major sectional interests. There is manifestly some merit in this claim. The Republicans might have replied that a good working combination of two major sectional interests forms a more serviceable instrument of government than a more nearly universal combination which does not work so well. As long as the two wings of the Republican party did work well together while the Democrats were torn by such dissensions as were revealed in the Smith campaign, there would have been some merit in this reply.

Certain conclusions are clear. The failure of the Republican party to obtain any substantial support in the South has been a grave defect in the constitution of that party. On the other hand, in the past the Tammany wing of the Democratic party seems to have been attracted to that party less by the prospect of obtaining a due influence in the conduct of national affairs than by the hope of securing a freer hand in local affairs than under Republican rule. Indeed, the solidarity of the Solid South was originally brought about by precisely such considerations. The Republicans might plausibly have argued that the Democratic party was less an instrument of national government than a group of instruments of sectional and local government. To this the Democrats might have replied that the charge was not altogether inapplicable to the Republicans also. On both sides the possibility exists of creating a more serviceable instrument of popular government than either of the major parties in its traditional form.

The adjustment of conflicting sectional and class interests is not enough to justify the function of major party leadership. In many cases, as Madison pointed out long ago, such an adjustment cannot be made "without taking into view indirect and remote considerations, which will rarely prevail over the immediate interest which one party may find in disregarding the rights of another or the good of the whole." It is necessary, as Turner said, that statesmen not only should represent the special interests of their own section—or, it may now be added, class—but also should find a formula that will bring together the different sections, and classes, in a common policy. It is necessary, too, that statesmen should be able to appeal to more general interests than those of any particular combination of sections or classes. Herein lies the essential difference between successful party leadership and true statesmanship. Major parties, reflecting in their characters the dominant traits of independent small farmers and even-tempered middle-class city-dwellers, may offer the closest approach to ideal instruments of government that modern democracy can reasonably expect to obtain. But the ideal party would be devoted to the common good regardless of section or class.

There can be no such party, in reality. All the more important is it that party leaders should cherish proper political ideals. This obligation seems to be recognized by many politicians. Both the Republican and the Democratic parties profess their devotion to ideals. But they are devoted to the same ideals. They are both Democratic-Republican parties. Hence the temptation to fall into the wearisome repetition of truisms and platitudes which so tries the patience of many well-wishers of popular government. The history of our times reveals the widespread craving for more inspiring leadership. The apparent popularity of single-party systems of government in certain foreign countries challenges the pretensions of double-party systems like our own, which seem to many citizens to subordinate principle too much to expediency. Interests, as has been shown, play an indispensable part in the political scene. But the drama cannot satisfy the spectators unless, somehow, principle also can play a major rôle. The great party leaders must be able to rise above the characters of their several parties and assume the character of the whole people—or what may be cherished as the character of the people—for whom the parties hold their vast powers in trust. The popular instinct is sound which insists that there is a real difference between the mere politician and the statesman. The American people rightly demand that there be more statesmanship in national politics.

In a presidential campaign a number of parties take the field along with the two major parties. In the 1932 presidential campaign there were, besides the Republican and the Democratic parties, the Socialist, Prohibitionist, Communist, Socialist-Labor, Farmer-Labor, Jobless, and Liberty parties.

The Republican and the Democratic parties dominate the political scene, largely determine the policies to be put into effect, and fill the public offices. In the 1932 election these two parties received 38,583,000 votes, 97 per cent of the entire presidential vote.[1] A vast amount of management is necessary to accomplish these purposes; and to furnish that management elaborate machinery has been developed. A clear view of the thoroughness of the organization of the major parties will help to explain how they achieve their aims.

The organization in the two major parties is similar. Both are organized nationally, with a national committee and a senatorial and a congressional committee; each party is organized on a state-wide basis with forty-eight state committees; each party is organized with a county committee in practically all of the 3000 counties in the United States and with committees in practically all of the 119,643 precincts throughout the United States. In addition, the two major parties have separate city organizations in most of the 191 cities of 50,000 population or more.

It is to be noted that the organization of the two major parties conforms to the political divisions of the country. This is a convenient arrangement and at the same time a logical one, because in practically all of the districts one party has control of the government of the district, while the other is striving to gain control. The party in a given district exists to control the government of that district, and in a real sense, as will be seen later, the government supports the party which is in control. Therefore, in examining the thoroughness of the organization

[1] The vote polled by the other parties in the 1932 presidential contest was as follows: Socialist, 884,781; Communist, 102,991; Socialist-Labor, 33,276; Farmer-Labor, 7309; Prohibitionist, 81,869; Jobless, 740; Liberty, 53,425.

Chapter II: Party Organization in the United States

by EDWARD B. LOGAN
Associate Professor of Political Science, University of Pennsylvania

IN THE United States forces are constantly at work determining the public policies of the country and determining which officials shall be placed in positions of responsibility to carry out those policies. These forces operate and their influence is oftentimes unobserved by the people generally—unobserved except by those who make searching inquiry. The political party, the organized pressure groups, the press, educational institutions, at times the church, individual leaders, public office holders, all are forces joining to mold our political life.

The strongest of these forces is the political party which nominates and elects candidates to public office, organizes legislative bodies, formulates public policies, and operates the government, national, state and local. It is proposed to make here an analysis of the organization of this institution, which day in and day out is on the alert, shaping our public policies and placing men in public positions.

A good time to make an analysis of a political party is during a presidential year when the whole organization of the party is astir, when from the top of the organization to the bottom the various parts of the machine are working in harmony to win the big prize in the party battle, the election of the President. Then can be seen not only the machinery which has been established in these nation-wide organizations but also the functioning of the organization, the methods of securing cooperation among the various parts of the organization, and the ways and devices used to attain its objectives.

of a party, there is need to go much further than the party committees. But first a brief examination of these committees should be made.

The national committees of the two major parties are similarly composed, with representatives from each state, one man and one woman from each, and from the District of Columbia, Alaska, Hawaii, the Philippines and Puerto Rico. The Democratic national committee allows representation from the Canal Zone and the Virgin Islands as well. This aggregation makes up a body of one hundred and six members to constitute the Republican national committee, and one hundred and eight for the Democratic national committee.

The members of the national committees have four-year terms. New committees are formed at the national convention, the members being chosen by one of four methods—by the delegations from the states to the national convention, by state conventions, by state committees, or by direct primary elections.

At the present time, in about a third of the states the members of the national committees are chosen by delegates to the national convention, in another third by state conventions; the other third of the states is about equally divided between the method of choosing the members by the direct primary or allowing the state committee to choose. Members from Alaska, Canal Zone, Hawaii, Puerto Rico and the Virgin Islands are selected by the convention method, the members from the District of Columbia by the direct primary.

Of the present membership of the Democratic national committee, thirty-two were selected by the delegations from the states, forty-four by state or territorial conventions, eighteen by state committees, and fourteen by direct primary elections, and the situation is practically the same in the Republican national committee. While the members of the national committees are chosen for four-year terms, many members continue as members for term after term, making the committees in a very real sense continuing bodies.

An analysis of the membership of the committees shows that

many members hold public positions. Many are United States Senators or ex-Senators,[2] many are Representatives in Congress, and a large number of the chairmen of state committees help to compose the committee. Practically all are leaders or bosses in their own states.

Further analysis shows that nearly all of the members of the national committees have done years of service for their parties. Most of them have come up through the party ranks from the local committees to the state committee before arriving at the national committee.

The national committees elect their own executive officers, with the important exception that the presidential nominee of the party names the chairman of his party's national committee. Since this man manages the campaign, the candidate is allowed to choose the chairman in order to obtain a manager in whom he has full confidence. The usual practice is for the candidate to name as chairman the man who has managed the nomination campaign.

Because of this practice of changing chairmen, most of our presidential campaigns are directed by men little experienced as national campaign managers. Even when a President is a candidate for a second term, his party manager often is changed. For many years in the Democratic party there was a practice of keeping an experienced man in the office. August Belmont served as chairman from 1860 to 1872, William H. Barnum from 1876 to 1892, James K. Jones through two presidential terms from 1896 to 1904. But not since that time has there been a chairman who served more than a four-year term.

The function of the national committee is, broadly speaking, the promotion of the interests of the party throughout the nation. The committee operates through the chairman, and the chairman for the party in power usually holds an important government position—oftentimes the postmaster generalship,

---

[2] Writing in 1923, Frank R. Kent said that close to a majority of the membership of the national committees was composed of United States Senators or ex-Senators.

to be in direct charge of the postmasterships which constitute the most important block of patronage among the federal positions.

The chairman has charge of the national headquarters of his party. The whole committee meets a short time after the national convention to ratify the candidate's choice for chairman of the committee, turns over the management of the campaign to him, and then rarely meets again until about the first of the year preceding the presidential election. The primary function of the members of the national committees during the intervening years is to keep the chairman informed of the welfare of the party in their particular states, and to give advice. The chairman makes use of them to help strengthen the party organizations in the states, to help raise funds, to make contacts with party leaders in the states and in general to direct the activities of the national committee in the states.

The responsibility of protecting and promoting the party's interests is very largely that of the chairman and his staff. If the chairman's party is in power he is in a much more advantageous position to promote its interests than he is when his party is out of power. When his party is in power the chairman's chief means of consolidating the party's strength are the use of patronage and propaganda, and the direction of legislation and administration into channels that will win support for the party.

The patronage which is available for party purposes is, as will be seen later, very great. It is customary for the chairman to bring about the replacement of a large part of the federal office holders outside of the civil-service system with those who are sympathetic to his party and who are valuable politically.

Policies are established which inure to the special benefit of large numbers of persons throughout the country. Several examples of the establishment of such policies have been seen during the present administration—the Federal Relief Organization, the Agricultural Adjustment Administration, the Federal Home Loan Corporation, and the Reconstruction Finance Corporation, to mention a few of the most important. Through the establishment of such agencies through which individuals receive direct aid from the government, although they are administered non-politically, the party which is in power possesses a great advantage over the other party in promoting its cause. If used politically, then, the party in power possesses a tremendous advantage.

The chairman of the party which is not in power, not possessing these advantages, plays the rôle of critic of the party in power, works with state and local organizations to maintain and strengthen the party's organization locally, and attempts to increase the party's strength in Congress.

The work of the national committees was, until a few years ago, very largely confined to the presidential year—except the patronage surveillance of the chairmen—but through the national chairmen and their staffs at headquarters the committees are becoming, more and more, permanent working organizations. During the four years prior to the presidential election of 1932 the Democratic headquarters inaugurated an especially active rôle for an opposition party by setting up a publicity bureau to furnish constant criticism of the party in power. The party members in the Senate and House were kept active; material went constantly to the members of the national committee and the chairmen of the state committees for use in the states, and the newspaper men were well supplied.[3] Feeling the effects of this Democratic propaganda campaign, the Republican national committee followed the example of the Democratic committee, and established its own publicity bureau. Since the 1932 election both headquarters have continued their activities.

[3] For a description of the work of the Democratic publicity bureau during the four-year period, see the articles by Thomas S. Barclay in the *National Municipal Review* for February, 1931, pp. 68-72, and February, 1933, pp. 63-65.

In an address before the American Political Science Association members in Philadelphia, Chairman Farley said: "There can be no doubt that the information service maintained at Washington from 1928 to 1932 by the Democratic national committee under the able leadership of my predecessor on the committee, John Raskob, and his colleague Jouett Shouse, had much to do with laying the basis for the Democratic victory of last November."

The two other committees which operate in the national field, the senatorial and the congressional committees, are similar in composition for the two parties, the Republican senatorial committee being composed of seven members appointed by the chairman of the party caucus, the Democratic senatorial committee of six Senators chosen in like manner, all for two-year terms. To retain political experience in the committee the practice is to reelect the members, except when they are candidates for reelection. The chief function of these senatorial committees is, as the name implies, to promote the reelection of party members to the Senate and to increase the party's representation.

The congressional committees of the two major parties, formed to promote the election of party members to the lower house, are similar in composition, being made up of one member, elected for two years, from each state delegation. At present there are twenty-three states from which the Republican party has no delegation,[4] and three from which the Democratic party has no delegation.[5] There, too, through the practice of reelecting members, many members have continuous service on the committees.

The national committee has no direct authority over the congressional committees, but there is close cooperation. Especially is this the case during the presidential year, when the fate of congressional candidates rests in no small measure upon the fate of the presidential candidate. The congressional committees raise funds on their own account, but rely primarily upon the national committees for funds. In 1920, the treasurer of the Republican national committee testified that his understanding was that a loan of $200,000 was to be made to the senatorial committee and $500,000 to the congressional committee.[6] The

[4] Alabama, Arizona, Arkansas, Colorado, Florida, Georgia, Idaho, Louisiana, Maryland, Mississippi, Montana, Nevada, New Mexico, North Carolina, Oklahoma, South Carolina, South Dakota, Texas, Utah, Virginia, Washington, West Virginia, Wyoming.

[5] Delaware, North Dakota, Vermont.

[6] Presidential campaign expenses; Hearings before subcommittee of the committee on Privileges and Elections, United States Senate, 66th Congress, 1921, p. 1199.

chairman of the Democratic national committee reported in 1924 that the work of the senatorial and congressional committees had been virtually merged with that of the national committee.[7]

These three important committees—the national, the senatorial and the congressional—function in the national field in taking the responsibility for the election of the President and Senators and Representatives. But these committees would be practically helpless were it not for the aid they receive from state and local party committees.

The state committees function to elect the governor and all other state officers, aid at times in the election of local officers where the positions are important to the party organization, and cooperate with the national committee and congressional and senatorial committees in electing the President, Senators and Representatives.

The state committees are composed of representatives from subdivisions of the state, with counties, congressional districts, state senatorial districts and state assembly districts serving as the units of representation. The representatives are chosen generally by two methods, the direct primary and the convention, with the states about evenly divided in using these two methods.

The state committees vary greatly in size, from eleven members in Iowa to five hundred and seventy-four in California. In New York, with the state assembly district as the unit of representation, both parties have three hundred; in Pennsylvania, with the state senatorial district as the unit, the Democratic state committee has one hundred and thirteen, the Republican two hundred and twenty-six; in New Jersey, with the county as the basis, the Republican state committee has forty-five members; in Indiana, with the congressional district as the unit of representation, the Republican committee is composed of twenty-six members, the Democratic of thirteen.[8]

In the state committee the chairman is the important character. Chosen usually by the members of the committee, he domi-

[7] *Proceedings of National Convention of 1924*, p. 1092.
[8] See R. C. Brooks, *Political Parties and Electoral Problems*, p. 165.

nates it in determining policy and activities. The factional divisions within the party usually manifest themselves by a fight to elect the chairman of the state committee. Often these fights are so bitter that the bad feeling engendered carries the state committee into nomination campaigns, contrary to the proper rôle of state committees, and often contrary to law.

An examination of the membership of state committees shows that most of the members have served many years of apprenticeship in local party positions. Many members continue to hold their local positions while serving on the state committee. Often state committeemen hold public positions, many being members of the state legislature or incumbents of other state and local positions.

In analyzing the party organization a great deal of emphasis must be placed upon the position of the state committees in the structure. These committees, being the supreme governing body of the party in the state, maintain a general oversight over the welfare of the party in the state. The chairman is either a member of the national committee or cooperates closely with the chairman of that committee. He puts forth special efforts to maintain close contact with the chairmen of the local committees.

Those who seek to control the politics of the state set out to establish their control over the state committee. The chairman of the state committee may be the dominating figure, but usually control lies outside of the committee. Frank Kent asserts that in ninety-nine out of a hundred cases the state chairman, instead of being the real leader ". . . is simply a figurehead, a politically dominated man, controlled by the real leader, whose influence made him chairman and who can as easily retire him."[9]

Control of the state committee is the special aim of a political boss. With control of the committee, which has members in the local districts throughout the state, he has an excellent organization for dominating the politics of the state. Local party workers look to the state committeemen for advice, and the state committeemen usually have much to do with the distribution of state

[9] Frank R. Kent, *The Great Game of Politics,* p. 143.

positions and other patronage and campaign funds in the local areas.

Quite often the state committee is the dominating factor in operating the state government, controlling legislation, appointing the personnel, and playing an important part in the day-by-day administration. When Boss Platt held power over the New York state committee, its members were considered to be far more powerful factors in determining what should be the policy of the state than anyone in the public service of the state.[10]

The state central committees rest heavily upon the county and city committees—and quite naturally so, for these latter committees are composed of the politicians who come into direct contact with the voters. Usually the state committees have no direct control over the local committees, but have little difficulty in getting effective cooperation.

The county committees are usually composed of representatives from each precinct within the county. These representatives are required by law, in most of the states, to be elected by the voters; in others they are chosen in conventions, and in others the choice is left to the party rules. In a number of the states which use the convention method for choosing state committeemen, the primary has been established to select the county committeemen. Giving representation to all precincts results in large committees; in the larger, more densely populated counties some of the committees have several hundred members. Because such large committees are unable to function, the control of the committees falls into the hands of a small executive committee, and often into the hands of one man.

On these committees will be found the politician precinct leaders. A high percentage of them hold county or other public positions. Most of the members of the county committees are reelected over and over again to the committee as long as they are able to control their precincts. While the system is, in form,

---

[10] H. F. Gosnell, *Boss Platt and His New York Machine*, chap. v, p. 73, well shows the importance placed by Boss Platt upon the control of the state committee.

one of election, in actual practice it is usually appointive, for the county leader dictates who the candidates shall be in the election.

The parties reach their greatest thoroughness of organization in large cities. There the organization takes on a military aspect with a system devised for enforcing rigid discipline from the top to the bottom. A description of the Philadelphia Republican organization will show the character of political organization in large cities.

At the bottom of the organization are the qualified voters of the party who constitute the division committee. These voters elect, for a two-year term, two representatives to the ward committee. The ward committees, composed of two representatives from each division, range in size from twelve to three hundred and thirty members. The ward committee selects one of its members to act as ward leader. Each ward committee also selects one member of the central campaign committee, the one member usually being the ward leader. The central campaign committee of the city is made up, therefore, of one member from each of the fifty wards. This committee selects its chairman and other officers. The chairman may be the "boss" of the organization, but not necessarily so. William S. Vare, the "boss" for many years, held an honorary party position only. As far as there is a "boss" at the present time, the chairman of the central campaign committee can be said to be the dominant figure.

This form of organization, provided by law, presents a perfect hierarchy and has the appearance of being democratically ordered. But it does not function democratically. The organization is under the strict control of the city committee, which dictates the selection of the ward leaders. The ward leaders, in turn, govern the election of the division committeemen.

In New York City the Democratic organization matches in perfection the Philadelphia Republican organization at its best. Tammany Hall differs from the Philadelphia Republicans chiefly in the method of selecting the precinct leaders. In the Tammany organization the precinct leaders are appointed by the leaders of the assembly district committees, of which there are twenty-three in New York County. But although the precinct leaders are elected in Philadelphia and appointed in New York, the actual result, from the standpoint of control of the selection, is practically the same.

City organizations form an important part of the structure of the political parties. They are, for the most part, strong, smoothly functioning machines efficiently producing votes for the parties. As is shown later in this chapter, the principal source of strength of the city bodies lies in the fact that so many of the members hold public positions.

At the bottom of the party organization are the precinct leaders. Throughout the country they number more than two hundred thousand in the two major parties. With the precinct used as the basis of representation including some five hundred voters, the party is able to establish very close contact with the voters. How this is done is described in the following chapter.

These division leaders constitute the infantry in the party. They work day in and day out to achieve the chief purpose of the party, to control the vote. They gather around themselves a group of party workers who can be counted upon at all times, they establish a personal relationship with the voters, they grant favors, they give help where needed, they pull doorbells and have a car at the voter's door to take him to the polls on election day.

The foregoing shows in brief the thoroughness of the organization of the parties. It describes the permanent personnel of the two major parties, the standing army. In each major party the number will total somewhere around one hundred and fifty thousand. This number includes only those who hold party positions. There are many others who are regular party workers; they render regular valuable service, and might well be considered a part of the organization. They hold no party positions, but in season and out they can be counted upon to serve it. They are relatives or friends of the committeemen, they are public office holders, they are business associates of committeemen, they secure favors in one way or another, and many of them are paid for the services they render. The number of such workers varies from year to year and from campaign to campaign, but it has been estimated to be seven hundred thousand, and sometimes it reaches a total of more than a million.[11]

It is characteristic of American parties that often control is held not by those at the head of the formal organization but by persons outside it who hold no party office. The President holds no party office, but he controls the party which elected him. United States Senators and governors often rule over their state organizations. Industrial and financial leaders often constitute the power back of the throne, and govern the activities of those who hold the high party positions. The leaders of organized groups—labor, industrial, agricultural, social—exercise an ever-increasing power over the party.

Control of city organizations often lies outside of the circle of party officers. Charles F. Murphy, boss of Tammany Hall for more than twenty years, held no party office, and John F. Curry held only a minor position in the organization. William S. Vare, boss of the Philadelphia Republican organization, held only an honorary party office. Mayors, councilmen, county commissioners, township commissioners, judges, often govern the local organizations. The real headquarters is many times not the party headquarters, but is found in city halls, in court houses, in township buildings, or elsewhere.

In the United States, during most of our history, political parties were allowed to form and exist without any governmental regulation. They established their committees, prescribed the methods of choosing the committees, defined membership, and established methods of selecting candidates for the elective offices without any regulation by the states.

During the long reign of freedom the parties built up forms and engaged in practices which did not harmonize with democratic theory; membership on party committees fell under the

[11] Charles E. Merriam and H. F. Gosnell, *The American Party System*, p. 70.

control of a few leaders, and the committees gained power over the policies of the party and the choice of candidates. The people generally found that they had very little voice in shaping party activity. Accordingly, the states began to throw restrictive laws around the practices of the parties.

Regulative laws were passed to break up this close control which the parties had established. The laws struck out in two chief directions: to secure more popular selection of the party officials who composed the membership of the various committees and conventions, and to regulate the functioning of those officials and committees. These laws strove for more popular control over the selection of candidates and the determination of policy. Looking over the whole field of state regulation of the selection of party candidates, one sees that the first important fact is the transformation of the political party, within a short period of time, from a voluntary association to a semi-official agency, with many of its activities regulated by state law. The second outstanding fact is the almost complete sweeping away, in the states, of the convention system for making nominations, and its replacement by the direct primary. In forty-four states the direct primary has been substituted for the convention method of making nominations, and with the exception of three states has been applied to the selection of candidates for all public offices.[12] In three of those states, New York, Idaho and Kentucky, the convention system has been re-established for making nominations for the state-wide offices.

The third outstanding fact to be noted is the regulation of

[12] The Pennsylvania primary law is typical of those which extend the direct primary to the selection of candidates for all elective offices. It provides that "Hereafter all candidates of political parties for the office of the United States Senate, for the office of Representative in Congress, for elective state, county, city, ward, borough, town, township, school district, poor district, and election divisions or district offices, and for all other elective public offices except that of presidential elector, shall be nominated, and delegates and alternate delegates to national party conventions, state committeemen, and party officers shall be elected at primary elections held in accordance with the provisions of this act and in no other manner."

the convention system, in many ways, by state laws, where this system is used by the states. Much of this regulation has to do with the selection of delegates to conventions, a number of states requiring that the delegates be elected. The general election laws regulating ballots, time of holding elections and methods of conducting them, have been made applicable to the primaries. The expense of the primaries, in practically all the states, has been made a public one;[13] in some states the unit of representation is defined, the use of proxies is strictly regulated, and provision is made for the instruction of delegates for certain candidates.

It should be noticed, too, that some of the states have extended their regulations to the national field by prescribing the manner of electing delegates to the national conventions. At the present time sixteen states provide for the election of such delegates. Besides requiring that the election method shall be used in selecting delegates, various other regulations are imposed, governing the method by which a candidate for delegate has his name placed on the ballot, the basis of representation, and the methods of controlling the action of the delegates in the convention. In the states which use the convention method for selecting delegates to the national conventions, many regulations are provided for holding conventions similar to those discussed above for the nomination of candidates for state and local offices.

It is noteworthy, also, that while the convention reigns supreme for nominating the party candidates for the Presidency and vice-presidency, that method has been very largely swept away in the selection of party candidates for the United States Senate and House of Representatives. All of the states but three which have adopted the direct primary system have applied it to the selection of candidates for the United States Senate and House as well as for state and local offices. Thus the parties are compelled to make their choices for the legislative branch

[13] Except in Arkansas, Georgia, Mississippi, South Carolina and Texas, where the expense is still carried by the party.

at Washington in a different manner from that by which they make their choice for chief executive.

Along with the attempts to increase popular control of the selection of party candidates went the movement to gain more power over party policy. In establishing more direct regulation of conventions, the dual purpose was served of establishing more control over both the selection of candidates and the framing of the party program. As long as the convention method is used, the two considerations can be dealt with together; but when the states abolished the convention system and replaced it with the direct primary they provided only a method of selecting candidates, and the manner of preparing the program was abolished. Program-making then became a separate problem.

Some of the states have provided for delegate conventions to act in drafting platforms, some have provided party councils, some use a combination of party council and delegate convention, and one state allows the candidates to place a short statement of their platform on the ballot. In several states no provision whatever is made for framing the party platform.[14]

The other direction which state laws have taken, in democratizing the parties, has been toward the regulation of the selection of party officials. There was widespread feeling that those who held the party offices were hand-picked by political bosses or the dominant political group in the jurisdiction, and that the people had no effective voice in the undertaking. Those seeking to control the government would establish their control over the party committees by dictating the selection of members of the committees. "The key to the political machine, the hall mark of the boss, the sign that he is in the saddle," says Frank Kent, "is control of the state central committee."[15]

Once the states had begun to require the use of the elective method for selecting delegates to conventions, it was not long

---

[14] See Charles E. Merriam and Louise Overacker, *Primary Elections*, p. 85 ff.
[15] Frank R. Kent, *The Great Game of Politics*, p. 142.

PARTY ORGANIZATION

until that method was provided for selecting party officials, and legislation was enacted regulating the organization of the party in other respects, the powers of party officers, terms of office, activities, and the like.

Now in most states the standing committees of the parties are selected by direct vote of the people, and in a number of states the elective method has been provided for selecting the national committeemen. The Pennsylvania law previously quoted is typical of those laws which require the election of party officials. The membership of all state, county and ward party committees is selected by direct action of the voters. The only party committee members in Pennsylvania who are not selected by the voters are the members of the city committee in Philadelphia, which party officials are selected indirectly by members of the ward committee, and committeemen appointed to fill vacancies which occur between elections.

The question arises whether this broad attempt to gain more popular control over the selection of party candidates and officials has brought about the result intended, whether it has succeeded in democratizing the parties. It will be better, in considering this question to treat separately the regulation of the selection of party candidates and the selection of officials.

It is now quite clearly seen that neither the regulated convention nor the direct primary has fulfilled one of the hopes of those who promoted such legislation, that the powers of the boss and the machine would be destroyed. With his smoothly working organization establishing daily contact with the voters, the boss continues to control the election of delegates to conventions and the selection of candidates in direct primaries.

Money expended for organization and propaganda plays a vastly larger rôle than was foreseen. Quite often money expended for these forms of control is decisive in determining the selection of the party candidate. It can be said that usually, in the selection of delegates to conventions or candidates in direct primaries, control goes with the political machine and use of money. It was expected that control would be placed in the hands of the voters, but in most cases it comes from the top down rather than from the voters at the bottom. Power lies with the voters, it is true, but methods have been devised to direct its use into the desired channels.

In another important respect these attempts to secure more popular control have not given good results. The attempts to control the actions of delegates in the convention have been almost a total failure. The dominant political leaders in the state find little difficulty in governing the action of the delegates by controlling their election.

The methods adopted in regulating the selection of party officials have not worked as intended. Most of the shortcomings of the direct primary laws described above are found to exist here as well. To a much greater extent, however, there is control from above in the organization, or by those outside the organization who are powerful politically, over the selection of those in minor party positions. Especially is this true in cities and counties with highly developed party machines.

The groups or leaders who seek control over the functioning of the government in the jurisdiction concerned adopt as a method the control of the party organization. It was to break up such control that state laws were passed providing for the election of party officials. But in spite of these laws, these groups and leaders are seeking control as before. They spend a great deal of energy and money in managing the election of members of the state committee, in order to gain control of that committee. They work with their political lieutenants in the counties and the cities, furnishing funds, distributing propaganda, giving jobs or promises of jobs, in order to secure the election of favorable members to the state committee. In areas with highly developed political machines under the control of a boss, the selection of the state committeemen is made by the boss through his control over the voters and the election machinery. The dominant political leader or group in the area selects the candidate for state committeeman and manages his election. Rarely is there a contest.

PARTY ORGANIZATION

When the situation in the local areas is examined, the control from above is found to be much more complete. City and county bosses exercise almost complete control over the selection of ward leaders, precinct leaders and county committeemen. The situation can be seen in Philadelphia; this city has in form a thoroughly democratic method of choosing the party officials. As already described, the voters in each election division elect two members to the ward committee. The members of the ward committee choose their own chairman, who becomes the ward leader and is usually the representative of the ward on the city committee. The dominant authority controls the selection of the ward leaders through his power to recognize or not to recognize them as members of the city committee. If he chooses not to recognize a man, someone else in the ward becomes its representative on the city committee. Because of the favors the boss is able to bestow upon the ward leader, and he in turn upon the division leaders of the ward, the division leaders are careful to select a ward leader acceptable by the boss. And the same system operates with the ward leader in the election of division leaders. If the person elected is not suitable to the ward leader, he is not recognized. Without recognition from the ward leader the division leader is not in position to obtain favors and privileges for his constituents or for himself; he soon finds himself so weakened that he cannot control his own election, and he is displaced by one who has been recognized. With the recognition of the ward leader the division leaders control their own election through the system of favors and personal work which is described in the following chapter, a method which in many cases has nothing to do with the opinions of the voters of the division.

This same sort of control from the top down goes on in thousands of local districts. The county boss, who may be the chairman of the county committee or someone entirely outside the party organization, uses his authority to recognize or not to recognize the county committeemen selected in the election divisions of the county, in controlling their election.

The system does not operate as intended. Instead of working from the voters up, it operates from the top of the organization down. In its results in most jurisdictions, it is the same as the system which this elective system was supposed to displace. In actuality the party officials are still chosen by bosses, small caucuses, professional politicians, and the politician public office holder. In most jurisdictions popular choice of party personnel is only in the statute books.

There is a serious question whether such laws, providing for popular selection of party officers, are not an absolute detriment, and this applies to state and local jurisdictions as well. The law establishes a recognized party authority in the jurisdiction, with the intent that it shall be one popularly selected. By prescribing a means of selecting this authority the law gives to it a preferred position—in fact, an exclusive right to direct and speak for the party in the jurisdiction. Other groups which would like to compete under the same party banner find themselves excluded. Their only method to secure a position of influence is to gain control of this machinery established by law, and they find that a practical impossibility because of the control from above which has already been described.

It appears that by means of laws providing for the election of party officers we have given political bosses and their lieutenants a monopoly of the party, and have provided them with a system which effectively shuts out opposition. The question is raised whether it would not be better to scrap these laws providing for the selection of party officers, especially in jurisdictions subject to boss control, and return to the system of free play of competing groups. Without a method established by law the party would set up an authority in the jurisdiction, but competing elements would be free to set up rival authorities. There would be no one authority which had upon it the seal of the state.

There is another practice of which these party authorities are guilty which gives point to this question of repealing laws providing for the election of party officers. It has now become the established practice for party committees to participate in primary elections and actually to support candidates for nomi-

PARTY ORGANIZATION

nation. This practice is usually forbidden by state law, but state committees as well as local party committees are regularly using their influence and resources to nominate the candidates of their choice. Sometimes these committees act as committees in promoting candidates in the primaries; at other times, where there are prohibitive laws, they make some pretense to conceal the identity of the committee, but it actually exerts as much control as if it acted openly. The situation is that the weight of the party organization is being thrown into the direct primary, the system set up to afford more popular control of the selection of candidates. Because of the great advantage which the party organization has in controlling elections, its support determines the choice of candidates in most instances. The question then arises, whether by law a party organization should be constituted to which is given a preferred position and which is able to enter nomination contests, giving advantages to the candidates whom it supports. It appears that by laws governing the selection of party officials, party machines are being aided to dominate primary elections and the selection of party candidates. The party organization which has control of the government thereby has a means of perpetuating its control. Bosses and groups seeking to control the activities of the government know well this preferred position which the organization has, and accordingly exert strenuous efforts for control of the party organization.

There is still another factor which raises the question of the wisdom of attempting to maintain popular selection of party officials, and that is the existence of the spoils system in most of our jurisdictions. Under this system the organization which has control of the government uses the public jobs to strengthen itself. Many of those who hold party positions fill public positions also, often when forbidden by law to do so. In many jurisdictions it is largely through the judicious awarding of public jobs that bosses control the selection of the party officers under them. In turn, these jobholders, because of their public positions, are possessed with so many favors which they can grant to constituents, and are able to spend so much time in political work, that they have a great advantage in running the elections in their divisions, including their own election. It is questionable, therefore, whether popular choice of party officials should be attempted as long as public positions can be used by the organization to great advantage in perpetuating itself. It would seem that it might be better to take the preferred standing away and give other groups an opportunity to contend for power.

In examining the organization of the political party, an analysis should be made to determine the extent to which the organization is composed of public office holders if one is to understand one of the chief sources of its strength.

Fortunately, information is available so that the situation can be examined in its broad outlines. In the United States as of June 30, 1932, there were, it was estimated, 3,278,500 public employees, of which number 934,000 were federal, 252,000 state, 591,500 municipal, 302,000 county, township and district, and 1,189,000 engaged in public education.[16]

Of the 934,000 federal employees, 456,096, or 48.8 per cent, were under civil service; 266,379, or 28.5 per cent, were chosen by fixed standards, primarily the military forces. Of the 252,000 state employees, it was estimated that 96,750 were under civil service; 59.2 per cent, or 350,000 of the 591,500 municipal employees, were under civil service; and 14.4 per cent, or 45,000 of the 302,000 county, township and district employees. None of those employed in public education are under civil service, but all are chosen by fixed standards.

Another way of expressing the above figures is that 22.7 per cent of the federal appointive positions, 211,525 in number, are available for political appointment. In the state governments, 61.6 per cent of the positions, or 155,250, are subject to political appointment; in municipal, county, township, and district positions 85.6 per cent, or 302,000, fall in that category. There are, then, in the public service, 875,275 positions subject to political control. In addition, it can be said that political control extends to a percentage of those included under civil

[16] Better Government Personnel, Report of the Commission of Inquiry on Public Service Personnel, p. 92.

PARTY ORGANIZATION

service and those included in the group chosen by fixed standards through violations of civil-service laws, evasion of civil-service systems, and violation of established standards, but how large a percentage cannot be said. It is safe to say that the number of positions subject to political control will total a million—probably more.

The parties, then, have before them upward of a million appointive positions to help to strengthen the party organization. These positions can be given to party workers as rewards for party service; they can be controlled to grant privileges and immunities to party members; and they can be obtained by party leaders and party workers for the purpose of furnishing them a living, giving them prestige and experience, and also a vantage point from which they can carry on their work in the party organization.

The extent to which the available public positions have been usurped by the party organizations differs in the various jurisdictions. In the federal service it is customary for a party, when it gains control of the government, to see to it that the positions not in the classified service are held by party supporters. This practice can be seen upon a change of parties in control of the government, for then a large number of changes are made in personnel. When Harding came into office in 1921 after eight years of Democratic administration, thousands of changes were made in personnel and it was seen again when President Roosevelt came into office after eight years of Republican rule.[17]

It is customary for the party to place its supporters in all cabinet positions. These appointees are nearly always outstanding leaders in the party organization. Ambassadorships and ministerial posts are given to persons in high standing in the

[17] The following figures show a comparison of the number of first-, second-, and third-class postmasters confirmed during the administration of President Harding and President Roosevelt:

Harding Administration	Roosevelt Administration
1921 1385	1933 90
1922 7492	1934 4698
1923 3140	1935 3369
1924 4289	

organization, or those who finance the party generously. The other positions for the most part are given to party supporters upon the recommendation of the Senators or Representatives. In many cases these appointees are members of the party organization in the states; if not, then usually they have been regular party workers.

Postmasterships especially are used to strengthen the party organization. Until 1908 postmasters were subject to appointment without restrictions, fourth class by the Postmaster General, and first, second, and third class by the President with the approval of the Senate. In 1908, by executive order, Theodore Roosevelt transferred all fourth-class postmasterships in the fourteen states north of the Ohio River and east of the Mississippi River to the classified service, thus adding 15,488 positions to the competitive service; and in 1912 President Taft extended the classification to the fourth-class postmasters in other states. First-, second-, and third-class postmasters remained subject to appointment by the President with the consent of the Senate, without restriction, until 1917. The system that prevailed was that the Representatives and Senators nominated the candidates, and the President ratified them. Those recommended were strong party men or men valuable to the party.[18]

In 1917 President Wilson by executive order provided that vacancies by death, resignation or removal or changes made for the good of the service in first-, second-, and third-class postmasterships should be filled by the nominations of the highest eligible obtained by civil-service examination. In 1921 President Harding changed this order by allowing selection from the highest three eligible and extended the system to vacancies by expiration of term. Under this system Representatives and Senators were successful in nearly every case in having selected a Republican from among the highest three eligibles. In 1933 Franklin D. Roosevelt by executive order gave the Postmaster General power to disqualify any certified candidate at will, a

[18] See Frank M. Stewart, *The National Civil Service Reform League—History, Activities, and Problems*, pp. 115 ff.

provision which allows as many examinations as desired for the same vacancy. The President's order also disqualified incumbent postmasters from competing at the end of their four-year term, and excluded classified employees in the presidential postoffices from competition. Of the 46,000 postmasterships in the United States in 1933, approximately 13,700 were not included in the civil-service system and were open to appointment by the President with the consent of the Senate. These positions constitute an important part of the patronage used to strengthen the party throughout the country. The party in power selects for these positions members of that party, or party supporters who have the political influence, prestige and time to maintain the party's strength in the locality.[19]

Positions in state governments are used generally to support the party organization. Only ten states have civil-service laws, and in one of them, Kansas, the law is inoperative because of lack of appropriation. It is estimated that about a third of the state employees are subject to civil service.[20]

Great reliance is placed upon the state positions by those responsible for maintaining the party organization. A description of the system used in Pennsylvania whereby the party makes use of these positions will serve to indicate the emphasis placed upon them by party managers.

The system is based upon a county sponsorship system. The party leader of the county is the recognized sponsor for the county. Often he is a member of the governor's cabinet, or

[19] An executive order issued in July, 1936, provides that vacancies in first-, second-, and third-class postmasterships shall be filled by one of two methods: the Postmaster General may recommend to the President the appointment of the incumbent or the appointment by promotion of a classified employee in the postal service after being found eligible by the Civil Service Commission by non-competitive examination; or upon request of the Postmaster General the Civil Service Commission shall hold an open competitive examination to test the fitness of applicants, and the President must appoint the highest eligible unless it is established to the satisfaction of the Civil Service Commission that the character or residence of such eligible disqualifies him for appointment.

[20] Better Government Personnel, p. 92.

a legislator, or he holds some other state position. It is customary for the party official responsible for maintaining the party organization to hold an important state position, such as the governor's secretary, personnel secretary, secretary of state, or other cabinet position.

When a vacancy is to be filled, the party authority at the state capital asks for a recommendation from one of the county sponsors. Rarely is an appointment made from one of the counties without the approval of the county sponsor. County sponsors have many promises of jobs charged up to them by those who have been doing the party's political work in the county, and to those the jobs go.

Once a man is appointed, neither the county sponsor nor the central party authority loses sight of him. The county sponsors remind the employees, if they need reminding, that their services are needed during political campaigns, and call upon them to perform services in their official capacity for county party members. The party official at the state capital "expects" in strong terms that "voluntary" contributions will be made to the campaign fund as election day nears, and takes it for granted that the employees will be faithful to their county sponsors in doing political work.

And so throughout these state departments, and holding membership on boards and commissions, are to be found the important party officials and many of the minor party officials, as well as many others who regularly work for and support the party.

In many local jurisdictions the party organizations and the public positions have become greatly intermingled. A study completed in Philadelphia in 1935 shows in that city a situation which in all probability exists in many cities and counties throughout the country.[21] It was discovered that of the 3132 precinct committeemen, 1828, or 58 per cent, were holding public positions. In some wards the percentage of committeemen on the public payroll was much higher—93 per cent in one

[21] David H. Kurtzman, *Methods of Controlling Votes in Philadelphia.*

of the wards, 90 per cent in two of the wards, 85 per cent in another, and ranging down to 30 per cent, the lowest.[22] The public positions held were federal, state, city and county. Most of them were county positions because most of the city jobs are under civil service and there is a law prohibiting city employees from holding party positions. These were the precinct committeemen. The study reveals also that of the fifty members of the city committee, nearly all of whom were ward leaders, forty-six were holding public positions, appointive or elective.

A still better way of realizing the extent to which the party organization has taken over the public positions is to examine more closely the situation in some of the county offices. In the Bureau of Weights and Measures, of 118 employees 98, or 82 per cent, were party committeemen. In the office of the Board of Revision of Taxes, 43 of the 53 employees, 81 per cent, were committeemen. In the office of the Clerk of Quarters Sessions, 88 of the 110 employees, 80 per cent, were committeemen. In the Sheriff's office, 133 of the 170 employees, 78 per cent, were committeemen. In the office of the Recorder of Deeds, 209 of the 279 positions, 75 per cent, had been appropriated for party purposes.[23]

The study shows clearly that in Philadelphia public positions have become the main framework upon which the party organization is built. They are made to serve the party in many important respects. In the first place, the salaries become the compensation for the party officials; the 1828 committeemen holding public positions in Philadelphia received $4,090,086 in total yearly salary. The forty-six city committee members mentioned above received yearly salaries of $253,400. And in other important ways these public positions are made to serve the organization, in obtaining other positions for party workers, in overlooking violations of the law, in imposing lower real estate assessments, in securing release from jury service, in directing welfare aid, and in other ways.

[22] *Ibid.*, See p. 48.
[23] *Ibid.* See table opposite p. 55.

It appears that the theory held by many practical party men—that patronage is essential to the maintenance of virile party organization—is holding sway in this country. That patronage is the price of democracy is believed by many. Recognizing the situation, the Commission of Inquiry on Public Service Personnel stated that in great sections of the United States, and in other democracies of the world, democracy exists, political life is maintained, parties thrive, without the spoliation of the appointive administrative services. The Commission asserted: "The truth is, as Theodore Roosevelt once observed, that patronage is the curse of politics. It is the selling-out price of democracy, because of itself it turns the political party into a job-brokerage machine, creating a mercenary army of occupation, which under the guise of democracy, robs us of self government."[24]

From both the party and the public standpoint there is good reason to urge the prevention of this intermingling of party and public positions, because this condition places parties on an unequal basis. The party in control of the administration has a great advantage over the opposing parties which have no such control. With parties on so unequal a basis, it cannot be known which principles, policies and candidates have public acceptance. Often a party oligarchy is built up which battens upon the public positions and is able over a long period of time to maintain a monopoly in the area in which it operates. Opposing parties find mere existence a difficult matter, and at times exist only because by law the dominant party has been prevented from throwing its tentacles around all of the public positions.

After the foregoing discussion, some observations about party organization in the United States can be made. One of the outstanding characteristics of the situation is that only two parties, the Republican and the Democratic, have nation-wide organizations. Both of these parties are organized nationally, in each of the forty-eight states, in each of the counties, in the larger cities, and in practically all of the precincts. No other

[24] *Better Government Personnel,* p. 18.

PARTY ORGANIZATION

political party approaches these two in the extent of their organization. The Socialist party is organized nationally, state and locally, but it falls far short of the two major parties in the extent of its organization. The smaller parties are very limited in the extent of their organizations.

It is noticeable, too, that the organizations of the two major parties are similar in form. They run in terms of the governmental divisions—federal, state, county, city, ward, township and precinct. The chief reason for the existence of the party organization in any governmental district is control of the elective offices and policies in that district, and accordingly the party organization is made to conform to those districts. It has developed that in many districts there is now a strong secondary motive, the desire to control the appointive offices as well as the elective. One of the outstanding characteristics of the parties today is the great extent to which they have built the public positions into their own framework. The truth of the matter is that taxpayers are, in large measure, maintaining the political parties by means of salaries to public officials who are at the same time party officials, and by providing patronage. The amounts contributed to the parties in the form of campaign funds is small compared to the regular support which comes from the public treasury.

While both parties have nation-wide organizations and are similar in form, the organizations are not equal in strength in all areas. In the first place, there is advantage, from an organization point of view, to the party which controls the government within the area in which it operates. When in control of the governmental offices in a district, the party not only has its officials as leaders in the elective offices, but has secured control over the much more numerous appointive positions. In practically all governmental jurisdictions these positions are used to compensate those who are in the organization or are needed in building it up. The truth of the matter is that the party which controls the government brings a large army of public officials into its organization.

And then, too, the party in control of the government is in a position to appropriate funds for undertakings which inure to the benefit of the party, and to dispense services and grant privileges in many forms. The Democratic party has had tremendous advantages over its rival during the past three and a half years in developing its organization because not only has it been in control of the federal government in both the executive and legislative branches,[25] but it has had control of more than three-fourths of the state governments and has made great gains in establishing control of local governments. A good illustration of the development of the Democratic organization in a district which for years had been overwhelmingly Republican is seen in Philadelphia. There, for many years, only a few thousand were registered as members of that party, and only a skeleton organization existed, principally built around those holding the minority public offices provided by law. Only a small part of the divisions (precincts) of the city were organized. Now the Democratic party has registered as members about three hundred thousand voters. It has its city committee, a ward leader in every ward, and a committeeman in every division in the city. It is now as thoroughly organized in Philadelphia as is the Republican party. Many other similar illustrations of the development of the Democratic party in local areas are to be found throughout the United States.

Huge federal and state appropriations, with billions of dollars given in direct payment to individuals throughout the country, to the farmers, to those working on relief projects and to those receiving direct aid, and many others, have brought into the Democratic party workers and membership; and thousands of Democratic party officials have received positions as compensation for their political work and to secure their continued support. The Republican party has had the problem of maintaining its organization, although its officials and workers by

[25] In the Senate there are 69 Democrats, 23 Republicans; in the House 318 Democrats, 104 Republicans. The Republican party has no representation in the House from twenty-three states, the Democratic party has representatives from all but three.

the thousands have had their means of support taken away and the party has had little appropriating powers at a time when the needs of the people have been most urgent. Whatever strength is to be gained through control of government must be gained by the Republican party primarily in its control over local governments, where, outside of the Southern States, it is still considered to have an advantage over the Democratic party. Readers may recall the consoling message given by William Allen White to his fellow Republicans after the Roosevelt victory in 1932, wherein he reminded them that there were still a great many Republican court houses.

The organization of the two major parties is very unequal in a large section of the United States comprising ten Southern States. Writing more than thirty years ago, an outstanding observer described the situation there as being, from the point of view of party organization, abnormal. At that time he said: "There are no fairly balanced party forces, and this because there is no free voting constituency to which the two parties have access upon equal terms, and to which each may appeal by argument in fair debate for political support. Instead are two sharply distinguished constituencies, one of which belongs, as it were of right, to the Democratic party and the other to the Republican. The former party, having the command of the sources of political power, is, in effect, the actual government of the states, and under the guise of party, has supplanted both the former state governments and true party government also."[26]

The situation which he described exists today as it did then. The Democratic party is strongly organized not so much to maintain Democratic supremacy as to maintain white supremacy in controlling state and local offices. The Republican party is not considered a serious contender for state and local offices or for the electoral vote. Although in 1928 the Republican party won the electoral vote of Florida, North Carolina, Tennessee, Texas and Virginia, this was due, primarily, to the prohibition and

[26] Jesse Macy, *Party Organization and Machinery*, p. 186.

religious issues raised, not to improvement of its organization in those states.

The Republican party has in each of the Southern States a state committee, but very little in the way of local organization. The state committee organization is maintained primarily by federal patronage in those states when the Republican party is in control at Washington; when it is out, the organization continues upon the hope of the party's return to power. But with no state and local patronage the party has not been able to build effective units in local districts of the states. Little attention is given by the party to building up its organization there because of the remoteness of the possibility of capturing the electoral vote of any of these states. Instead, the party acts upon the belief that more can be gained by concentrating its attention upon other regions where its handicap is not so great.

Another characteristic of the two major parties is that they are loosely knit, with no direct lines of authority running from the top of the organization to the bottom. The national committee has no direct authority over the state committees, nor have the state committees authority over the county and city committees. It is only within some of the county and city organizations that there is direct authority; but even there laws prescribing the election of committee members have attempted to break up strict control. These great machines must be operated without direct lines of authority such as are found in large businesses. They are managed by securing cooperation among the various units, and practical methods have been established for this purpose.

One of the chief methods used to secure cooperation is through overlapping membership on committees. State committeemen are often members of the national committee, and on the state committees will be found many members of county and city committees. In some states the state committee is composed of the chairmen of local committees. County committees are usually made up of the precinct committeemen, and city committees usually comprise the chairmen of ward committees which latter committees are, in turn, composed of precinct committeemen.

Another great force for making the unwieldy organization operate is the use of public positions to insure party service. For faithful party service, men are supported for the elective offices, or receive appointive positions. Retention of the positions depends upon their continued party service.

The organization must be made to function in spite of the fact that the party provides no direct compensation for any of its officials. One of the reasons why it functions is that there are numerous forms of indirect compensation. One of these forms, public positions, has just been mentioned. To many men the only reason for serving a party is to get compensation in the form of a public job. Another form of compensation lies in the privileges and immunities which can be granted if the party controls the government, another in exercising control of legislative enactments, another in business which the party can be instrumental in giving to those who serve it, and some will help to make the party function because the prestige and honor of party positions are a compensation to them. The traditions and the principles of a party play a part in making it function, but to those who serve in the party offices year after year they play a minor rôle.

Another observation which stands out is that the party organization often functions in the nomination process as well as in promoting the election of candidates. This is true, although nominations are made by the direct primary method; perhaps it is not true to so great a degree as when nominations are made in conventions.[27] Because party organizations are entering the nomination contests, candidates do not stand on an equal footing. It was thought that the situation had been corrected when

---

[27] An outstanding example of the party organization functioning in the nomination process was seen in Pennsylvania in 1930, when the Philadelphia Republican organization supported Francis S. Brown for the Republican nomination for governor, against Gifford Pinchot. When Pinchot won the nomination the organization threw its support to the Democratic candidate in the election campaign.

the states provided primary elections, provided for meeting all expenses from the public treasury, and enacted laws forbidding the parties to enter the nomination process; but the most that can be said is that the situation has been only partially corrected.

It is noteworthy that the nomination process has been made a public expense in most of the states, but remains a party responsibility or partly a party responsibility in a few states, as well as does the process of nominating the candidates for the Presidency. It seems that the assumption of the responsibility for the nomination expenses by the state helps to keep the party organization out of the nomination process. The question of public financing of the presidential nominating process should be seriously considered.

It should be observed that the organizations of the parties are only the principal bodies; there are many auxiliaries clustering around them. There are scores of organizations outside of the parties whose primary purpose is the support of one or other of the parties. They are not provided for by either party rules or state laws, and usually they escape regulation by the states. There is, too, a large number, commonly called pressure groups, described in a later chapter, that are nonpartisan and will be found supporting one party or the other, depending upon the candidate and the issues. These organizations cannot be considered a part of the main body, but contribute a great deal of strength to it. Some of them cooperate so closely and so regularly with the parties that they in fact might be considered adjuncts.

A characteristic of the party organization is that it carries the national principles and purposes of the party down to the state, county, and the smallest units, the precincts, in order to insure the success of the national ticket. "To insure the success of a certain candidate for the Presidency," says Ostrogorski," it was necessary to have a national convention favorable to it; this could only be attained if the state convention from which the latter emanated were composed of members ready to choose

PARTY ORGANIZATION

their delegates from that point of view, and so on. In this way national politics, that is, relating to the presidential election, became the aim of the whole convention system, making all the elections, even the strictly local, purely municipal ones, contests of political parties waging war for the possession of the White House."[28] State and local candidates are carried along into office on the strength of the national ticket, and not placed there according to the voters' judgment on state and local issues. State and local politics become infused with national politics. This feature gives a character of unreality to state and local politics and greatly interferes with the decision of issues on their merits.

Some attempts have been made to alter this situation. Nonpartisan elections have that aim. While retaining the identity of the party organization, state and local elections in some states are held on different days and in different years from national elections.[29] Still another method of breaking up the influence of the national parties over local affairs is the formation of citizen organizations to deal only with local government problems. In his book on the Cincinnati experiment, Charles P. Taft asserts his belief "that a citizen organization can establish good local government and maintain it permanently on a business basis without patronage, without yielding to either national party, and without injuring either."[30]

In a democracy, organization is indispensable. Any group adopting principles and feeling that those principles should be established for all of the people of the state finds that without organization it is helpless in effectively promoting those principles. Organization is needed to establish a solidarity of interests among the members of the group. It is necessary to maintain a unified fighting front against those who oppose the principles which are being promoted. It is only thus that resources can

[28] M. Ostrogorski, *Democracy and the Party System*, vol. ii, p. 69.
[29] On this subject, see the article, "National Parties and Local Politics," by Ellen D. Ellis, *American Political Science Review*, February, 1935.
[30] Charles P. Taft, *City Management—The Cincinnati Experiment*, p. 5.

be pooled for use in the methods of party warfare. Democracy functions through leaders, and only through organization can leadership be made effective.

The true development of party organization, then, requires that it be made the means to the end and not the end itself. It should be developed to attempt to secure the adoption of principles which the group believes to be desirable.

The present-day major parties do not disband. They have become great permanent institutions with highly developed organizations which continue on and on, whether or not the principles advocated by them have been adopted. Often the party picks up new issues to keep the organization alive. In a very real sense party organization has become an end in itself. It may be argued that there is always a rôle for the party out of power to criticize the party in power, but much of the opposition has for its chief purpose the maintenance of the organization of the party. Thousands of persons secure their livelihood from the party organization, and to them it is an end in itself.

The question arises, whether, when our political affairs and our governments are managed by the great and highly organized permanent party institutions, democracy really exists. According to Michels, organization inevitably leads to oligarchy. "It is organization," he says, "which gives birth to the dominion of the elected over the electors, of the mandatories over the mandators, of the delegates over delegators. Who says organization says oligarchy."[31]

In this chapter have been discussed some of the attempts to break up oligarchical control within the party organization and to prevent such control from developing. The direct primary, popular election of party officers, prevention of the use of public positions for party purposes, all have that purpose. Some measure of success has been achieved, but constant vigilance and greater efforts are needed to make and keep the party organization responsive to the will of the people.

---

[31] Robert Michels, *Political Parties*, p. 401.

Chapter III: The Politician and the Voter

by J. T. SALTER
Associate Professor of Political Science, University of Wisconsin

I

THE politician is usually a specialist in the art of governing, either in a neighborhood or in a nation. He is a person who takes a hand in nominating and electing himself or someone else to public office and who spends his time between elections in exercising and maintaining whatever political power he has cornered. He usually campaigns because he definitely wants to direct the course of local, state or national government. In the majority of cases, however, the politician is as much interested in getting public recognition and in the excitement of political life as he is in the job itself; and his interest is neither casual nor spasmodic. Politics with him not only amounts to a profession, but actually *is* one.

It is a profession whose subject matter is human nature, whose data, like the lore of the medicine man among the Indians, are retained only in the minds of the living. Sometimes it is passed from father to son, or from friend to friend; but much is irretrievably lost whenever a politician dies. This body of knowledge that *is* politics, is the folklore of all the city halls of the land; it is the living language of the county court houses, the vivid and real talk in the corridors of state legislatures, and the personal conversations on the fringe of Congress. Much of it is as evanescent as smoke or as plum blossoms in the spring, but sometimes a word, an expression or an idea is permanently fixed in the annals of the craft.

The politician learns not only through the traditional apprentice-craftsman relationship, but also through direct contact with the people. His constituency is his test tube and the voters are the chemicals—or the voters, in relation to symbols and privileges, are the chemicals. The devotee of politics, like the neophyte in chemistry, must carefully observe his experiment under different temperatures or conditions, and learn what symbols and techniques will win a plurality of votes to one banner. The main thing for either the beginner or the old-timer in politics is to be able to look at life exactly as it is, and without a shudder. This qualification is common to the successful politicians of all ranks.

Moreover, the greater part of the body of knowledge that *is* politics is descriptive of all politics, whether urban or rural, local, state or national, for there is a constant—human nature —that is forever present. The stage setting varies, the lines are changed, but the actors are the same. As Colonel House said in the 1932 campaign: "The secret of success in a presidential election is to forget that it is a presidential election. There is a technique for electing a village constable. And there is a technique for electing a President. The formula in both cases is practically identical."[1]

II

Unfortunately for both the public and the politician in America, the term "politician" has evil connotations for the vast generality of citizens. In his Fourth of July oration Artemus Ward embodies this idea in his statement, "I am not a politician, and my other habits are good." An American of a very different sort, Henry Adams, tersely observed, "In politics, no man should be trusted."[2] Shakespeare expressed it not only for his age but apparently for our own when he applied the epithet, "scurvy politician,"[3] and again, "A politician . . . one

[1] "How to Make Either Candidate the Next President," *Cosmopolitan*, September, 1932.
[2] Henry Adams, *The Education of Henry Adams*, p. 151.
[3] *King Lear*, Act III, Scene 6, Line 175.

that would circumvent God."[4] Yet the feeling of distrust and smoldering suspicion we have for the species is truly remarkable in a land where the people fill more offices by popular election than does all the rest of the world combined, and, furthermore, when it is plainly evident that the people have the power to relegate any politician to private life by merely refusing to vote for him or his party. It is also remarkable that those politicians who are most roundly denounced from press and pulpit are invariably individuals who have been elected to public office not once but many times; in some cases these targets of the public's ire have been elected to a lifetime of offices. As Dean Inge once remarked, "There is no gratitude in politics"; and the American public does indeed seem to have no permanent feeling of gratitude for those doing her public business.

Either this is true, or else those who speak and write about politicians are expressing something other than the general view. Or, what is more reasonable to believe, a stereotype has been fashioned of the politician horrible! This stereotype, like a coin, is freely passed around without thought, and it may not at all correspond to a politician whom one knows personally. Moreover, the majority of citizens suffer either from envy or a holier-than-thou attitude when thinking of this creature who has won the people's mandate. They may attempt to justify their own unfulfilled ambitions or to bolster up their egos by loudly damning him (though these critics are not likely to give even a superficial thought to the resemblances between their own more secret actions as business or professional men and the loudly publicized activities of the politician). Whatever the reasons may be, there is little doubt that he has become a veritable whipping boy for the American people.

Those who scorn the politician and who consider him and his activities beneath their notice are answered once and for all by Walter Lippmann in a brilliant article in *Vanity Fair*, in which he cites a remark of George Jean Nathan, the dramatic

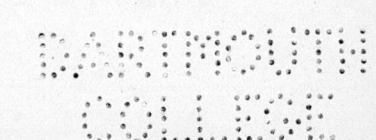

[4] *Hamlet*, Act V, Scene 1.

critic, to the effect that politics is a "low concern" for which he and his friends have no time. Lippmann contrasts the ease there is in coming to grips with a play in which "a creative mind has intervened between the audience" as compared with the ordeal of coming face to face "with what William James used to call the 'blooming, buzzing confusion of reality.' In politics you have to take reality in the raw. For the spectator and the reviewer the theatre is relatively effortless, because the creative effort has been made in advance. But when Mr. Nathan picks up a newspaper, he is driven, if he is to make head or tail of it, to know much that is not apparent, to disentangle the sense from the nonsense, in short, to do his own creative sweating. . . . Now the art of governing happens to be one of the most difficult arts which men practice. It is more difficult, I think it is fair to say, than reviewing plays. It may even be more difficult than writing plays. At least there have been more masterpieces produced in the theatre than in the chancelleries. The art of governing is often practised by absurd amateurs. Like all the arts, especially the theatre, it attracts a host of second-raters and fakers. I do not think Mr. Nathan could surprise me with any new stupidity in politics. But when I am told that this art is a low concern, I set down the man who tells me that as just a trifle dumb."[5]

Mr. Dooley, the wise and humorous political commentator of the period around the turn of the century, presents another slant on the art of politics in its typical American sense. "Politics 'ain't bean-bag.' 'Tis a man's game; an' women, childher and prophybitionists'd do well to keep out iv it." And although women have not kept out of politics, and more women are entering it every year, it still is a most strenuous trade. At another time this political philosopher made an observation about politics that is as valid today as it was in 1900: "Th' reason th' New York jood thinks marrid men oughtn't to be in pollytics is because he thinks pollytics is spoort. An' so it is. But

[5] "The Enormously Civilized Minority," *Vanity Fair*, March, 1928.

it ain't amachoor spoort, Hinnissy. They don't give ye a pewter mug with ye'er name on it f'r takin' a chanst on bein' kilt. 'Tis a profissional spoort, like playin' base-ball f'r a livin' or wheelin' a thruck. Ye niver see an amachoor at annything that was as good as a profissional. Th' best amachoor ball team is beat be a bad profissional team; a profissional boxer that thrains on bock beer an' Swiss cheese can lam the head off a goold medal amachoor champeen that's been atin' moldy bread an' dhrinkin' wather f'r six month, an' th' Dago that blows th' cornet on th' sthreet f'r what annyman'll throw him can cut the figure eight around Dinnis Finn, that's been takin' lessons f'r twenty year. No, sir, pollytics ain't dhroppin' into tea, an' it ain't wurrukin' a scroll saw, or makin' a garden in a back yard. 'Tis gettin' up at six o'clock in the mornin' an' r-rushin' off to wurruk, an' comin' home at night tired an' dusty. Double wages f'r overtime an' Sundahs."[6]

F. S. Oliver, the biographer of Robert Walpole, the great English politician of the eighteenth century, recently had this to say about the nobility of politics: "It is this uncertainty, with its various consequences, that makes politics the most hazardous of all manly professions. If there is not another in which a man can hope to do so much good to his fellow-creatures, neither is there any in which, by a cowardly act or by a mere loss of nerve, he may do such widespread harm. Nor is there another in which he may so easily lose his own soul. But danger is the inseparable companion of honour. The greatest deeds in history were not done by people who thought of safety first. It is possible to be too much concerned even with one's own salvation. There will not be much hope left for humanity when men are no longer willing to risk their immortal as well as their mortal parts. With all the temptations, dangers and degradations that beset it, politics is still, I think, the noblest career that any man can choose."[7]

[6] *Mr. Dooley's Philosophy*, p. 142.
[7] *Politics and Politicians*, p. 82.

III

There are certain unique factors that have, generally speaking, determined the class of men that have gone into politics in this country. Civilized man has never found a land so rich in natural resources as was the United States of the eighteenth and nineteenth centuries; and at first the individual was free to exploit the prodigality of nature as he would. The less government the better, was the idea. The early American learned to fend for himself and he took what he could hold. The interests of the whole were sacrificed to the enterprise of the few. This was thought to be the way of progress, and those who took the most were given the most prestige in the community and the nation. The most enterprising and ambitious youths in the land were, naturally enough, under the great incentives of possible wealth and social recognition, drawn into the private worlds of commerce and finance. The dollar sign, not public service, was the mark of sterling worth. And the result was that the less gifted or adventuresome turned to politics. Furthermore, about the time that Andrew Jackson was elected to the Presidency, the general idea was stated, and later widely accepted, that anyone was worthy of any public office that he could get. The bars were down. The average man turned longing eyes toward politics. The people recognized him as their own—denounced him and gave him their votes. Since that time the American voter has tended to vote for someone like himself and to ignore the candidacies of his betters. The successful candidates were born in log cabins, or they pretended that they were. There was no leisure class; and when American society included men independently wealthy, they were more likely to buy yachts than to campaign for aldermanic posts. That office carries prestige and ceremonial dignity in England, but not here; and since men work for recognition as well as cash, the urge to go into public service in this country is weakened right at the outset. Those in public office lack the support of great traditions, and they know there is no "sense of state" in the American people. It is an interesting reflection upon the attitude of the "rich and well born" among us to remember the remark of Sarah Delano Roosevelt, that when her son Franklin was first elected to the state senate in New York a number of her friends sympathized with her as though some dire calamity had come upon the family. She herself felt differently, and was proud of her boy for entering the public service. Of 614 Harvard men of the class of 1911 who are now alive, 500 recently replied to a question as to what they have done with their lives. John R. Tunis, in analyzing their answers, had this to say about their attitude toward politics: "Most of us have done nothing for good government except vote once a year; those evincing a desire to improve the lot of the community are in the minority. . . . We are almost barren of leaders of public life. We have produced no mayors of cities, no state governors, no members of Congress in the past twenty-five years."[8] When Theodore Roosevelt was a young man and about to enter politics, he was warned off by men in his social class who told him that his kind of people did not go into politics. "I answered that if this were so it merely meant that the people I knew did not belong to the governing class, and that other people did— and that I intended to be one of the governing class; that if they proved too hard-bit for me I supposed I would have to quit, but that I certainly would not quit until I had made the effort and found out whether I really was too weak to hold my own in the rough and tumble."[9]

Political life and attitudes do not exist apart from the other interests of man. The mores of men in politics are naturally identical with their mores in business, the professions or in their private dealings, save, as Delisle Burns says, that "there is more room for quackery in politics, since the problems are more complex and our ignorance more complete than in the case of

[8] "Twenty-fifth Reunion," *Scribner's Magazine,* vol. xcix, no. 6 (June, 1936), pp. 325-326.
[9] Theodore Roosevelt, *Autobiography,* p. 56.

medicine."[10] And since more than half a million persons are sentenced to one penal institution or another in this country every year, it is reasonable to believe that there are crooks in public as well as in private life. Thomas M. Farley, Sheriff of New York County, was found by the Seabury Committee to have deposited $396,000 in a six-year period in which his estimated total income was $90,000, and he could (or would) not explain the source of the other $306,000. In the spring of 1936 an investigation of the Highway Committee of Dane County, Wisconsin, disclosed the fact that county officials had paid a number of highway bills twice, and that the county had been paying premiums on compensation insurance for phantom employees. Great publicity was given to the Farley and other findings of the Seabury Committee in New York. The newspapers of Dane County fully reported the revealed shortcomings of the Dane County Highway Committee. In each case the public doubtless chalked up one more black mark against the politicians. Yet during the past few years bankers in both New York and Wisconsin have been sentenced to the penitentiary, and although the arrests and convictions of these men have been reported in the newspapers, the public in neither case has reached a point where it is condemning bankers generally (although in 1933 it was approaching it. Roosevelt probably saved the bankers from the fate that has befallen the politician). The bankers and business men escape public censure when they are revealed in anti-social acts because the public has not yet come to see the fundamental relationships between the banker and the public that it sees between the politician and the public. The people vote for the politician; he, the man in public office, is their man—or he got in over their opposition. The politician makes promises, and the promises are often capable of various interpretations. Or the individual voter may suffer in a period of economic distress and blame the politician, even though the man in public office is doing all that anyone can do. It is obviously true that what the politician says and does depends

[10] Delisle Burns, *Political Ideals*, p. 335.

THE POLITICIAN AND THE VOTER

usually on what the people demand of him; and since it is easier to think in terms of a personality than in terms of a social and economic situation the generality of voters may never know that "it is a system that confronts the people, not an individual."[11] As F. S. Oliver has so well said: "And in justice to him [the politician] and also to ourselves whose servant he is, we should not lay the whole blame on *his* shoulders, or on our own peculiar system of government, *but on the unchangeable conditions of the art of governing men.*"[12] Earlier he refers to the stream of detraction in these words: "What humbug it is, for the most part! And what a welter should we be in, if the politicians, taking these lectures to heart, were to hand over the management of public affairs to their critics!"[13] Welter, I think, is too mild a term—revolution is more descriptive of what would happen in our democracy. And after the forces of chaos had been spent or brought under control we would again find politicians in the saddle.

This derogatory attitude toward public officials is not only "the most expensive luxury in America,"[14] but it is as unwise

---

[11] J. T. Salter, *Boss Rule: Portraits in City Politics*, p. 249.
[12] F. S. Oliver, *Politics and Politicians*, p. 79. (Italics mine.)
[13] *Ibid.*, p. 78.
[14] "I do not hesitate to say that the most expensive luxury in America today is the widespread opinion that government is necessarily weak, ignorant, corrupt and contemptible. This attitude costs not only millions, but billions of dollars annually because it poisons the springs of governmental interest, enthusiasm and service.

"This boycott of government and public life makes difficult the recruitment of the personnel necessary for government. It invites spoilsmen and racketeers and drives away many of those who might best serve the state. It produces higher costs and lower achievement levels.

"Government is not a pest or a blight or a necessary evil—it has an important and real function to perform in modern life. Men are not paid merely in dollars and cents, but in terms of social regard and respect. They will work as hard to be well thought of as to be well paid. The continuing denunciation of the uselessness of government and its agents will tend to discredit the public service at the very moment when it might well be built up and made still more serviceable to the community. Out in the country we used to have fires where the volunteer firemen sometimes did more damage than the flames." "Boycott of Government Costly," *Public Management*, vol. xiv, no. 4 (April, 1932), p. 115.

and illogical as the belief that all people living in odd-numbered houses, or on the west side of the street, are dishonest. There are obviously both kinds on both sides, and there are both kinds in public office. Lincoln and Theodore Roosevelt were professional politicians. Whenever we in the United States have had a great President we have had in him a great political leader and a successful politician. And these politicians are not Houdinis who can take votes out of a big black hat where none exists. Rather, as I have said elsewhere, the politician is "a natural phenomenon, not a legal device; and he is a prototype of his people, not a 'sport' or a freak. In fact, in viewing a politician that has been representing the people for ten, twenty, thirty, or more years, I have often felt that I was seeing his constituency in miniature—not all of it, but its basic quality. In normal times he is the expression of the general tenor of his people."[15] The LaFollettes are descriptive of Wisconsin, William Borah of Idaho, Carter Glass of Virginia, Jack Garner of Texas, Key Pittman of Nevada, Pat Harrison of Mississippi. And in the recent past Alfalfa Bill Murray was Oklahoma, Vare was a basic expression of Philadelphia, Jimmie Walker of New York, Big Bill Thompson of Chicago. Still earlier in our history Theodore Roosevelt was the America of expansion and the square deal following the turn of the century; Wilson was an expression of the new freedom and the crusading America fighting for world justice and world peace; Harding expressed the America home from the wars—the return to normalcy; Coolidge, the idea of minding our own business and conserving our resources; Hoover, business efficiency and two chickens in every pot. Then came the crash, and the mood of America changed. The 'let well enough alone' philosophy disappeared with prosperity and in its place the American people demanded action on the part of their government. Franklin Roosevelt met that demand so adequately that in 1933 and 1934 Roosevelt was America—so much so, in fact, that the New York *Times* editorially characterized the 1934 election as "an individual triumph

[15] J. T. Salter, *Boss Rule: Portraits in City Politics*, p. 244.

for the President such as never came to any of his predecessors, whether in peace time or in war."[16]

This next election is the reagent that will measure the extent to which the President still expresses the mood of America. If he does express it he will be returned, and if he doesn't he will be supplanted. This is quite elementary, and I think that the logic of Huey Long's statement to a reporter about himself, "Say, I am *sui generis*," is almost as inescapable. And I think that it also follows that the politicians that have repeatedly been elected by the voters in a certain constituency are a cross-grain of the majority of citizens in that constituency. Although the people do not select someone like themselves when they want a doctor or a lawyer, they do when they are voting for a public official. And perhaps this may be one reason why the politician is criticized, as an unretouched photograph is protested against by the subject. In some cases, the more faithful the likeness the more vigorous the protest. (The lady wanted her picture taken while she was under a soft light and in the midst of her most satisfactory smile!) If the American voter does not recognize his politician, it may be because this particular voter is extraordinary and in no sense an average voter; or if he is average and fails to recognize the politician as his own, then it follows that he does not know himself or his kind. (Of course, this would not be true in a land where votes were cast solely because of the merit and integrity of the candidate.)[17]

IV

The career men in politics, as I have said before, are often colorful figures. They are the most out-and-out human beings I know. Many of them are characters, even as Tracy Tupman, Augustus Snodgrass, Nathaniel Winkle and their friends in *Pickwick Papers*, are characters. They have been stained by their perpetual quest for votes—the imprint of democracy is on

[16] November 8, 1934.
[17] When the Republicans nominated Landon, William Allen White described him in these words: "Kansas is Landon and Landon is Kansas incarnate. . . ."

them, and therein they are much alike; but in their ways, their personal appearance, their individual habits, there is entertaining and endless variety. Moreover, theirs is a picturesque speech filled with arresting metaphors, similes and colloquial idiom. The man on the street recognizes the language as his own—it is "United States," not Europe.

Furthermore, one who knows politicians intimately is often reminded of Lincoln Steffens' comment about Charlie Prodger: "He was something of a politician, and I was made to feel that there was something bad about a politician. I did not know what it was that was bad, but I did not care in the case of Charlie Prodger. I loved the sight of him coming, dapper and handsome, smiling, toward me; and I had, and I have now, a deep, unreasoning respect for him. *What grown-ups call good and bad are not what us boys call good and bad.*"[18]

And one might add that what the writers, preachers and orators call good and bad is not always what the majority of people call good and bad. For the politicians are judged by both an indoor and an outdoor code—one that is private and personal and used by the insiders; another that is public, impersonal and formal. The second code holds with the League of Women Voters, "Not the job for the man, but the man for the job"; the first code is the cornerstone of our major parties—the man who brings in the most votes deserves the best job.

Politicians have certain fundamental characteristics in common. All of them, for example, are rigorously contemporaneous. They are concerned not with the ultimate verdict of history, but rather with the election returns today. They, unlike the poet or the philosopher, must be recognized by the people between 7 A.M. and 7 P.M. on a certain day, or their capacity for governing will be of no avail. Johann Sebastian Bach died in comparative obscurity, and today no name is brighter than his in the world of music. But there is no such postponing of glory in the field of politics. The person must be indorsed when the ballots are marked, or he can never be known in the annals of statecraft.

[18] *The Autobiography of Lincoln Steffens*, p. 15. (Italics mine.)

This applies to workers in townships and wards as well as to candidates for the Senate and the Presidency.

Furthermore, the politician, unlike certain bank presidents I know, is a personal individual. He is not like the figure on the cover of the *Saturday Evening Post*—all guff without substance. He has three dimensions. He sees "you" and "me"—he is aware of people. He naturally (or so it seems) meets his casual constituent with a smile, and a pleasant greeting, and often a chat. He is a specialist in personal relationships. He is doubly appreciated in a world that is too vast for the individual—in a great society in which all of the members are strangers or act as though they were. The more lowly the person, the more certain is the attention of the politician. And of course, the politician is *necessarily* in this business of making friends, for friendship is his capital; strangers do not vote, and enemies vote for someone else. I cite the letter of the Hon. John Steven McGroarty of California to one of his constituents as the *antithesis* of the typical correspondence of a Congressman. This Congressman is the poet laureate of California (the legislature so proclaimed him) and is different.

"One of the countless drawbacks of being in Congress is that I am compelled to receive impertinent letters from a jackass like you in which you say I promised to have the Sierra Madre Mountains reforested and I've been in Congress two months and haven't done it.

"Will you please take two running jumps and go to hell?"[19]

The more characteristic attitude is the one we find attributed to President F. D. Roosevelt in the following statement:

"One thing which handicaps the President in maintaining discipline and harmony among his official family is his deep love of people because they are people. This love is genuine and profound. He may disapprove of their actions, he may resent the fact that they cause him political difficulties, but he tolerates them. Time after time the President has shown the temerity to

[19] *Time*, March 25, 1935.

break with tradition, but he is a coward when it comes to breaking with a friend."[20]

Another identifying characteristic common to politicians as a rule is a marked willingness to talk. Talk is certainly a staple of the trade, and they are usually eager for it. Given a good listener, a comfortable chair in City Hall, an office, a club, a home, and a cigar to smoke or break in the middle and chew, and the flow of conversation will continue until there is some decisive interruption. In many departments of the city government official duties are not pressing and conditions are ideal for leisurely conversation—so satisfactory that long ago I learned never to make a call on a politician without a full stomach. He is no respecter of the luncheon hour, and I am always loath to end a good story. A politician who would not think of lending an individual a dollar bill or a greater sum might willingly spend an hour or two talking to him. He gives one a feeling that there is ample time, that the day is spacious, and that the present moment is really satisfactory for conversation.

Furthermore, let me repeat, the politician is "of the people." One might imagine a great mass of pliant clay, all of the same texture, and call it a constituency; and were one to pinch a piece off from the mass he might call this the politician. He is just like the rest of the mass (so far as his moral taste and general attitude are concerned); the only difference is that he is only one and therefore easier to see. And just as the politician is part of the people, he almost invariably has a realistic and positive knowledge of the people. He is usually interested, for one reason or another, in their personal problems. If he were not, the countless demands upon him would be intolerable. He is, above all, a social person, and thrives on the warm embrace of the crowd. He likes to be with folks and feel that he is important to them. He is not a thinker, a reader, or a dreamer in an isolated study. He is available to any person in need whenever he can be found; he has no office hours. He is, moreover,

---

[20] Drew Pearson and Robert S. Allen, "How the President Works," *Harper's*, June, 1936.

a dramatist who captures the attention of the electorate; he is a diplomat and an empirical psychologist; he is a man of action, and the possessor of a tough skin. Usually he is one who can forgive and forget, and he understands that he cannot indulge in the luxury of personal hatreds. He is a social worker not interested in reform. And he is most often the special agent of a vested interest—the party organization; and the party organization may, in turn, be controlled, or markedly influenced, by economic interests in the constituency.

The greatest politicians must have the flair for characterizing a social or political situation in a flash. My best illustration of this concerns Gandhi. A few years ago an elaborate address was delivered in his honor before some thousands of persons at Lucknow. It happens that at Lucknow the purest Urdu is spoken. Immediately after the address, Gandhi rose to his feet and in the most dramatic manner said, "What, you of Lucknow, in the land of the classic Urdu, speak to me in English?" and indignantly sat down. He had made his point against the British. He refused to say another word to the people assembled. The effect on the thousands was electric. The fact that this was a self-made situation against the British and that those in India who are most anti-British, and even Gandhi himself, speak English most of the time did not change this situation from being a most dramatic one.[21]

If the politician is an orator or an effective public speaker, he has an additional and invaluable string to his bow. This ability to speak interestingly to large groups is indispensable in some constituencies that are not larger than assembly districts but where traditions of oratory have been built up; in a wider number of districts this quality is especially important in times of economic depression, when increasing numbers of voters turn questioning minds toward politics. And, finally, the larger the constituency the more essential the persuasive speaking voice. It is a possession more essential to aspirants for the Presidency than it is to contenders for the mayoralty. But even here, party

[21] Conversation with Professor Philo Buck.

organization and money have elevated more men to the Presidency than has eloquence. Bryan, the silver-voiced orator, was three times defeated. O'Brien was elected mayor of New York in a depression year because he had the backing of an effective party organization and in spite of abysmal shortcomings as a public speaker. Roosevelt's friendly and persuasive voice will count for much in the election just ahead, but so will the minutiae of political organization, perfected by Farley and some hundreds of thousands of lesser individuals. The gist of the matter seems to be this: The problem confronting a candidate for public office is to capture the attention of a controlling number of the voters in his constituency—to carry his message to every single one of them, to motivate the voter so that he will first actually vote, and, secondly, vote right. Sometimes this is done through the magic of a single voice, but usually an army of sales agents known as political workers or neighborhood canvassers is required. To win in a constituency of any size, a candidate must have one or other of these supports, and often he has both. The LaFollettes have them in Wisconsin. Both the Senator and the Governor are most effective public speakers, but neither of them neglects his party organization. And finally, in addition to the various characteristics that I have just cited, the politician usually has political "it." Sometimes a leader may lack this quality and yet succeed because of his superior political judgment or wealth, but the majority of politicians that succeed have some flavor or quality about them that commands attention. They are usually persons of higher electrical voltage than the casual outsider—people who radiate some electric or psychic charge that attracts attention; they are probably more of a human dynamo than are their neighbors.

V

The lifelong politician wins elections not because he is mentally superior but because of his indefatigable energy and his willingness to stay close to the people. A prominent politician once told me, "To be successful in politics, you mustn't count

THE POLITICIAN AND THE VOTER

the hours; you go into the day and into the night." And in view of the time that the politician gives to his subject, it is surprising that his political judgment is not better. He can be far more adequately explained by his mental limitations than by his mental superiority. Politics is a life where lungs, liver, a strong stomach and a tough skin are primary requisites; if, in addition, a person has keen intellectual power, that may be an advantage to him. But such power is more apt to lead the possessor to other fields of activity where reason counts for more and where one can maintain his own identity and his own individual will. The great majority of lesser politicians are essentially individuals with single-track minds, and their success is more clearly grounded in leg work than in brain work.

The politician is the great promiser. Countless persons ask countless favors of him, and he, by his very nature and the nature of the work he is in, is interested in agreeing to all possible calls that come to him or demands that are made of him. The requests usually have something to do with the future; and unless the politician has learned by painful experience, he is likely to assume that he will be in a position to grant the favor asked. Then when the future comes he may be unable to carry out the promise he has made, and this discredits him. The clearest-headed politicians are most careful about the promises they make; the weaker ones are likely to err, not because they intend to deceive but rather because they are afraid or lack the sternness to say no. (The fact that so many more favors are asked of politicians than of professors or business men again intensifies this handicap against the former.) In his campaigns the politician may promise the people what he is going to do when he is elected to public office. But, logically, no man can really say what he is going to do in a given situation until he finds himself in that particular situation. The politician in office may view the problems confronting the electorate quite differently from the way he viewed them as an outsider. He may attempt to do the things that should be done, in spite of contrary promises that were given on his way to power. As prime minister, Gladstone once made a speech concerning an important governmental policy. After he had spoken, a close friend reminded him that five years before he had spoken very differently on the same issue. Gladstone merely remarked, "I was not prime minister then."

Nevertheless, the great majority of strong politicians are distinguished by a habit of not breaking their word to each other or to those with whom they have personal dealings. They are loyal men, although their loyalty is of a circumscribed and personal sort. Their relations are personal throughout, as were those of an old feudal state. There are serfs, barons, princes. They can grant one high favors or consign one to a dungeon. Their loyalty is often of the party or organization, and usually takes the form of loyalty to a leader, or to a controlling economic or psychological interest in their district. It is not primarily to the city or to an intangible ideal; and even though it is an immature and unenlightened loyalty, it (unless the electorate's pocketbook nerve has been painfully touched, as in the present economic crisis) appeals to the rank and file of the voters; a majority of them prefer a friend to a principle. Immediate concrete benefits and personal recognition weigh heavier with them than abstract canons of justice.

This loyalty pattern is unusually well developed in organizations under strong leadership. There it often seems the better part of valor to obey implicitly the instructions of the boss, lest one be cut off from the pay roll or denied all chance of getting on it. Emotion or friendship for a person, and this economic consideration combine to create a loyalty comparable to that found in a military organization. A few years ago a powerful ward leader sat in his ward club on election night waiting for his lieutenants, the division leaders, to bring in the election returns. It was the year in which the former district attorney, Angus Terrell, was a candidate for the municipal court. (A little more than five years before, while acting as district attorney, he had succeeded in obtaining a conviction and a five-year sentence in the penitentiary for John Flint, who had, less than a year before, been released from the "big house," and was now back in this, his old division, shepherding the voters.) Because of his commanding presence and the record he had established in his division, he was the one who controlled it. Flint's six-foot-two frame appeared in the room where the ward leader was waiting, and when the leader asked, "What did you give Angus?"—Flint, in spite of the bitter resentment felt against the former district attorney, replied, "The ———— gave me five years!—I gave him 500 majority!"

The great generality of politicians are conservative and reactionary so far as the machinery of government is concerned and so far as many social questions are concerned as well. Their interest or stake is in the present order. They always do their best to maintain the *status quo*, and they never champion reforms in government unless by so doing they think that they can cripple a rival or because they no longer can safely ignore an increasingly insistent public opinion. They are skilled in running the governmental machinery as it is now constituted, but any improvement must come from energy and plans supplied from the outside.

Moreover, politicians may sacrifice the interest of the many for the few. The reason is simple. The few are usually better organized and possessed of more wealth and intelligence than the general public. And furthermore, they (the private interests) pay closer attention to what the politician does, once he is in office, and they usually provide the necessary cash for the campaign that takes him there. Those who pay the fiddler often have a good deal to say about the tune.[22] When the public pays

[22] Mayor Daniel W. Hoan of Milwaukee has just written me a letter concerning "the tremendous influence of the underlying conditions and causes of things on the politician himself." I quote: "Take for example the split in the Protestant churches at the time of the Civil War. How can anyone explain that the preachers of the South would use the Bible to vindicate slavery and those just north of the line, to castigate it? There is no other explanation than an economic one. The source from which the funds to support the church came directly or indirectly influenced the message they gave. This is exactly what happens in politics and to the politician . . . the old maxim, that whoever puts up the money for the

the cost of the campaign and closely follows the official acts of its public servants, then, it can be unequivocally stated, the politicians will zealously safeguard the public interest; but until then many politicians will continue to serve some fraction of the people instead of all of them, for this fraction of the public—not the general public—may hold the power of political life or death for the elected person. If he wants to continue in power he is going to work for the master who is most appreciative. This idea is handsomely illustrated by the following passage in the *Autobiography* of Theodore Roosevelt:

"Peter Kelly's fate was a tragedy. He was a bright, well-educated young fellow. . . . We began to vote together and act together, and by the end of the session found that in all practical matters that were up for action we thought together. He was ardent and generous: he was a young lawyer, with a wife and children, whose ambition had tempted him into politics, and who had been befriended by the local bosses under the belief that they could count upon him for anything that they really wished. Unfortunately, what they really wished was often corrupt. Kelly defied them, fought the battles of the people with ardor and good faith, and when the bosses refused him a renomination, he appealed from them to the people. When we both came up for reelection, I won easily in my district, where circumstances conspired to favor me: and Kelly, with exactly the same record that I had, except that it was more creditable

---

campaign funds of the politician will dictate the music he will play. Senators coming from the cotton states, where the business of cotton finances the Senators, will surely cast their ballots pro-cotton. Aldermen, Congressmen or Senators, elected with campaign funds coming largely from utility sources, are sure to fight municipal or public ownership. Politicians elected with money gathered from gangsters or racketeers are sure to represent them in office. In these days, when there is such a tremendous struggle being waged by the working people to shorten their hours, to increase their pay, and to improve their conditions generally, while on the other hand the employing classes wish to increase their profits and oppose those things that labor wants, is it not important to bring out that politicians in public office who receive their campaign funds largely from reactionary interests are bound to support these interests in their votes and actions?" (May 4, 1936.)

because he took his stand against greater odds, was beaten in his district. Defeat to me would have meant merely chagrin: to Kelly it meant terrible material disaster. He had no money. . . . He had lost his [law] practice and he had incurred the ill will of the powerful, so that it was impossible at the moment to pick up his practice again . . . he had stood up for the rights of the people of Brooklyn and . . . the people had failed to stand up for him . . . he was punished precisely because he had been a good citizen and acted as a good citizen should act."[23]

It is true that some politicians, men like Theodore Roosevelt and the elder LaFollette, have enough dramatic ability, energy, intelligence and courage to capture and hold the attention of the people, and to serve them faithfully. (This is more easily done in comparatively sparsely settled states and communities.) This year, for example, Dan Hoan was for the sixth time elected mayor of Milwaukee; he is an excellent example of a politician devoted to the public interest. The only condition under which a President can possibly serve the people instead of special interests in America is to strive unceasingly to keep the people interested in what he is doing. Without their interest supporting him, he cannot serve them. This is doubtless the reason why President Roosevelt has spoken over the radio so frequently concerning the work of his administration. But there are a great many more Peter Kellys in America than there are Dan Hoans and F. D. R.'s—and there would be still more Peter Kellys were it not for the unerring eye with which some of the weaker and more vulnerable men in politics recognize their masters, and follow orders without question.

The politician is usually one who has no opinion on public questions, or, if he has, he hesitates to disclose it.[24] He has

[23] Theodore Roosevelt, *Autobiography*, pp. 74-75.

[24] There are undoubtedly both brilliant and notorious exceptions to this statement, and this is particularly true in a depression era; it is generally true in a state like Wisconsin, where for forty years the LaFollettes and other progressive leaders have been campaigning on issues among the congenitally liberal Scandinavians, and a particularly liberal set of German *émigrés* and their descendants. It is also true that some politicians adver-

learned that his own power is most likely to be maintained by concerning himself with a multitude of individual services that specific persons demand of him, and, as long as he is able, he postpones action on the major questions that necessarily involve differences of opinion. He often believes, and rightly, that questions that are of general interest are less worthy of his attention than those questions that appeal to specific individuals and groups, since there is no such thing as a general voter. A general voter, for example, would not require food, but an actual voter does. The politician's strength comes from the support of concrete individuals whose specific wants he has satisfied, and not from an anonymous public.

Furthermore, a politician in America must identify himself with some fixed spot on the earth's surface. He must be one who is here today and here tomorrow too. He must become identified by a controlling number of persons in his constituency, and this means either being born in the district whose support he is seeking or moving there as early in life as possible. Van Buren's parents must have had this in mind when they contrived to have their son, who later became President, born at a polling place. Other successful politicians have become interested in the polling place very early in their lives. Another requisite is living in a community that has the same general racial, nationality, and religious affiliations as the politician. It is often true that voters prefer to vote for one of their own rather than for a member of a different nationality group. This is one reason why no Jew, Roman Catholic, or child of immigrant parents has ever been elected to the Presidency. Our

---

tise themselves through the issues they champion. However, this may be a minor issue rather than one with fundamental implications. For example, a state senator in Wisconsin noticed that restaurants in Madison advertised Idaho potatoes on their menu cards. He thereupon introduced a resolution in the senate calling upon the farmers of the state to boycott the restaurants that advertised Idaho potatoes. The resolution was discussed in newspapers in different parts of the state. It got as far as the committee in the legislature and the senator asked to have the resolution withdrawn. The restaurants stopped advertising Idaho potatoes, and the senator received much publicity.

Presidents have thus far come from the same sort of stock as constitutes a controlling number of voters.

Although there are widely different types of individuals in politics, as Al Smith, Alfred M. Landon, Governor LaFollette, and Franklin Roosevelt reveal, the successful ones, as I have said elsewhere, invariably have the following traits: "(1) they stick everlastingly at it; (2) they know that the Kingdom of Heaven is taken by violence; (3) they live decades among their people and learn to judge their wants; (4) have a flair for getting along with people; (5) have problem-solving ability; (6) understand that politics is a science of the possible"; (7) are able to dramatize their appeal so as to effectively capture favorable attention; (8) often have an unusual memory for names and people; (9) can gauge public sentiment and strength of various groups attitudes; (10) have the kind of courage that enables the possessor to risk all on the outcome of an election and then be able to start building anew in case of defeat; and (11) have enough vision and imagination to see over the district for which they are candidates, whether this be a township or all forty-eight states. They understand that in politics the race is not always to the swift nor the battle to the strong, and that a smile and a genial manner may be more convincing than logic unadorned. "And finally it may be added that in temperament politicians are more likely to be like Aaron Burr than John Quincy Adams; and, furthermore, it cannot be said of politicians, as is so often remarked of other arresting personalities, that their bark is worse than their bite."[25]

In conclusion I might add that, though the majority of politicians are lock, stock and barrel for the *status quo* (and this is largely because the controlling interests or groups in their constituencies are for the *status quo*), yet there are brilliant exceptions among the realist political leaders. Such men are on the march. They have an objective, or they seem to have one, and they are actively on the way toward it. One cannot follow a squatter, and one cannot follow a person who seems undecided

[25] J. T. Salter, *Boss Rule: Portraits in City Politics*, p. 10.

as to what he wants—but one *can* follow someone who marches. He may be heading out over the brink of a precipice, but none the less he is heading out, and it is that quality in him—in the LaFollettes, or a Roosevelt, or a Huey Long—that awakens response in the electorate and creates followers.

VI

The politician is as inevitable in a democracy like ours as are actors in the theater, editors on newspapers, physicians in hospitals, promoters, managers and salesmen in life insurance companies, bankers in financial institutions, professors in universities, or leaders in orchestras. He is inevitable and necessary because he has much work to perform, work that requires vast energy and time, and no little degree of skill. We have generally failed to provide some official agency for doing this work—the work inseparable from self-government in a republic that covers a continent and involves more than 125,000,000 persons—and the politician has become the self-nominated custodian of the people's business.

We may now briefly consider the outstanding concrete needs that the politician satisfies in our present-day democracy. First of all, we must remember that the world and the society in which we live is altogether too vast, too complex and too fleeting for direct acquaintance. "The world that we have to deal with politically is out of reach, out of sight, out of mind."[26] Therefore the politician's first service is to make this incomprehensible political world meaningful, if not intelligible, to the voter. He serves as a bridge—though sometimes a most inadequate one—that spans the gap between the unseen outer environment on one hand, and the casual voter in his workaday world on the other. The great majority of voters have little more than an inkling—and some millions do not have that—of the implications of even such major pieces of legislation as the Smoot-Hawley tariff law, the Emergency Railroad Act, the Securities and Exchange Act of 1934, the Social Security Act, the Holding

[26] Walter Lippmann, *Public Opinion*, p. 29.

Company Act, the Guffey Coal Act, the Vinson Naval Act, or the Executive Order taking the United States off the gold standard.[27] Supreme Court decisions of recent months have inspired much discussion, but the significance of even these decisions is not clear. The Constitution and its relation to our times is a most fundamental question, and yet it is one to which the great majority of voters can bring only a feeling of reverence or frustration; the materials for a carefully reasoned decision are wanting.

A similar confusion and lack of definite knowledge exist with regard to the work of most of our governmental agencies. Here is where the political party and the politician come in, and it is here that they (along with other agencies such as the press, the radio evangelists and commentators, the American Liberty League, and myriad pressure groups that mold public opinion) render their first great service. They take their stand on specific issues and they suggest remedies for social disease; "the suggesting of remedies is the office of specialists."[28] One remedy may be urged as the solution to the problem, by one group of political specialists, and a different remedy by another group; or a very similar remedy may be advocated by the other major group. "The true function, then, of political parties is that of formulating and presenting the alternatives between which the people are to choose."[29] By the very nature of the case, in a country as

---

[27] The fact that Congressmen and professors may not understand the nature and significance of major pieces of legislation does not weaken, but rather strengthens, the argument concerning the complexity and vastness of the political world in which we live. Space does not permit an enumeration of state, county or municipal legislation that is beyond the grasp of the casual voter.

[28] Delisle Burns, *Political Ideals*, p. 333.

[29] A. L. Lowell, *Public Opinion in War and Peace*, p. 187.

Lowell has most clearly stated two functions of a political party in the United States: "The propositions which this chapter seeks to set forth are that, whether for good or for evil, political parties in every large democracy are, under ordinary circumstances, unavoidable; that this is the more true the larger the size of the electorate, if the holders of the chief political offices and the policy to be pursued are to be determined by public opinion; that the normal function of the parties is to present for popular

heterogeneous as ours, where there are vast differences both in cultures and in degrees of civilization, as well as in economic interests, and where because of our electoral college there are only two major parties, the party itself is filled with men of various shades of opinion, and is asking support of most incongruous groups of voters (millionaires and millions on relief, white-collar workers, miners and farmers); it prefers to ignore many controversial issues, and takes unequivocal stands on the generally accepted measures. We believe that this course of action is necessary if a controlling number of diverse voters or interest groups are to be brought under one banner. And, since all the issues for which a party stands cannot be reduced to one

---

choice alternative candidates and policies; and that public opinion on these matters is on the whole most truly expressed if the choice lies between a single pair of alternatives. It was pointed out that everywhere the parties perform this function imperfectly, sometimes very imperfectly; and that the extent to which they perform it varies a great deal in different countries. In the United States the parties are more concerned with nominating candidates for office than with presenting definite alternative policies; in England as a rule they deal at elections more with questions of policy and less with the personal matters; while in France, the groups in the Chamber of Deputies, which determine the character of the ministry and the course of legislation, are not national parties in the same sense, and hence public opinion has a less direct influence upon national affairs than in either the United States or England." *Ibid.*, p. 219.

Edmund Burke's classic statement on parties should be noted. It is as fine as anything ever written on this subject: "When bad men combine, the good must associate; else they will fall, one by one, an unpitied sacrifice in a contemptible struggle. . . . Party is a body of men united, for promoting by their joint endeavours the national interest upon some particular principle in which they are all agreed. For my part, I find it impossible to conceive, that any one believes in his own politics, or thinks them to be of any weight, who refuses to adopt the means of having them reduced into practice. It is the business of the speculative philosopher to mark the proper ends of Government. It is the business of the politician, who is the philosopher in action, to find out proper means towards those ends, and to employ them with effect. Therefore every honourable connexion will avow it as their first purpose, to pursue every just method to put the men who hold their opinions into such a condition as may enable them to carry their common plans into execution, with all the power and authority of the State. As this power is attached to certain situations, it is their duty to contend for these situations." *The Present Discontents—The Works of Burke,* vol. ii, *The World Classics.*

principle, like Liberty or Planned Economy, it must hold various positions, not all of which are compatible. The present campaign, however, is one in which there is likely to be a clear-cut issue, with those favoring a government actively interested in the social security of the people supporting one candidate, and those who are more generally interested in individualistic freedom supporting the other. It will be an election in which the voter will be definitely able to say whether or not he favors the present tendency in American government.

But in spite of the speeches, newspaper items and propaganda concerning issues, and the varying amounts of discussion given to them in a political campaign, there will remain in many, if not all elections, a substantial part of the electorate whose minds have not been touched. Public affairs to them remain dull and uninteresting until some political artist dramatizes the issue so vividly that the voters' attention is captured. Roosevelt's smile, the magic of his voice over the radio saying, "My friends," won more millions of voters in 1934 than did his policies; and the same thing may happen again. In Roosevelt America has a politician whose personality is big enough to cover the length and breadth of the land. For people not attracted to Roosevelt, a Borah or a Landon or a LaFollette may represent in his personality all that is to be decided in an election. Or, again, some politician in a township or precinct may embody, in his face-to-face contact with a constituent, all the issues in a campaign. The importance of the human equation in American politics cannot be easily overemphasized.[30]

The politicians are naturally the ones who form the board of directors and the permanent personnel of the political party. Just as the party is the agency that runs the government, the politician is often the intellect and the guiding energy that motivate the party. This is as inevitable as is the power wielded by the dean and a few of the older members of university faculties who give time and thought to questions that later come up for vote in faculty meetings. The power is certainly not exer-

[30] J. T. Salter, *Boss Rule: Portraits in City Politics.*

cised by professors who rarely go to faculty meetings or who never discuss the questions before the meetings. The same situation is found in church affairs when one considers the influence of the rector and the board of vestrymen. They are able to determine the outcome of questions that confront the congregation because they have given their time, energy and thought to the work in hand.

The party is not only concerned with issues but with candidates, and the magnitude of this task of selecting issues and candidates is not easily grasped. On paper, and often in reality, there is a party committee for each district that elects a candidate to public office. There are, for example, no less than 175,418 governmental units in the United States.[31] This does not include voting precincts, state representative and senatorial districts, judicial districts, etc., from which there are either elected or appointive officials chosen, and sometimes both. The large number of offices in the United States is exceeded only by the large number of voters.

The exact number of elective offices in the United States is not known, but Professor Merriam has estimated the number to be approximately 700,000 to 800,000.[32] If there are 800,000 elected officials, there are necessarily several times as many candidates. The magnitude of the task of not only getting candidates to run for this multitude of offices, but of supporting them in the campaign, is gigantic. It is so great that in many sections of the country it is a full-time job. Moreover, in addition to the candidates for public offices, a veritable army of minor public officials (often party workers) is required to conduct the balloting on election day. According to Brooks, in 1932, there were 119,643 precincts in the United States.[33] There are usually polling places in each or nearly all of these precincts. There are several election officials in each polling place—a judge,

[31] William Anderson, *The Units of Government in the United States*, p. 1. (Public Administration Service, No. 42.)

[32] C. E. Merriam, and H. F. Gosnell, *The American Party System*, p. 242.

[33] R. C. Brooks, *Political Parties and Electoral Problems*, p. 158.

THE POLITICIAN AND THE VOTER

ballot clerks, inspectors, etc. There is also the registering of the voters prior to the election, which is in itself a sizable task.[34] The majority of private citizens care little for this type of work, save at extraordinary times while a revival or wave of reform is in progress; the major part of the burden of election work, rain or shine, is shouldered by the politician.

In addition, the politician himself, either stands for office, or supports someone who does; and this in itself is an indispensable, expensive and laborious service in a democracy (especially one with a long ballot and short terms of office). He discusses the contest in terms of symbols[35] and expressions. And what these are necessarily depends on the quality of the electorate being addressed. The elder LaFollette said: "I have always felt that the political reformer, like the engineer or the architect, must know that his foundations are right. To build the superstructure in advance of that is likely to be disastrous to the whole thing. He must not put the roof on before he gets the underpinning in. *And the underpinning* is the education of the people."[36] For more than thirty years he gave the people solid argument, statistical information and facts. For four hours, without stopping, he would speak compellingly to his people about railroads, taxation and other authentic issues. Today, although his sons do not speak for four hours in an afternoon, they are carrying on the great tradition of dramatizing the facts for the electorate. This is one clue to the explanation of some of the outstanding excellencies of Wisconsin's government.

In contrast to the LaFollettes is Big Bill Thompson, who was on three different occasions elected mayor of America's second city. His best-known campaign cry had to do with the king of England keeping his "snoot" out of our affairs. In his last campaign I heard Chicago's Falstaff say to a large audience

[34] This statement is not descriptive of communities that have adopted permanent registration, but those communities are comparatively few.
[35] "What privileges do within the hierarchy, symbols do for the rank and file." Walter Lippmann, *Public Opinion*, p. 234.
[36] *A Personal Narrative of Political Experiences*, pp. 240-241. (Italics mine.)

—and an appreciative one, too—"Give the English hell; there ain't many of them here." Whether the candidate will offer the voter a social program or a cigar or a recipe for making bread-and-butter pickles[37] will depend on what it takes to win the support of the voter.

Edmund Burke once told his constituency: "I could hardly serve you as I have done, and court you too. Most of you have heard that I do not very remarkably spare myself in public business; and in the private business of my constituents I have done very nearly as much as those who have nothing else to do. My canvass of you was not on the 'Change, nor in the county meetings, nor in the clubs of this city: it was in the House of Commons; it was at the custom-house; it was at the council; it was at the Treasury; it was at the admiralty. I canvassed you through your affairs, and not your persons. I was not only your representative as a body; I was the agent, the solicitor of individuals; I ran about wherever your affairs could call me; and

---

[37] In the 1934 election for the state senate in Wisconsin a Norwegian candidate sent to the voters in a rural district a small campaign card bearing his picture and name on its face, and a recipe for preparing bread-and-butter pickles (one quart sliced cucumbers, six small onions; one cup, etc.) on its back. However, this candidate was defeated by a man who discussed issues. Dickens describes a campaign appeal that is not unknown to voters in the United States: "The breath was scarcely out of the body of the deceased functionary, when the field was filled with competitors for the vacant office, each of whom rested his claims to public support, entirely on the number and extent of his family, as if the office of beadle were originally instituted as an encouragement for the propagation of the human species. 'Bung for Beadle. Five small children!'—'Hopkins for Beadle. Seven small children!!'—'Timkins for Beadle. Nine small children!!!' Such were the placards in large black letters on a white ground, which were plentifully pasted on the walls, and posted in the windows of the principal shops. Timkin's success was considered certain: several mothers of families half promised their votes, and the nine small children would have run over the course, but for the production of another placard, announcing the appearance of a still more meritorious candidate. 'Spruggins for Beadle. Ten small children (two of them twins), and a wife!!!' There was no resisting this; ten small children would have been almost irresistible in themselves, without the twins, but the touching parenthesis about that interesting production of nature, and the still more touching allusion to Mrs. Spruggins, must ensure success." Charles Dickens, *Sketches by Boz*, pp. 17-18.

THE POLITICIAN AND THE VOTER 119

in acting for you, I often appeared rather as a shipbroker, than as a member of parliament. There was nothing too laborious, or too low for me to undertake. The meanness of the business was raised by the dignity of the object."[38] But the voters of Bristol did not reelect him; however, Malton did, and this is one great advantage that an English politician has over his American counterpart—he can stand for election to Parliament in any constituency in the United Kingdom, regardless of where he happens to live. In this country there is only one avenue open to the candidate for Congress—the district in which he lives, and this usually means the district in which he has lived for many, many years. A Labor candidate for Parliament in 1935 issued a circular captioned, "'The world is my parish' should be the motto of statesmen." Here a candidate's parish is not the sphere of his duties, but the exact geographical district that elects him. The brilliant Penrose understood this when he explained why he was not concerned with the great issues that might be of interest to members of the United States Senate: ". . . he 'was swamped in the machinery we won the privilege of directing and ruling.' . . . 'There are about five thousand election divisions in this state,' he said. 'They hold from twenty thousand to twenty-five thousand Republican workers who carry the division and bring out the vote. I must know all these men. They must know me. . . . I must know what they are, what they want, and how and when. My hand must always be on the job. I can never take it off. All my time goes to the task, and must. If I take my hand off, I am gone. . . . As for great measures and great issues, no Senator of a state of this size, run as it is, has the time to take them up.'"[39]

As I have already indicated, the politician stands as a buffer between the official government and the voter. The government creaks; the politician supplies the oil that helps it function more

---

[38] Speech at Bristol. *The Works of Burke,* vol. iii, p. 6.
[39] T. Williams, "After Penrose, What?" *Century,* vol. cv. (November, 1922), cited in R. C. Brooks, *Political Parties and Electoral Problems,* pp. 207-208.

smoothly. The government is rigid, impersonal and unable to meet officially many of the problems that vitally concern the citizen in the Great Society. This is true today in 1936; it was doubly true before the official government so directly concerned itself with the immediate personal security of the citizen. The politician makes up this lack. His knees are supple; he can stoop right down to where the voter lives and help him with the task in hand. He can cut corners and act on the instant. The government is more ponderous and slow-moving. The official eye of the government cannot see a single concrete individual in distress; the human eye of the politician can, and he can hear even a whisper. Furthermore, the politician's helping hand is not limited by any equal-protection clause.

What are these wants supplied by the politician? This question can be answered only in terms of the economic and cultural status of the people in a given constituency and the efficacy of the official government in meeting the wants in the chosen constituency. A Negro leader in a colored precinct in a great city is concerned with different problems (because his people have different wants) from those of a state senator from a rural district in Wisconsin.[40] Here may I quote two statements prepared for me by two state senators in Wisconsin concerning the personal service that each has given or been asked to give his constituents during the past twelve months? The first statement is from Senator A, who represents a district that is largely urban; the second statement is from Senator B, whose district is primarily rural. I need not say that these statements only faintly indicate the range of a politician's private services. They are by no means complete.

A Representative Number of Senator A's Personal Services to His Constituents

1. A gentleman by the name of A calls frequently to complain about his relief budget. He has a wife and five

---

[40] See J. T. Salter, *Boss Rule: Portraits in City Politics,* for an extensive discussion of this service phase of a politician's life.

children and he is always complaining of harsh and discriminatory treatment by relief officers. On one occasion I visited relief headquarters with him, and took his part in urging that he be allowed to buy his own coal with cash which he earned on work relief. We urged this on the ground that he could buy coal more cheaply than the relief department. Later, in an unguarded moment, he informed me that he was accustomed to stealing his coal.

2. Mr. B has been after a job for many months. I have been able to get him some temporary work, but he always turns up about once every three weeks.

3. Mr. C is a janitor in a school in a village about twenty miles from Madison. He has been seeking work in Madison, where he hopes to educate his son. Recently Mr. C's father had a golden wedding, and I spent most of one Sunday at this ceremony. I have been at two golden weddings during the past year, and should have gone to a third.

4. Mr. D, a negro, requested my assistance in adjusting a criminal case in which one of his race was being prosecuted for rape.

5. Mr. E, a WPA worker, requests my signature upon a note which he seems never to get paid.

6. Mr. F is much concerned over a row in a local political group and calls me up at all times of the day and night asking for my services as a mediator.

7. Mrs. G requests my assistance to get her relief money directly instead of through an abusive husband.

8. Mr. H, a labor union leader, requests advice for assistance in settling a labor row at the French Battery Works where he has been fired for insubordination.

9. Mr. I, a state employee, requests advice concerning how he may properly administer the barbers' code.

10. Mr. J, a farmer, comes in with his son, and hopes that

I can furnish his son with a dishwashing job so that he may attend school next year.
11. Mr. K wishes my assistance and recommendation in securing a student scholarship.
12. Mr. L calls for aid on behalf of a friend of his who has been committed to the state prison for two years and for whom a pardon is being sought.

A Representative Number of Personal Services by Senator B to His Constituents

1. Requests for jobs. During the past four years I believe I have received approximately 2,000 requests for assistance in securing work.
2. Letters of introduction and recommendation. This is somewhat related to number 1, but these letters are requested for many different purposes.
3. Assistance in procuring concessions from Commissions and Boards. For instance, when a ruling was made for fire escapes on three apartment buildings, I was called upon to try to secure a different plan of construction from the one ordered by the Commission.
4. Requests for talks usually made by organizations such as Farmers' Union, Parent-Teacher Associations, Game Clubs, etc.
5. Numerous requests for proposed bills when printed.
6. Numerous requests for printed acts or bills after they have been passed.
7. Assistance in securing rerouting of bus service in District.
8. Support for movement to relocate highway or secure new road or new surfacing from Highway Commission.
9. Assistance in securing establishment of Fish Hatchery in District, from Conservation Commission.
10. Assistance in securing favorable action from Conservation Commission for location of State Park in District.

11. Numerous requests on explanation and assistance in securing Old Age Pensions.
12. Numerous requests for explanation of Unemployment Insurance Act, and other laws.
13. Requests to attend Booster Programs, and other public functions of like nature within the District.
14. Requests for information concerning the securing of informative agricultural pamphlets and other printed articles from the State and Federal Government.
15. Requests for assistance in securing favorable action on Work Projects within the District.
16. Requests for assistance in securing relief from Relief Administrative bodies, or for securing reinstatement when laid off.
17. Numerous requests to use influence with Governor on appointive positions.
18. Requests for articles for local newspapers on laws or other matters of public interest.
19. Requests for advice on how to secure introduction and passage of legislation or resolutions for investigation of public officials or commissions.
20. Requests for interviews for consideration of ideas for World reform or establishment of Utopia.[41]

[41] A veteran Congressman from Oklahoma recently (July 7, 1936) told me that he now receives 50,000 letters per year. "Ten years ago I got less than 5000 letters per year—so the people are becoming more interested in government." Congressman Will Rogers, who represents the entire State of Oklahoma, told me that he receives 400 letters a day while Congress is in session and on some days he has received as many as 9000 letters. He added, "All are answered." A member of the State Assembly in Louisiana, writes (July 21, 1936):

"My office is crowded all day with all types of individuals. In the waiting room there are never less than three people and sometimes up to 20 waiting to see me. They want jobs, political jobs, private jobs, or want me to call this party or that for them. They want me to use my influence to get them state sales in the various institutions, or to get some loved one out of the pen, or out of the mental hospital, or to get some special consideration. For the past two days over 180 L. S. U. students have called me to get me to O.K. scholarship blanks for a work-

He who writes about politics and politicians in America must be prepared to write about life, for one can understand the politician only by considering him in the light of the kind of civilization, traditions and governmental arrangements that we have here. Space does not permit any further comment on this fundamental aspect of politics. Neither have I mentioned those lone generals, the reformers, who contribute much to the progress achieved in governing and in governmental institutions. Their greatest service has been in calling the electorate's atten-

---

ing scholarship (if this were put through the Legislature—by its workings over 1000 students would get to go to L. S. U. practically free)."

A Congressman from Mississippi has recently (July 7, 1936) made the following statement concerning the way he serves his people:

"With the depression, personal services and departmental activities in behalf of constituents have vastly increased. It is my thought that for the past four years probably 75 per cent of the actual hours of a Member's time is devoted to these personal services. In response to your inquiry as to concrete illustrations, typical or characteristic of personal services, I may mention the following:

"1. Personal consideration of applicants for governmental appointments that are within the recommendations of Members of Congress, including postmasters and rural carriers.

"2. Consideration of applications for emergency employment and for relief work under the emergency legislation.

"3. The unemployed take much of a Member's time with complaints as to inequalities and discriminations in administration.

"4. The veterans of the World War and of the Spanish-American War with their claims for pensions and disabilities occupy much of a Member's time.

"5. Departmental inquiries respecting the provisions that have been made in assisting youth in school and college and inquiries from young men desiring to enroll in the CCC camps consume their part of one's time.

"6. Then a constituent writes he will be in Washington and will be glad for me to arrange to show him the principal places of interest. When he does come to Washington he always calls and it is the pleasure of the Member to show him and assist him in seeing principal items of interest.

"7. In my district I have many public improvements—flood control work along the Mississippi River obtains, and there are many applicants for this type of work that do not obtain in other districts.

"8. Assistance in collecting the benefits of the Cotton Reduction program consumes much time."

tion to pathological conditions in the state of public affairs and the specific shortcomings of certain public officials, rather than in holding office themselves. (The voters evidently agree with part of the foregoing statement, at least, for in normal times the reformers are seldom elected to office, and even more seldom reelected.) The reformer is, usually, one who profoundly believes in some great issue, and just as profoundly in his own sovereign self. Garrison's words indicate this attitude: "I am in earnest—I will not equivocate—I will not excuse—I will not retreat a single inch—and I will be heard." There are, however, increasingly large numbers of reformers who are tolerant and capable of compromise and who have a realistic conception of human nature in politics; but many of them "do not encounter humanly in the flesh, but inhumanly upon paper."[42] Their knowledge of what is good for the voter may be impeccable, but their insight into who the voter is and what he wants may be inadequate. It is inevitable, before we conclude, that we at least mention a distinction that may be made between politicians and statesmen. One way of putting it is that the former are primarily concerned with private purposes, and statesmen with public ones.[43] "The former 'do a little service for a lot of people on a lot of little subjects,' while the latter try 'to do a big service out there in the void.' That is, the politician devotes ninety per cent or more of his time and thought toward getting Tom, Mary, and Bill a job or an exemption from some governmental rule that is about to oppress them; but the statesman, though he must give a varying amount of his time to the individual constituent's demands, attempts, nevertheless, to centre his best thought on an employment program that will provide work generally, or on humanizing the official government so that the individual's needs in the great society will be satisfied; and he does this as a matter of public duty rather than as a special favour. The statesman

[42] F. S. Oliver, *Politics and Politicians*, p. 87.
[43] For a more complete discussion of this difference, see J. T. Salter, Roosevelt and the Higher Politics, in the Dalhousie Review. Volume XV, Number 1 (April, 1935).

is distinterested, in the sense that he strives to serve the entire electorate rather than a fraction of it. And he knows that only by serving the whole group can he permanently serve himself. He is an architect of an organic social order. And he must be both a dramatic artist and a practical student of human nature in politics; for this more perfect vision is useless unless he can compellingly bring the ideal he has before him to the attention of a people that will not feed on pale theory.[44]

[44] Space does not permit a discussion of the technically trained man in governmental service—the expert. In the words of one observer, he should be always on tap but never on top. The politician is in the seat of authority, but the increasingly technical nature of the problems that confront the state forces the politician to rely more and more on experts. The rôle of the latter is to make available the findings of science in any field of governmental activity; the function of the politician is to educate the public mind and to support what it will accept. This is a significant check-and-balance system (the voter—the politician—the expert) in our political process today.

Chapter IV: Presidential Campaigns

by Harold R. Bruce
Professor of Political Science, Dartmouth College

DURING a national history of nearly a century and a half the United States has been developing political processes and institutions notable among the governments of the world for their originality and distinctiveness. None is more outstanding among these than the campaign that precedes the quadrennial election to the office of President. Strictly regarded, the campaign begins in late June or early July of the election year, after the national conventions have adopted the party platforms and have nominated the party candidates for the November election. Actually, however, the campaign begins in the preceding mid-winter, and the great forces of the parties begin then to gather momentum that increases in speed and power through the summer and early autumn months.

The presidential campaign presents an unparalleled example of national absorption and concentration of interest. No other event can compare with it in public interest, enthusiasm and participation. Part of this is traditional; part of it is developed by skillful promotion and advertising; part of it is due to a proper appreciation of the importance of the office. The Presidency, the supreme objective of political careers and political ambition in this country, is the most powerful, and capable of being developed into the most influential, office in democratic governments throughout the world today. It is only natural and fitting, therefore, that the quest of this office by individuals and by party organizations should develop struggles of unique intensity and magnitude. In business circles the campaign is of special significance because of the general belief that "business is always bad in a presidential election year." So strongly rooted is this belief that it will doubtless be of considerable general surprise to learn, from a study recently made at the University of Chicago, that business averages only two to four per cent worse in election years than in non-election years, and that the investigation shows about as many "better-business election years" as it does "bad-business election years."[1]

Judged by every criterion, measured by every standard, of popular participation, American presidential campaigns far outrank any similar political procedure anywhere else in the world. English parliamentary election campaigns may be confined to a short period of three weeks, and rarely extend over six weeks or two months. Campaigns for the election of new members to the French Chamber of Deputies are of similarly brief duration. But in the United States, where elections follow a regular time-table schedule, year after year, quadrennium after quadrennium, plans are laid many months ahead. The campaign forces are called into activity in early spring; they are enlarged in number and their efforts are intensified as late summer brings the "Tuesday following the first Monday in November" nearer to hand. These forces comprise a wide variety of partisans: national committeemen; state committeemen; county, city, town, ward and precinct committeemen; men and women; the professional and the amateur; the party "war horses" and the occasional workers; the salaried and the volunteers—by October, a small army. From national headquarters down through the state offices to the smallest election precincts the organization of the forces is carried and directed, to the accompanying expenditure of millions of dollars, in order that party control may be fastened, primarily, upon a single office, and, secondarily, upon the national Congress and the various state governments.

Arrangements for the Conventions

The two major parties, Democratic and Republican, select their candidates for President and Vice-President at quadren-

[1] "Business Conditions in Presidential Election Years," by W. F. Ogburn and A. J. Jaffe, of the University of Chicago, reported in *American Political Science Review*, April 1936, vol. xxx, pp. 269-275.

nial national conventions composed of delegates selected in the various states. The arrangements for these great gatherings are made by the national committees, which, in turn, have been elected by the preceding national conventions. The course of events follows a traditional sequence and is the same for both parties, except as otherwise noted.

The national committees meet in mid-winter, usually, as a matter of convenience, in Washington, to take the first formal steps in arranging for the national conventions. To plan for the conventions of 1936, the Republican national committee met on December 16, 1935, and the Democratic on January 9, 1936. The committee performs four important services at this meeting: it fixes the date of the convention, selects the convention city, decides on the number and apportionment of delegates, and issues the formal "Call" for the convention. (This is the formal notice issued to the state party organizations to send their designated delegates to the convention on the specified date.) Of these matters, three are substantially formal and traditional now; only the selection of the city is a matter of real discretion.

The Republican convention of 1936 met in Cleveland on June 9; the Democratic convention, in Philadelphia on June 23. This sequence of dates is traditional. On only three occasions, in 1856, 1860 and 1888, since the present major parties have competed against each other from 1854 to date, has the Democratic national convention preceded that of the Republicans. National political conventions are eagerly sought by all large cities, as are national gatherings of all large organizations such as the American Legion, the Elks, the Mystic Shrine, etc., for the income to be derived by local business concerns from the expenditures of those who attend the gatherings. This results in "bidding" for the convention by the offering of large sums by the various cities, to be used by the party in paying the expenses of holding the convention and adding to the party campaign funds whatever balance may remain. The national committee auctions off the convention, commonly "knocking it down" to the highest bidder. For the conventions this year, Philadelphia paid the Democrats $200,000, and Cleveland contributed $150,000 to the Republicans.[2] Other factors of occasional importance in selecting the city are its strategic political position in the campaign (that is, in a "doubtful" state or section that the party is very desirous of carrying), the presence or absence in that state of a leading candidate for the nomination, its geographical or central location, the auditorium facilities, etc. Chicago is the great convention city; the Republicans have met there eleven times and the Democrats five. The Republicans ruled out Chicago this year because of the prominent candidacy of Colonel Frank Knox, a resident of the city, and went to Cleveland for "neutral territory."

The apportionment of delegates among the states has followed a traditional practice: twice the number of Senators and Representatives in Congress, with an equal number of alternates, and a small courtesy allotment to the territories and dependencies. The four delegates corresponding to the two Senators are known as delegates-at-large, and the two for each Representative as district delegates. The Democrats follow this practice without deviation—twice the congressional and senatorial membership from each state, plus six delegates from each of the territories and dependencies, making a total of 1100 members in the 1936 convention. The national committee recommends to the state organizations that twice that number be sent from each state, half of them to be women, and then each delegate has one-half a vote in the convention.

The Republicans have wrestled for several years with the problem of southern delegates. It has been felt that the Republican organizations in the Democratic states of the Solid South should not have representation in the national convention on the same apportionment basis as those states in which the party has a real chance of winning electoral votes. The rule followed this year was that which was adopted for the 1924 convention and was used in 1928 and 1932. It allots delegates as follows: four

---

[2] When the Republicans opened their meeting in Cleveland, it was estimated by the local committee on housing that the convention had brought to the city 50,000 persons who would spend about $250,000 a day while there.

at large from each state (two per Senator); three additional at large from each state that cast its electoral vote for the Republican presidential nominee in the last preceding election; three each from Alaska, Hawaii and the District of Columbia; two each from Puerto Rico and the Philippine Islands; one from each congressional district; and an additional one from each district that cast at least 10,000 votes for Republican presidential electors in the last preceding presidential election or for the Republican nominee for Congress in the last preceding congressional election. This plan gives the "Republican states" a bonus of three votes, and "Republican congressional districts" the full representation of two delegates; and cuts down "Democratic districts" to one delegate each. The 1936 convention had 1003 delegates. This practice operates to produce fluctuations in the size of Republican conventions. A Republican landslide, such as Hoover's victory in 1928, increases the membership of the next convention (1154 in 1932) and a Democratic tidal wave, such as Roosevelt's victory in 1932, wipes out the bonuses in so many instances as to reduce sharply the size of the next convention, as down to 1003 in 1936.

Selecting the Delegates

Delegates are selected in the states either by conventions or by direct primaries, as the laws in the respective states may provide. In a few of the southern states the laws permit the parties to decide which of these two methods shall be used. Ordinarily, when the convention system is used, all of the delegates of that particular state are chosen by the state convention, but occasionally conventions are held in the congressional districts to select the district delegates. Primaries were used in sixteen states this year, and the convention system in all of the others.[3] Selection by either method may produce "uninstructed" or "instructed" delegations; in other words, delegates

[3] New Hampshire, Massachusetts, New York, New Jersey, Maryland, Pennsylvania, West Virginia, Ohio, Illinois, Wisconsin, South Dakota, Nebraska, Oregon, California, Alabama and Florida.

may go from their states "unpledged" to any aspirant for the nomination or as "pledged" to a particular man. Under the convention system, the convention may not only select the delegates but it may also "instruct" them to support and vote for a particular man in the national convention. To the simple direct primary method of popularly electing delegates, Oregon added in 1910 a provision for expressing the voter's preference as to the party nominee, thus "instructing" the delegates to support and vote for a particular man in the national gathering. This system is called the presidential preference primary.

Although there is neither party rule nor general practice as to how long "pledges" or "instructions" must be followed by the delegates in the national convention balloting on candidates, it is, obviously, greatly to the advantage of any man who seeks the party nomination for the Presidency to enter the convention with as many pledged delegates as possible. Consequently, the primaries and state conventions become battlegrounds for the contenders for the party nomination during the weeks immediately preceding the national conventions. Although only one-third of the states use the Presidential primary system, this group comprises the larger states with the large delegations: New York—90, Pennsylvania—75, Illinois—57, Ohio—52, California—44, Massachusetts—33, New Jersey—32, etc., with a total of 505 delegates (in the Republican convention of 1936) or over half of the entire convention. Public attention is, therefore, especially focused upon the pre-primary campaigns in these states.

The campaign that precedes the November election is a *party* campaign, in which the full organization of the party—national, state and local—is utilized, but the campaigns preceding the national conventions are *personal* ones. Men who actively seek the nomination must develop an organization to carry on the campaign for pledged delegates in those states that it is thought desirable to enter. The common procedure is to appoint a general campaign manager, who obtains state managers and plans the strategy to be followed in the various states. The most

PRESIDENTIAL CAMPAIGNS

spectacular developments arise in those preferential primary states in which two or more of the leading candidates clash in their quest of delegates. In the campaign of the present year President Roosevelt had so clear a field for renomination that public interest centered entirely on the Republican race. Senator William E. Borah and Colonel Frank Knox waged aggressive primary campaigns, and met in sharp clash in the Illinois primaries in April. Governor Alfred M. Landon not once personally asserted his candidacy, but his campaign was very skillfully directed by John Hamilton and two newspaper friends, Henry Haskell, editor, and Roy A. Roberts, managing editor, of the Kansas City *Star*. Their strategy was to avoid open clashes with the other leading candidates, to refrain from assuming the open initiative, and to secure the selection by conventions or primaries of "unpledged" delegates who were clearly favorable to Landon's nomination. For this reason the Republican convention seated far more uninstructed delegates than usual.

If the parties had "social registers" the names of most of the delegates would be found therein. Barring factional strife within a party, all of the important, leading, outstanding members of the party, from Maine to California, are at the national convention. United States Senators and Representatives, governors, state and local political bosses, prominent party men and women from all walks of life are there, and the chief members of the administration will be especially prominent in the convention of their party to direct the course of its action as the President dictates. A great mass of federal office holders supplies the voting force for the President in the convention of his party. The great throng of delegates and alternates makes a colorful, noisy, bustling, impressed-by-their-own-importance mob. Only one group is traditionally absent—the leading candidates for the nomination themselves![4] They remain at home,

[4] At Cleveland this year this tradition was rudely broken by Messrs. Borah, Knox and Vandenberg, all of whom were present. But the absentee (Landon) ran away with the convention and the nomination. And Knox

with the radio, telegraph, and telephone bringing the open convention developments and the under-cover negotiations to them, and with the aid of direct wires to their managers they direct their convention forces and strategy. The speed of air transportation has opened a new development in making it possible for the successful candidate to fly to the convention to accept the nomination while the delegates are still present in the auditorium. Mr. Roosevelt set this precedent at Chicago in 1932. Factional strife in a state may cause the defeat of some of the leading party men in primary or convention contests for delegate seats, but this need not necessarily cast them into outer darkness,—witness the defeat of James M. Curley, as a Roosevelt man, in Massachusetts in 1932, and his subsequent occupancy of an alternate's seat as from Puerto Rico! One of the marks of a politician is never to accept defeat.

The National Convention: Preliminaries

There is in the whole world of politics no spectacle to compare with an American national convention. Nowhere is its counterpart to be found; it is unique to American political life. Not all of the conventions in this country are of the roof-raising, heart-throbbing, pulse-stimulating variety. Many are of that type, to be sure, as witness the titanic Democratic struggle in Madison Square Garden in New York City in 1924 and Bryan's "Cross of Gold" stampede in Chicago in 1896. But some are so cut-and-dried, so dreary and mechanical, as to be positively funereal in character, as were both the McKinley and Bryan conventions of 1900 and the Roosevelt Republican convention of 1904. This latter was described as "the tamest, most soporific one ever held." Thus there are "drab conventions" and "jazzy conventions," and the prospect in the early spring of 1936 was that there would be one of each this year. The administration forces in complete control of the Philadelphia convention could scarcely make of it anything more than an orderly testimonial meeting

---

had departed for home before he was nominated for the second place on the ticket.

for President Roosevelt. It looked for some weeks in advance as though the Republicans would put on a good show for the people of Cleveland, to make amends for the disappointing Coolidge convention held there in 1924, but the sharp conflicts among the forces supporting the leading candidates, threatened in early spring, failed to materialize, and the gathering was dull, monotonous and tedious, for the most part.

The national conventions are laws unto themselves; they are wholly extra-legal in character; they know no regulation whatsoever, of law, court, sheriff or policeman. Just as state party conventions have been held to be the final authority of state party organizations, so the national conventions are the supreme power in the national party organizations.[5] They make their own rules, adopt their own procedure and practices, and enforce them in their own way. But all of this cannot well be left to the inspiration of the moment upon the convening of this vast assemblage, so the national committee is charged with arranging in advance a temporary organization. This involves the selection of a temporary chairman and other convention officials (secretaries, clerks, sergeants-at-arms, doorkeepers, etc.) and the determination of a temporary list of members of the convention. The officials are selected early enough to enable them to prepare for their activities. The Republican committee on arrangements selected Senator Frederick Steiwer, of Oregon, on April 21, to be the temporary chairman this year and to deliver the opening or "keynote" address of the convention, and Representative and Floor Leader Bertrand H. Snell, of New York, to be permanent chairman. The Democrats selected Senator Alben W. Barkley, of Kentucky, for the position of temporary chairman, a post

[5] In the case of Grovey v. Townsend, 295 U. S. 45, the Supreme Court held, on April 1, 1935, that a state party convention possesses "whatever inherent power a state political party has to determine the content of its membership." The case arose out of the action of the Democratic state convention in Texas prescribing the qualifications of members of the Democratic party in that state, for the purpose of voting in primary elections, to include only whites in the party membership. The Court upheld the action.

he held also in 1932. This selection is often of more significance than the mere naming of an effective speaker, for it may indicate some factional control of the party or the convention and the general position of the party in the campaign, its general line of attack or defense. Senator Joseph T. Robinson, of Arkansas, was the permanent chairman.

A much more important preliminary proceeding is the preparation of the temporary roll of members from the credentials sent to the national committee by the delegates. When delegates are selected in primaries, the secretary of state certifies the validity of their election and no question arises about their right of admission to the convention. But under the state convention system, factional strife within the party may reflect itself in contesting delegations. A minority may withdraw from a state convention, alleging misrepresentation of the party by the dominant faction, hold a convention of their own, select a body of delegates and dispatch their credentials, signed by the chairman and secretary of the seceding convention, to the national committee. Inasmuch as parties are extra-legal bodies, there is no court process available for determining which is the authentic party organization in the given state. The national committee, at its meeting just preceding the national convention, thus faces the problem of deciding which set of credentials to accept, which delegation to seat in the convention. After hearing the claims of each group it may seat one or the other of them, or it may dodge the issue by seating both groups and assigning to each delegate half a vote. The factional character of the majority of the committee ordinarily determines its action on credentials. In the 1912 Republican convention nearly 250 seats were contested, and the action of the Taft-conservative-Old Guard forces in riding, in steam-roller fashion, over the Progressive delegations was a prime factor in producing the Republican-Progressive conflict in the campaign. The number of contests has notably declined in recent conventions, only two state delegations being contested in each of the 1932 conventions. The seats of 57 delegates in this year's Republican convention were contested, most of these contests being conflicts between white and Negro delegates from southern states. The committee seated the "lily-white" group in every case. This action was in conformance with current Republican efforts to strengthen the control of white leadership of the party in the southern states. Inasmuch as the delegates first seated by the national committee vote on all questions of temporary and permanent organization and comprise the important convention committees, the preliminary action of the committee on credentials is virtually decisive in all convention actions.

The National Convention in Session

At length the great day arrives when the thousands of delegates and alternates, the party leaders, politicians, visitors, newspaper men, and all others who have been able by various and sundry means to secure tickets of admission gather in the vast auditorium for the opening session. Elaborate press, wire and radio facilities have been installed to give publicity to the proceedings, and from 1000 to 1500 publicity people take up the task of spreading every minute of the convention's activity to the four corners of the nation.[6] Literally, a national convention dwarfs every other public event in the nation in popular interest and provision for publicity.

After the preliminaries are concluded and the temporary chairman has delivered his "keynote" address, the four great convention committees are elected, one member from each state delegation having been selected by the delegation itself for each committee—the committee on rules and order of business, on permanent organization, on credentials, and on resolutions or platform. The work of the first two is formal: to recommend to the convention the adoption of the rules of the preceding convention, and the names of the temporary officers for permanent officials, save for the position of permanent chairman, which commonly goes to another prominent party man, in part to pass

[6] In Cleveland seats were provided for over 700 metropolitan newspaper men and over 350 representatives of country weeklies.

the honors around and possibly to secure a more experienced parliamentarian to preside over the hectic sessions of the assembly. The credentials committee will review the contests again and recommend a final disposition of the rival claims, but the original action of the national committee is almost sure to be followed.

The resolutions or platform committee has the difficult task of framing the platform, and even with such preliminary work as may have been done on the various planks in advance of the meeting, its problem is a serious one. Public hearings are commonly held to enable various non-party groups and interests to present their planks and requests; and finally, after much argument, compromise, weighing of appeals and effects, balancing of force against force, and (in the case of the Republicans) considering what the other party is likely to do and (in the case of the Democrats) what the other party has done, a report is ready for convention adoption. The Democrats in 1932 broke with tradition by adopting a "tabloid" platform of only 1350 words of explicit, succinct declarations; but the usual platform is a long, dull, cautious statement of criticism of the other party and adroitly phrased forecasts of party action. Convention adoption of the platform precedes the selection of candidates, because of the loss of interest in proceedings after the party standard bearer has been chosen, and so it may be said that the nominee accepts the nomination on the basis of the platform adopted by the party as its program of action and policy.[7] Party platforms so seldom represent original thought or honest convictions that they have fallen into disrepute among most voters. They are put together because of outside pressure and for reasons of political expediency, in order to attract the largest number of voters and to render friendly to the party every big group of prejudiced voters in the country, to prevent them from

---

[7] In an unprecedented action Governor Landon wired the Cleveland convention a long statement of personal attitude on three of the platform planks, which was read to the convention before action was taken on the question of a party nominee.

flocking to the opposing party. Former Governor Alfred E. Smith recently proposed a change in platform-making. He suggested that the platform committee be named in advance of the convention and that it meet to work out and adopt a platform before the convention opens, thus being able to work in a quiet, leisurely manner and avoid the confusion, bustle, noise and pressure of the convention.[8] In this manner, he believes, the committee could "really make a satisfactory job and a finished product of a platform," whereas "the present practice almost invariably results in a compromise."

Selecting the Candidate

The names of the various candidates for the nomination are placed before the convention during an alphabetical roll call of the states. When "Alabama" is called, a speaker may mount the platform, and with a laudatory speech commending the political and personal virtues and record of his man, present his name to the convention. At the conclusion of his oration the carefully planned demonstration of the "popularity" of his man gets under way, and continues as long as the directors of it are able to keep his partisans aroused. The same procedure follows as each successive state is called. In case the state has no candidate of its own, but is favorable to the candidacy of a man from another state, it may yield its place on the roll call to a state alphabetically farther down the list. In Cleveland, Arizona yielded to Kansas to permit an early presentation of Governor Landon's name. After a man's name has once been presented, later states may "second" his nomination, thus showing the location and the amount of his support.

In the actual choice of a nominee there are several factors that go to make up his "availability." These are qualities of a nominee as a *candidate*, not as a President, a frank recognition that a campaign winner is the primary objective, not necessarily the man who will make the best President. The personal life and

[8] Alfred E. Smith, *The Citizen and His Government* (New York, 1935), pp. 117, 118.

public record of the man are scanned closely; his political opinions and acceptability to the dominant element in his party, as well as the public reaction to him, are carefully noted. Factors that may "make or break" a man are his relationship to some local party machine, his association with big business, his success or defeat in a recent state or national election, his religion, and the amount of his nomination campaign expenditures. Successful governors have held strong positions in the convention race of late. A man of real campaign ability and appeal is almost necessary. Until the World War a good military record was an asset. The candidate's residence is one of the primary considerations, if not the outstanding one, and this means residence in a large, doubtful, pivotal state or section. This latter element contributed strength to Governor Landon's candidacy from the beginning.

National conventions present various situations in the selection of nominees. Occasionally one man occupies the enviable position of "the favorite" and is nominated on the first ballot without opposition. The President, when a candidate for a second term, holds this status, as in the case of President Roosevelt at Philadelphia this year. In the 1924 Republican convention President Coolidge polled 1065 votes of the 1109 delegates on the first ballot, and in Chicago in 1932 Hoover had 1126½ votes on the first ballot out of 1154. In 1908 President Theodore Roosevelt dictated the nomination of his Secretary of War, Taft, who was named on the first ballot, and Hoover outstripped all competitors at Kansas City in 1928. When no candidate occupies the center of the stage alone, the pre-convention campaign produces a group of "leading candidates," each with a block of pledged delegates and general supporters. Landon, Borah, and Knox were examples of this type of candidate before the Republican convention met this year.

Nearly every convention sees a group of "favorite sons" paraded across the stage, receiving national publicity, convention acclaim, radio "time," and courtesy state votes in the early balloting. They have risen to political prominence in their respective states and are honored, or used for trading purposes, by being presented to the convention. It was anticipated that this year's Republican convention would record the following as of this type: Senator Vandenberg of Michigan, Senator Dickinson of Iowa, Senator Steiwer of Oregon, Governor Nice of Maryland, Judge Meekins of North Carolina, and Robert A. Taft of Ohio, but none of them was presented to the gathering. The Democratic convention of 1932 heard the qualities of eleven "favorite sons" extolled. A convention hopelessly deadlocked around a small group of "leading candidates" sets the stage for the "dark horse" to come to the fore and lead the candidates for the nomination under the wire. His managers have kept him discreetly in the background while they cultivated the good will and friendship of leaders in the convention and the managers of the leading candidates, biding their time until the psychological moment arrives to urge his acceptance as a compromise candidate. Harding was the "dark horse" of the 1920 Republican convention to break the deadlock over Lowden, Johnson and Wood. At Madison Square Garden in 1924 the Democrats fought (many of them slept!) through 102 ballots over Smith and McAdoo until finally, in desperation, out of utter exhaustion, and unable to pay hotel bills any longer, they compromised upon Davis on the 103rd ballot. Republican conventions never have seen the long-drawn-out factional contests that have rather frequently characterized Democratic gatherings. Fourteen times in the past twenty-two Republican conventions, the nominee has been named on the first ballot.

Final decision has always been made in Republican conventions by a simple majority vote, but until this year the Democrats have always held to a two-thirds vote. This requirement of an extraordinary vote, adopted by the Democrats in 1836, in part has offset the operation of the "unit rule." A state convention may direct its delegates, just chosen by it, to apply the unit rule in the national convention—that is, the entire delegation shall vote unanimously as a majority of it shall decide. The Roosevelt forces made a bold attempt to rescind the two-thirds rule in the 1932 convention (he held a simple majority of the delegate vote but not two-thirds at the opening of the convention); but when it began to appear that pressing for its repeal might act as a boomerang against him the effort was abandoned. The change was made by unanimous vote at Philadelphia.

The selection of the party nominee for Vice President often seems to come almost as an afterthought, so slight is the attention given to this act. A "bargain" may have been made in securing the presidential nomination; or a factional conflict may dictate a certain choice in the hope of uniting the two elements; or a sectional situation may direct the selection of an Eastern man as a running mate for a Westerner, or vice versa. With the adoption of the platform and the selection of the presidential nominee, the big work of the convention is done, and the impatient delegates quickly dispose of the Vice Presidency, often practically by acclamation, as was the case in Cleveland in the naming of Knox.

The national convention has come in for a good deal of justifiable criticism. Its confusion, noise, heightened emotions, "hurly-burly," under-cover negotiations, trades, manipulations, "deals"—the utter absence of anything resembling deliberativeness—make it a poor method for the parties to use in selecting a candidate for the highest and noblest public office in the nation. "National conventions are uncertain assemblies," says Frank R. Kent, who knows the inner workings of many of them from his journalistic association with them. "They are made up of delegates from every state in the Union, and the average delegation is a thoroughly bossed and controlled delegation. The average delegation is made up of hand-picked men who can be swung into line when the word is given out. . . . Such a convention is the super-market place for political deals and bargains, trades and treachery."[9]

[9] Frank R. Kent, *The Great Game of Politics* (Garden City, New York, 1926), p. 246.

Organizing the Campaign

The specialized work of a presidential campaign covers the four months of July, August, September and October, and the most important phases of it are organization, propaganda, and finance. In a sense, campaign activity is of a continuous character, year in and year out. Through patronage and appointments to federal office, through the personal and official prestige of the President, through the myriad channels of publicity especially available to him, and through the fear of removal from office attendant upon a change in administration felt by a great body of office holders—through all these and by other methods—the party in power solidifies its position, strengthens its organization personnel, arouses an enthusiastic *esprit de corps*, and endeavors to win increased popularity and good will throughout the nation. The party out of power rises to the traditional position and opportunity of the opposition, and conducts a continuous, systematic campaign of criticism. Much attention is given to "keeping fences in repair" and in maintaining state organizations in effective condition. The mid-term congressional elections afford an opportunity for heightened general activity and for arousing the party forces after a relapse of a couple of years.

The general direction of and responsibility for the campaign are in the hands of the national chairman. Technically, the campaign manager is elected by the national committee, but actually he is the personal selection of the head of the ticket as in the case of John D. M. Hamilton, Republican, this year. If he conducts a victorious campaign he may practically have his choice of Cabinet posts, and may either resign or retain his party executive office. James A. Farley, the skillful Democratic campaign manager of 1932, became Postmaster-General and has continued, under much criticism, to hold his office as national chairman. The political sagacity, intuition, skill and experience essential to a successful campaign manager could be dwelt upon at great length. He is the commanding general of the great campaign forces of the party, and the success of the campaign is very largely in his hands. One of his first acts is to set up national headquarters, usually in New York City, and occasionally with branch offices in other large cities. The office organization—personnel, staff and space used—increases as the campaign develops, until it is a large, highly integrated, smoothly working mechanism, operating intensively and at high speed. Prominent elements in the headquarters organization are the press bureau, publicity agents, speakers' bureau, purchasing department, congressional and senatorial campaign committees, research division, farm division, and assistants who organize clubs among such voters as college students, racial groups and colored people.

The regular party forces constitute the backbone of the campaign organization. They are ready at hand, cover the nation, and can be quickly galvanized into action by the proper directing agents and proper procedures. They are supplemented by the auxiliary, temporary forces. The conduct of the Roosevelt campaign of 1932 was probably a model of skill, technique and efficiency. It began as early as 1928, and was founded upon continuous, direct, personal contacts between Roosevelt and Farley, on the one hand, and over a hundred thousand election precinct party agents, captains and committee men and women. These "privates" of the party army were relied upon as the campaign "shock troops," with army discipline violated by the commanding officer as he went over the heads of national and state committeemen in direct, personal correspondence with these precinct workers. Through a personal correspondence of astounding magnitude a feeling of personal relationship and responsibility was built up between these 115,000 party workers and the nominee and his campaign manager. The same procedure had been followed by Roosevelt in his New York gubernatorial campaigns; it worked then, and it worked on the much broader national scale in 1932—and will be relied upon again this year.

The first task of the nominee and the manager is to bring

harmony among such clashing factions and personalities as may exist in the party or have been produced by the course of events at the national convention. The nominee's opponents in the convention, if such there were, must be conciliated, and the dissatisfied, critical groups brought into the supporting, active forces. No prominent leader or group must be allowed to "bolt the ticket" or "take a walk," if these actions can possibly be prevented. Then, enthusiasm for the ticket must be aroused all down the line, confidence inspired, and at least the illusion of victory created. The candidate "is faced with the necessity of making a favorable impression upon a large number of widely scattered, highly diversified groups of voters, notoriously swayed by prejudice, who are being fished for from every conceivable angle by his opponent. He has to watch his step with the utmost care. . . . The primary purpose is always to catch the votes. . . . Almost invariably expediency is the keynote of his every public utterance."[10]

Questions of general strategy or major campaign policy must be decided early. Various factors will influence the decisions: whether the nominee is the President seeking reelection, the personality of the nominee, the probable size of the campaign fund, the character of the leading issue or issues of the campaign, the type and program of the chief opponent, etc. The most important question is whether to send the nominee around the country on one or more extensive speaking tours, following a "swing around the circle" program, or to conduct a "front-porch campaign," keeping him pretty much at home and bringing delegations there to hear him discourse on the major issues of the day. It is traditional and really good technique for a President seeking reelection to maintain an air of dignity and an appearance of keeping at the nation's tasks by not going on extensive trips. Some candidates are much better adapted to the dignity and formality of a front-porch setting, and some elections turn on issues that require such skillful treatment as can only be guaranteed when the addresses are few and carefully

[10] *Ibid.,* pp. 197, 200.

written in advance. McKinley, under Mark Hanna's management, instituted the modern "front-porch campaign," and Harding followed the precedent. Both made impressive figures in such a setting. The fine distinctions that the Republicans made at the outset of the 1920 campaign on the League of Nations issue further counseled the care that could be given to Harding's speeches for the formal occasions of various pilgrimages to Marion, Ohio. But some candidates are of such personality and vitality that they refuse—and, indeed, should not be made—to stay at home. William Jennings Bryan, Theodore Roosevelt, Alfred E. Smith and Franklin D. Roosevelt simply had to take to the high road and meet the voters in the informal, casual manner that train stops in small towns, parades in larger ones, and monster mass meetings in the large cities provide on a coast-to-coast tour. It is not to be expected that President Roosevelt will do so much campaign traveling this year—he will not wish to appear as neglecting his official duty, and he has now amply demonstrated his physical powers. It is doubtful whether Governor Landon has the proper and sufficiently engaging personality to be a great success on a wide national stumping tour, and yet he will be on the offensive and must assume the initiative of attack, and the people will wish to see him. The situation raises some nice questions for his managers. The day following the convention he promised the party "a hard but fair fight" and began preparations for a vigorous campaign.

Campaign Publicity

A political campaign involves two kinds of activity: general publicity and personalized work. The former utilizes all known methods of propaganda: newspapers, radio, general literature, posters and lithographs, public meetings, rallies and parades, slogans, and the like. The latter is concerned with personal canvasses, personal and form letters, organization of clubs, and special efforts among new voters, racial groups, etc.

A good press agent and publicity bureau are essential to the success of any campaign. In fact, the really indispensable services of these agencies should be made available long before the national convention meets. Some of the most effective work can be done in the period between elections—during the second, third and fourth years of the administration, either in support of it or in criticism of it. The Democratic party held a notable advantage over the Republicans in the 1932 campaign because of the effective, constant "hammering" of the Hoover administration by the Washington Democratic press bureau under the direction of Charles Michelson. He has continued as director of publicity for the national committee, and this fact alone places President Roosevelt at a distinct advantage, for there is probably no more able and skillful political press agent in the country than Michelson. The Republican national committee or chairman has never shown, in this important matter, the smartness that the Democrats have exhibited. It is the task of the publicity bureau to prepare the news copy for the press of the country and act as the source of information for political reporters and newspaper writers. All kinds of matter are sent out: news stories of the progress and achievements of the campaign and of the nominee; human-interest stories of him and his family; speeches of all important leaders of the party; discussions of the platform; comments of prominent persons; reports of newly won support; forecasts of results; and criticism of the opposing party, its nominee, platform and record. Special racial and sectional appeals are devised and given appropriate publicity. Great sums are expended in display advertisements; editorial comment is supplied to the smaller papers. This is one of the most important, and in some ways the most significant, feature of the whole campaign organization.

The radio has increased in political publicity importance by leaps and bounds in the past decade, keeping pace with the amazing advance in this general field. To a considerable degree it has solved the problem of carrying the nominee directly to the voters by word of mouth without subjecting him to the strain and terrors of the country-wide tour. His voice, if not his face, may be carried to millions while he reads his carefully prepared speech in his own study and they listen in the ease and comfort of their own living rooms. The great broadcasting services treat the national conventions as news features to be put on the air at their expense, but from the close of the conventions to election day "time on the air" must be paid for as would be any other type of advertising. At prevailing rates, as quoted by the companies, it will cost $3095 per night-time hour for the four large stations of the Mutual Broadcasting System and $15,235 per night-time hour for a Columbia national hook-up covering stations in 93 cities. The rates on the National Broadcasting Company system are as follows: Blue network, 63 stations, $14,640 per night-time hour; Red network, 65 stations, $16,040 per night-time hour.

Campaign literature takes various forms—some, direct and unmistakable in their purpose; some, subtle and carefully disguised as partisan appeals. The *Campaign Textbook* is the party worker's "bible," with reprint and exposition of the two platforms, biography of the nominee, and scores of pages of argument, data, records and promotional matter, plus much criticism of the other party and its record in office. Pamphlets and leaflets are printed by the hundred thousands on a great variety of features and subjects prominent in the campaign. Biographical books on the candidates are written at the solicitation of the national committees, and often other supporting or critical studies appear. One of this latter type is James P. Warburg's *Hell Bent for Election*, severely critical of President Roosevelt and the New Deal, and reported by the publishers to have sold over 400,000 copies between publication in the autumn of 1935 and the middle of May, 1936. Outdoor poster and billboard advertising has its place in the publicity programs, especially in presenting large lithographed pictures of the nominee. When supplemented by some catchy phrase or slogan this is especially effective, as in the Wilson campaign of 1916 when every billboard from Maine to California drove home the statement, "He kept us out of war." Four years later they carried Harding's picture and the Republican slogan, "Back to normalcy." An effective slogan that says a little and suggests much more is a potent instrument in any campaign. Both parties are searching for one this year. Some of the best slogans have been the Republican "A full dinner pail" (McKinley); "The square deal" (Theodore Roosevelt); "Don't swap horses in the middle of the stream" (Lincoln); and the Democratic "16 to 1" (Bryan); "He kept us out of war" (Wilson); and "The forgotten man" (Franklin D. Roosevelt). Some have already been suggested for the Republicans this year: "Landon Knox out Roosevelt," "Land Landon with Landslide," "Off the Rocks with Landon and Knox." One of the points raised against the proposed nomination of Governor H. Styles Bridges, of New Hampshire, for the Vice Presidency in Cleveland, was the opening it would give the Democrats: "Landon Bridge's falling down."

Campaigns are filled with oratory, public meetings, rallies, parades and other demonstrations. The speakers' bureau enlists, supplies and instructs speakers of all types for all kinds of meetings. It is quite probable that as a vote getter the typical political speaker, especially of the "spellbinder" variety, has been overvalued, and of late years has suffered deflation. People want to hear and see the nominees, and personality impressions will produce results on election day; but it is not likely that campaign oratory, apart from the candidate's personality, ever changes many votes, whether it is of the emotion-arousing variety or the thoughtful appeal to reason. People like a good show and they will attend political rallies out of curiosity or a desire for entertainment, but the enthusiasm of a skillfully staged rally is deceptive as indicating the action of the same people at the polls. Public meetings, demonstrations and rallies, nevertheless, all have their proper places in a good campaign— they arouse party enthusiasm, they impress the laggard and wavering with the virility of the organization, they produce a big harvest of newspaper publicity, and they provide a setting for exhibiting the party candidates.

Practical politicians are convinced that, whereas the above

methods of reaching the voters in the mass are an essential part of every campaign, personal solicitation of individual voters is the best procedure and most certain of results. Direct personal approach through canvasses, personal letters, and personal work through clubs and small organizations are the most effective vote-getting methods thus far devised. Remarkable efficiency and thoroughness characterized the policy of "personal contacting" used by Jim Farley in securing the nomination and winning the election of Roosevelt in 1932. He made two extensive coast-to-coast tours in 1931 and 1932, compiled lists of all the Democratic workers he met, and during the campaign wrote over 3,000,000 personal letters to these people. Daily telephone conferences with his chief lieutenants in each of the forty-eight states characterized the latter part of the campaign. Roosevelt also flooded the mails with personal letters of appeal, guidance and encouragement to the party leaders in every election precinct of the nation. "And look at the result!" Farley declared with justifiable satisfaction as the election returns were tabulated. Much attention is also devoted to winning the votes of first-time voters by special organization and personal work among college students and racial groups. For the 1936 campaign both parties have established organizations for young people: the Young Republican National Federation, and the Young Democratic Clubs and the Roosevelt First-Voters League. It is estimated that 9,000,000 young men and women have come of voting age since 1932, and both parties are out to corral as much of this vote as possible.

No balance can ever be struck between appeals to emotion and appeals to reason in their effectiveness as campaign devices. Both will continue to play important parts in campaign strategy. Their effectiveness varies with voters' types, leading issues, general conditions of economic welfare and national tranquillity, the spokesman, and the channel of propaganda utilized. It is not likely, either, that with the passing of the years and the assumed general intellectual improvement of the nation there is much difference in the utility and the appeal of these two types of

PRESIDENTIAL CAMPAIGNS

propaganda. The influence of the radio is already being felt in shunting emotional oratory to the back of the stage and bringing into prominence more reasoned, dispassionate, less sensational public addresses. Whether the nation is "going intellectual" or not may be an open question, but with high-class entertainment available at the turn of the dial none but the most dyed-in-the-wool partisan will listen to a disappointing mixture of humor, pathos and reason, whereas a really good address on a high intellectual plane will hold millions in deep thought and contemplation.

A new nonparty device, the national poll or straw ballot, has come into prominence in the last three campaigns as indicating the relative strength of the two tickets and the course of the campaign. The most elaborate of these polls has been conducted by *The Literary Digest*. The names of 20,000,000 persons were picked at random from telephone directories and state automobile registration lists. Postal cards with detachable return cards, sent out in September, 1932, carried two questions: "Whom do you favor for President now?" and "Whom did you favor in 1928?" The poll gave Hoover 37.5 and Roosevelt 55.9 per cent of the popular vote, which proved to be 96.3 per cent accurate. The poll gave Hoover 57 electoral votes (he actually received 59) and Roosevelt 474 (he actually received 472) and was 99.6 per cent accurate in this forecast. This magazine has also conducted polls during the past three years on the status of the New Deal. The results of the last one were announced in the middle of January, 1936. It asked for a response to the question: "Do you now approve of the acts and policies of the Roosevelt New Deal to date?" Of the nearly 2,000,000 ballots returned, 37.3 per cent voted "Yes" and 62.7 per cent voted "No."

The party in power—that is, in control of the Presidency—always has a distinct campaign advantage over its opponent. Its partisans occupy thousands of federal positions all over the country, and it mans the important administrative offices in Washington. The entire body of that portion of the civil service that is within the spoils system constitutes a vast campaign working force. Furthermore, the Presidency is the most publicized office in the world, and the President is accorded radio time and newspaper space as befits the office and standing of the Chief Executive, privileges that give to his party and to himself a most important advantage in the campaign. In addition, there is a certain psychological advantage that accrues to the party in power. It is on the defensive, whereas the party out of power must lead the attack upon the established authority, and successfully promote an alternative program. Including this year's election, the Republicans have entered ten of the last fifteen campaigns in the strategic position of the party in power. Moreover, or as evidenced by that record, the nation is predominantly Republican.

The Splinter Parties

Discussion of the minor or third parties—called "splinter parties" in more recent discussions—has not been included in this chapter, largely because of their contemporary insignificance and their policy of following much the same campaign procedure as the major parties, within the limitations of their organizations and funds. Dominant as has been the biparty principle in the United States, there has been a succession of minor parties from the days of the Whigs in the 1830's and 1840's. The Civil War period brought out the Liberty, Free Soil, and Native American or Know Nothing parties; the Greenback and Populist parties expressed agrarian discontent in the last quarter of the nineteenth century; the Progressives of 1912 almost assumed the position of a major party in a single campaign. The leading present members of this group are the Prohibition, Socialist, Socialist Labor, and Workers' or Communist parties. Each has been identified with particular programs, and the supporters are people for whom principle takes precedence over expediency. The total vote of the minor parties in the election of 1932 was just under three per cent of the entire vote cast. Norman Thomas, third-time Socialist candidate this year, has

PRESIDENTIAL CAMPAIGNS

a very engaging personality and presents moderate socialism in its best form and most effective appeal, but disunity within his party, as was evidenced by the split in the Cleveland convention in May, weakens a force that has already shown its impotence in a time when economic discontent ought to play into socialist hands. The Socialist Labor, Workers' and Prohibition parties have too narrow a clientele and appeal to be significant factors in the present campaign. There was an earlier prospect of a radical movement to put a Farmer-Labor ticket in the field, but that has apparently been abandoned, along with similar earlier prospects of independent political action by Father Coughlin's National Union for Social Justice and Dr. Townsend's old-age pension movement. Something of this nature is seen in the Lemke-Union party, announced in June with the cordial approval of Father Coughlin, and subsequently apparently endorsed by Mr. Townsend. Independent action is restrained this year by the feeling that it is a case of "Roosevelt or reaction," and that liberal forces owe it to their ideals of social and economic justice to support the President rather than contribute to his defeat by dispersing the liberal vote.

Campaign Aspects of the General Situation

Presidential elections are much influenced, and often determined, by specific aspects of the general situation. Of first importance is the internal condition of the parties. Fortunate is the candidate who finds himself at the head of a vigorous, enthusiastic, firmly united party in which harmony and unity are actualities and the basis of energetic work in his behalf. Because of the diverse elements that comprise the two major parties, factional splits, dissatisfied groups, inactive elements and possibly even secession often endanger the success of the ticket. The regular Republicans went down to inglorious defeat with Taft in 1912 when the Progressive party drew off the liberals under Theodore Roosevelt's leadership. The disastrous Democratic convention of 1924 wrecked whatever chances John W. Davis might have had, and he was forced to lead a party so broken into dissatisfied elements and inactive factions that his poll of one-third of the popular vote was really a notable achievement. Just as the support of the state organizations is of great benefit to a man in the national convention contest for the nomination, so their immediate, whole-hearted support is of strategic advantage to the party nominee in the final campaign. When the President is a candidate for reelection, such support is practically guaranteed to him because of his hold on the state organizations derived from four years of federal patronage.

Political party fortunes rise and fall with the tide-like flow of prosperity. A party may ride the crest of the wave to reelection or go down to defeat in the trough of the waves of the ebbing currents. Nothing succeeds so surely in national elections as general prosperity; nothing is so hard to withstand as the absence of it. For decades the Republican party has been associated with national prosperity; the Democratic party, with policies that would endanger it. That the Republicans have no patent rights on prosperity or hold any magic formula for it was amply demonstrated during Hoover's administration, but the popular mind unthinkingly charged him and his party with large responsibility for the depression—or, at least, with inability to extricate the nation from it—and the voters turned to the other party for a hopeful alternative agency and program. The landslide that carried the Republicans out of office was not so much a vote against Hoover as it was a vote against hard times, against the persistent depression. It is almost impossible for a party to weather the storms of economic adversity and general economic discontent, as it is almost impossible to make any headway against a party in a time of rising or continued prosperity. This is the chief reliance for reelection of the Roosevelt administration at the time of this writing (July, 1936). The concrete gains and the definite business improvement of the past winter and spring breed confidence in the future, and counsel against change of policy, leadership, and party control of the government. Even if it be granted that to a large degree political responsibility for prosperity is a state of mind, it is, nevertheless, a fact that parties and political leaders are powerless when they go up against such a substantial and confirmed state of public mind as evolves from the existence of prosperity or the absence of it.

Every campaign brings forth several special phases—some, traditional in American campaigns, and some, unique to the immediate situation—that require special strategy and careful handling by the national chairman and the nominee. An effort is always made to reach out and get hold of the popular side of the most vital issue in the campaign, and to avoid being outmaneuvered by the opposition into an unpopular or unsound position on the less vital issues. This may dictate extreme caution, as in the case of Harding's statements on the League of Nations issue in 1920, or in a disregard of leading questions while dwelling upon a popular theme, as in Hoover's concentration on the prosperity of the nation in 1928 and his avoidance of the issues and tactics employed by Governor Smith. The campaign of 1928 was notable for the importance assumed by the religious and prohibition questions and the political associations of the Democratic candidate—issues that have very infrequently found their way into American elections. The Democratic party always faces a dilemma in Tammany: it is both a big asset and a big liability. Victory in New York (with its 47 electoral votes) hangs on Tammany's support, yet great public resentment among independent voters and in other Democratic strongholds, notably the South, is easily aroused by any particularly close relation between Tammany and the party nominee, as in the case of Smith's candidacy in 1928. Landon faced something of the same problem in the Republican primaries of this year, especially in California. As early as last December William Randolph Hearst made a special trip to Emporia, Kansas, with Arthur Brisbane and Paul Block, to secure an open avowal of candidacy from Landon and to proffer his very influential press and personal support. Landon parried the request and offer, and never openly committed himself on either matter. The closest that the situation ever came to a head was in the California primaries, where Hearst entered and supported a body of delegates pledged to the Kansan; but fortunately for the governor's peace of mind they were defeated by the Hoover delegates.

The support of one certain special interest is always sought and welcomed because today it carries no sinister implication or burden—and probably, it must be admitted, no great weight. Reference is made to the American Federation of Labor. Its traditional Gompers-established policy of nonpartisanship leads its president and executive committee to declare in each campaign which party it approves in that election. The stamp of approval has commonly been placed upon the Democratic candidate, and this is true this year, the decision having been reached even before the conventions were held, platforms adopted, or the Republican nominee was determined. On May 5, President William Green, speaking upon the political situation, declared in an address: "We cannot afford to make any change in the leadership of our present forward-looking social movement. We have been inspired and thrilled by the leadership that destiny has given us and we want to continue it without change."[11] After the meeting he was asked whether his statement was to be interpreted as meaning that he stood for the reelection of Roosevelt. "No other interpretation can be placed upon it," he replied.

The activity and the influence of the American Liberty League in this year's campaign are being watched with much interest and with some trepidation in both Republican and Democratic quarters. It is a new organization, founded in August, 1934, by a group of prominent men from both parties. According to its leaders and articles of incorporation, it is a nonpartisan organization formed to preserve fundamental American institutions and principles, to combat radicalism, preserve personal and property rights, and uphold and preserve the Constitution. Its leaders include Jouett Shouse, John W. Davis, and Alfred

[11] Address at Washington before the National Women's Trade Union League.

E. Smith, Democrats; Irenée du Pont, Nathan Miller, and James W. Wadsworth, Republicans. It has already amassed tremendous financial resources to be utilized in its educational and publicity activities, and such others as it may adopt. It was regarded at the outset as a crystallization of conservative sentiment, more or less nonpartisan, against some of the tendencies of the Roosevelt administration and the New Deal. Roosevelt twitted it with being a "lover of property" and with laying too much stress on the protection of property and too little on the protection of the average citizen. It will be an anti-Roosevelt force in this campaign, although its support of the Republican candidate may well prove a boomerang as indicating that he is the candidate of the moneyed, propertied, conservative elements of the nation. Certainly, Smith's demagogic address before it in Washington, on January 25, 1936, with millions of dollars of American capitalism represented among those seated at the tables, was of no aid to the Republican cause. His severe arraignment of the Roosevelt administration, his ill-advised comparisons with Moscow and communistic Russia, and his threat to "take a walk" after the Philadelphia convention—all of this in the atmosphere and setting of "predatory wealth and corporate interests"—has been held by many experienced political observers to mark the turning point in the political fortunes of the present administration in its reclamation of public support.

The political situation in a state often has a special bearing on the national campaign, because of the strength of the party's state ticket. At times a candidate for governor may carry so much prestige and vote-getting power as to insure the victory of the national ticket in the state when its success would be problematical if left to its own resources. In 1928 Smith personally appealed to Roosevelt to accept the Democratic nomination for governor of New York in order to strengthen the Smith national candidacy in the state. Roosevelt was elected governor with 2,130,194 votes, while Smith polled 2,089,863 and lost the state to Hoover. This year the New York situation recurred to give Roosevelt deep concern. Governor Lehman has shown himself in two gubernatorial elections to be one of the greatest vote-getters in the political history of the state—greater than either Smith or Roosevelt—polling from half a million to a million more votes than those popular candidates. Even in the Roosevelt landslide of 1932, Lehman's vote exceeded Roosevelt's by 125,000. In the present campaign, with popular sentiment running against the administration in the East and the Republicans all set to make a strong drive in up-state New York, Lehman's assistance on the ticket is especially to be desired by the President—and on May 20 Lehman delivered a body blow to the Democratic cause by announcing he would not be a candidate for reelection. Under much party and Presidential pressure, and after a great demonstration of his popularity in the Philadelphia convention, Lehman finally yielded and announced on June 30 his candidacy to succeed himself. This action will greatly enhance the President's chances in his home state.

Some Notable Campaigns

The election of Andrew Jackson, Democrat, over John Quincy Adams, Republican, in 1828 marked the beginning of party government and party politics as they are now understood. Jackson was swept into office by an enthusiastic, more or less unorganized mass movement, and his success was labeled by the old party bosses as "the triumph of the mob." His campaign really began immediately after the election of 1824 with the cries of "stolen election" and "cabinet bargain," because of the action of the House of Representatives in electing Adams in disregard of Jackson's popular and electoral vote pluralities. Jackson was "the people's candidate"; he appealed to the popular imagination; and the lowering of suffrage qualifications added great voting power to the masses that clung to him. He was a man of rugged character, tremendous courage and force, crude, without culture, full of faults, unforgiving, swayed by the violence of his own prejudices, a born leader and fighter, as relentless toward his foes as he was loyal to his friends, of absolute sincerity in his devotion to the masses and his belief in them. "Old Hickory," popular military hero of the battle of New Orleans, found no match in the aristocratic Adams, who was quite devoid of human appeal. There was a complete absence of issues in the campaign, or of any discussion of them. There was only one objective: the election of Jackson and the defeat of Adams. Men of every shade of opinion supported Jackson, but it was a picturesque contest between Southwestern democracy and New England aristocracy. Jackson's election, amid vast popular enthusiasm, partook more of the nature of a social and political revolution, bringing in its train changes in political party organization, control and procedure, and sectional dominance in governmental control.[12]

The "log cabin and hard cider" campaign of 1840 for the election of "Tippecanoe and Tyler, too" was unquestionably one of the most unique and picturesque battles in American political history. The Democrats confidently offered President Martin Van Buren for reelection, in the belief that the disunified Whigs would offer weak opposition with General William Henry Harrison. They proceeded to belittle Harrison by saying that he lived in a log cabin and drank hard cider—thereby unwisely setting the stage for one of the greatest campaign demonstrations of all time. All over the country, people gathered by the thousands at mass meetings, parading behind log cabins drawn by white horses, and singing songs written for the occasion. Harrison fitted into this picture admirably, he had gained great military prestige in a decisive battle over the British and Indians at Tippecanoe, and proved a great rallying center for the discordant elements of the Whigs. The Whig convention made no attempt to agree on a platform, but it did spend a great deal of time in cautious negotiation before it nominated the old Indian fighter. It was an amazing "hullabaloo" campaign, without

[12] See Claude G. Bowers, *The Party Battles of the Jackson Period* (Boston, 1922); Gerald W. Johnson, *Andrew Jackson* (New York, 1927); Frederic A. Ogg, *The Reign of Andrew Jackson* (New Haven, 1919).

issues, logic or coherence, but with tremendous fire and confusion, vast parades, furious denunciation, and enthusiasm. The Democrats, who said Harrison was elected by "noise, nonsense and numbers," were left stunned, crushed, angry and bewildered.

The campaign of 1860 was carried on in a country on the verge of great civil war, with the Southern states, led by South Carolina, straining at the leash, and the great slavery controversy gripping the nation in deep tension and ominous emotion. The new-born Republican party, militant, vigorous, imbued with a high moral purpose, entered the campaign with great confidence. The Democrats were split on the great issue of the hour, the extreme Southern pro-slavery and the Northern popular-sovereignty doctrines. They held not one or two, but several conventions, and finally presented Stephen A. Douglas as the Northern candidate and John C. Breckinridge as the Southern extremist leader. Ruined, exhausted by internal struggle, hopeless and helpless, the Democratic factions poured out more bitterness among themselves than they showed toward the Republicans. Douglas was a brilliant and eloquent speaker, a rough-and-tumble fighter, famed because of his debate with Lincoln, and he was the only candidate to take to the "stump" in the campaign. Lincoln had risen from obscurity as the "rail splitter" and "Honest Abe" to make a strong appeal to the common people, especially of the West, but he was regarded by the Eastern conservative Republicans as too unknown and inexperienced to deal with such a great emergency. There was great enthusiasm for him, especially among young men just out of college, and a marching organization, the "Lincoln Wide-Awakes," attired in oilcloth capes, carrying torch lights, and marching in military formation, proved very useful and effective in the campaign. Lincoln left Springfield only once during the campaign and made not a single campaign speech.[13]

[13] See William Starr Myers, *The Republican Party: A History* (2d ed., New York, 1931), chaps. i-x; Andrew W. Crandall, *The Early History of the Republican Party* (Boston, 1931); Frank R. Kent, *The Democratic Party: A History* (New York, 1928), chaps. xiv-xviii; Emerson D. Fite, *The Presidential Campaign of 1860* (New York, 1911).

PRESIDENTIAL CAMPAIGNS

The campaign of 1896 would be notable, if for no other reason, because it ushered William Jennings Bryan into American politics as a force to be reckoned with for the next twenty-five years. But it was also notable for other reasons: East *v.* West and South, sound money *v.* inflation, gold *v.* silver, business world *v.* the farmer, reason *v.* emotion. William McKinley, presented as the "advance agent of prosperity," of fine record in public office and as a soldier, student of the tariff and author of the McKinley tariff bill of 1890, was a fitting candidate to lead the Republican campaign for protectionism. But Bryan (dubbed by his opponents "the boy orator from the Platte"), having stampeded the Democratic convention for free silver, led the entire campaign into the money issue. His was the voice of social and economic discontent, of the common people. Here was a man of amazing ability in swaying the masses and influencing public opinion, of unquestioned honesty and sincerity, of good temper and genuine poise, in whom political convictions burned with religious fervor. He covered over 18,000 miles in speaking tours and made thousands of addresses, while McKinley made infrequent, dignified appearances to visiting delegations at the front porch of his Canton, Ohio, home. The real Republican power in the campaign was Mark Hanna, campaign manager, schooled in Ohio politics, who believed in the use of money, knew where to get it for this campaign, and went out and got millions of it. The Republicans matched Bryan's emotional appeals with tons of literature in an educational campaign, and the campaign lasted long enough for the voters to be instructed in economics—and education and organization won![14]

Herbert Hoover won the election in 1928, but the campaign will always be known as the "Smith campaign," even though the defeated candidate carried only eight states. None of the

[14] See Myers, *op. cit.*, chaps. xi-xiv; Kent, *op. cit.*, pp. 19-25; William J. Bryan, *The First Battle: A Story of the Campaign of 1896* (Chicago, 1896); Paxton Hibben, *The Peerless Leader: William Jennings Bryan* (New York, 1929); Herbert Croly, *Marcus Alonzo Hanna* (New York, 1912).

customary issues figured in the contest. Just four questions were raised: prohibition, religion, Tammany, and the personality of the two candidates. Both rose from humble origins, one from an Iowa village and the other from the sidewalks of New York, to highest positions of executive responsibility —one in world-wide activity and in Cabinet office, the other as governor of the most important state in the Union. Hoover, not a politician, was all that any voter could want in a presidential candidate—a sort of super-man in the performance of great tasks, a humanitarian, but lacking in the warmth of human appeal. Smith was the kind of man people fight over, a very human figure, schooled in New York politics and party-machine tactics, self-reliant and vigorous; he was presented to the Democratic convention by Franklin D. Roosevelt in a very able and effective nominating speech as "the Happy Warrior." The campaign saw religious antagonisms take an unprecedented importance in American politics, it saw the solid Democratic South rise in early rebellion with a sort of fanaticism for temperance and Protestantism. Smith made no effort to dissociate himself from Tammany's organization and support, and was unequivocal in his advocacy of the repeal of prohibition. His selection of John J. Raskob as campaign manager was an early blunder; there were many others in his campaign. Raskob is a "big business man," a member of the Philadelphia (Republican) Union League Club, a prominent Catholic, and with outspoken hatred for prohibition. Hoover made no errors, and gave Smith no opening to use his characteristic New York campaign methods. Hoover never once so much as mentioned Smith by name. Under such circumstances and conditions the Democrats never had a chance.

The 1936 Campaign

President Roosevelt has regained considerable lost ground since the opening of the present year—so much so that in some Republican quarters a defeatest attitude and hopelessness have been apparent. This is not due so much to a feeling that he has purchased reelection with AAA and PWA money as it is to Republican factionalism, the absence of a strong Republican alternative platform, the continuing improvement in business, the lack of a strong Republican candidate, and the President's own popularity and extraordinary political skill. As a master of practical politics he easily outranks all other Democrats and all Republicans, although he may not exhibit the same sagacity in the future, since he is now deprived of the notable counsel of Louis McHenry Howe. The President radiates confidence in the outcome of the election, just as he has evinced faith, throughout his administration, in the ultimate success of his program. He deliberately gives the impression that he regards the election as a mere formality. It is a clever move, good tactics, and by it he gets the jump on the opposition. In the first week of his term, back in 1933, he showed himself to be a man of action in a great emergency; he continues to show the same spirit in his partisan efforts for reelection.

Economic collapse is still possible in this country in the present situation, but there is abundant evidence that the nation is in the midst of an upsurge of business such as the country has not seen since 1929. If this continues to Election Day the administration is unbeatable. Yet there is a strange inconsistency and lurking danger in the situation: there are still about 20,000,000 persons on relief; and when government spending stops, as it must if solvency is to be maintained, and the bonus cash has left the pockets of the veterans, what then? The socialists contend that the New Deal is merely another capitalistic effort to satisfy the masses with half a loaf; conservatives and business leaders charge it with too much radicalism and unsound economic and fiscal policies. Let a prolonged business recession hit the country, and the administration would suffer grievously under a barrage from both fronts. As a matter of fact, there is not so much criticism of the New Deal's abstract ideals; it is the efforts and agencies to put them into effect that hurt. There is little quarrel with the theses that the hungry must be fed, child labor abolished, working conditions improved, farm prices raised, stock exchanges regulated, banking laws made more strict, and security in old age, illness and adversity provided. The objections arise out of the concrete legal procedures and governmental action taken to put them into effect. In answer, the New Deal partisans charge their critics with hypocritical advocacy of social ideals and opposition to concrete policies designed to put them into operation.

President Roosevelt is greatly blessed by the absence of a strong Republican candidate and a strong Republican platform. Granted that the country has grown tired and disappointed with the President, dissatisfied with his leadership, there is no great confidence in the "built-up" Republican candidate. None of the men considered before the Republican convention really measured up to the needs of the hour. There was an amazing bankruptcy of a great party, which even in the debacle of 1932 polled over 15,000,000 votes, and of which Elihu Root boasted some twenty years ago that it alone was fit to rule. It seems incredible that a party that holds in its ranks so many leading business men, bankers, professional men and great executives should have exhibited such a paucity of outstanding, available presidential timber in this year of extraordinary party and national need. The party has been in a similar plight as to program and platform, with no real agreement over the party position possible between the factional and sectional interests. Whether the platform as finally evolved and expounded during the campaign proves to be a conservative, liberal or middle-of-the-road program, the party will probably be as liberal, as near the New Deal, as the desire for victory requires. Moreover, such success as may be achieved will be hailed as an achievement of conservatism, no matter how liberal that conservatism may have to be. The most serious internal Republican problem centers in the necessity of uniting, conciliating or harmonizing the Middle West farm belt with the Eastern industrialists. Senator Borah's achievements in Illinois and Nebraska testified to the spirit of revolt present in that indispensable Republican territory against the traditional type of Republicanism found in the East and typified by the Hilles-Roraback-Brown-Schorr leadership.

Governor Landon's candidacy for the nomination presented a fine example of a political "build-up" and skillful management. Until last fall he was scarcely known outside of Kansas and the adjoining states, and prior to his nomination he had made just two political speeches and appeared in one radio interview. About all that was known of him was that he was in favor of balancing budgets! Farley unwittingly added to his publicity campaign by calling him "the governor of a typical prairie state!" He scrupulously followed a policy of noncommitment on the issues of the day; he said the Republican party must proceed on "sound and progressive" lines, that he would provide "humanitarian legislation," that he would remove the "disadvantages under which labor and agriculture suffer," and that he believed in government regulation of business that "protects, not hampers." Asked regarding social security, he replied, "I am for it!" Questioned on foreign affairs, he said, "As to our relations with other countries, it might repay all of us to read Washington's Farewell Address again." Campaign utterances are expected to be vague, but these set a high-water mark for noncommittal ambiguity. An extremely clever campaign was waged in his behalf, except in California where Hearst maneuvered him into embarrassment. He gave no offense to any other candidate and never broke with any of the party leaders, East or West. This largely explains the ease with which agreement upon him was reached in Cleveland. He is said to be very able in conciliating diverse groups and personalities. In his two addresses, in restrained language, he held the Roosevelt administration up to criticism and spoke in praise of simple, homely public virtues and personal idealism.

The Republicans in Cleveland made a supreme effort to establish and demonstrate a show of unity in the party. For the fourth time in the party's history a Presidential nominee was named by unanimous action on the first ballot, and all opposition withdrew from the balloting for both offices. The gathering was described as "a strange convocation of the quick and the dead"; this referred to the young Western liberals and the "Old Guard" ex-senators, respectively. It was a convention dominated by amateurs in national politics, giving rather more serious thought than usual to the platform, devoid of intense enthusiasm, and dependent upon Hoover for its only real show and upon Kansas sunflowers for its only color. The "stop-Landon" movement collapsed early, and the Kansan's nomination was conceded before Senator Steiwer began his less-than-average keynote speech. There were only two dramatic moments in the four days' sessions: those of Hoover's notable address and Landon's platform telegram. Former President Hoover rose to new party and oratorical heights when he called upon the party "to enter into a holy crusade for liberty," to "stop the retreat," and to "thank Almighty God for the Constitution and the Supreme Court." The "Grand Old Party" went West; it selected both candidates from the Mississippi valley—two ex-Bull Moosers who bolted the party in 1912. "Main Street" was in the saddle. The crusading young Kansas liberals took the party home to the Western prairies with them: Governor Alf M. Landon for President, Colonel Frank Knox, of Chicago, for Vice-President, and John Hamilton, of Kansas, chairman of the national committee and campaign manager.

The Democrats at Philadelphia were held by a veteran journalist to have contributed their portion to "the two least memorable major party conventions in history" and to have prolonged their gathering over five days and nights "for material reasons, until it became one of the greatest bores of its kind in American history." Completely controlled by White House strategy, it renominated President Roosevelt and Vice President Garner by acclamation and adopted a platform emphatically endorsing and continuing the New Deal in phrases of general terms that seldom go beyond a wide statement of objectives. The delegates became fatigued and bored as Chairman Farley overdid his showmanship and the leaders of the convention overplayed their hands in manufacturing synthetic enthusiasm and parading an almost endless stream of speakers to second the nominations of the party's standard bearers. Three events stood out above the week's lethargy: the unanimous convention vote to abrogate the century-old two-thirds rule in voting on nominees, the rioting in one of the galleries when banners were unfurled ("by some Republican hoodlums"!) for "Al Smith—we want Al Smith" that required police interference to quell the fist-fights and escort the demonstrators from the hall, and the stupendous acclaim given President Roosevelt by 80,000 rain-soaked people at Franklin Field stadium when he appeared Saturday evening to deliver his acceptance speech. The motion to rescind the two-thirds rule was adopted only after two days of debate in the rules committee, against strong southern opposition, and with the aid of a resolution that directs the national committee to bring in to the 1940 convention a plan for revising the apportionment system which will take into account the Democratic voting strength in each state. Any such change would not become effective before 1944. Just before the convention opened, an ineffective appeal was made in an open letter to the delegates to repudiate President Roosevelt and the New Deal or else change the name of the party. The authors of the appeal were: Alfred E. Smith, Bainbridge Colby, James A. Reed, Joseph B. Ely (former Massachusetts governor), and Daniel F. Cohalan.

A new character appeared on the scene on June 19th in the person of Congressman William Lemke, of North Dakota, who announced the establishment of the Union party, with himself as self-designated Presidential candidate, and Thomas Charles O'Brien, a Boston attorney, as Vice Presidential candidate. The program of the organization sets up "economic slavery" as the leading issue of the year and concentrates on policies for currency reform, agricultural restoration, and social security. Mr. Lemke received such an immediate and spontaneous blessing from Father Coughlin that their cooperation seems a matter of preliminary arrangement. At the Townsend Cleveland convention of the middle of July a grand, majestic union was ostensibly concluded that is designed to bring to the support of the Lemke Union party the anti-Roosevelt hordes of the Townsend Old Age Pension organization, Father Coughlin's National Union for Social Justice, and the Reverend Gerald L. K. Smith's (late Huey Long's) Share-the-Wealth Clubs. Father Coughlin launched the cooperative enterprise as he delivered a bitter, violent attack upon President Roosevelt, whom he called "the great betrayer and liar, Franklin 'Double-Crossing' Roosevelt." Led by such anti-administration critics, if the movement meets with any success it will be chiefly at the expense of the Landon-Republican forces.

The basic issue of the campaign will undoubtedly be unemployment and the problems that arise out of it and the policies followed to combat it. It is said that there are still nearly 12,000,000 workers unemployed today, and 20,000,000 on public relief. From this problem, as yet unsolved, flow the major questions of the day: relief policies, federal spending, public works program, farm relief, social insurance, and constitutionalism. The unbalanced budgets, the huge treasury deficits, the unprecedented national debt, will throw the national fiscal situation into bold relief. The states'-rights issue will raise its head again in political argument. This ancient shibboleth of American politics will be grasped, incongruously, by the Republicans, not so much for its reality (the Republicans would appear ridiculous in that light) as for its traditional appeal and emotional advantage. The resultant situation adds to the anomaly of American politics, for it is a direct reversal of party position. In this new alignment the Republicans have deserted the great Federalist jurist, John Marshall, precursor of Republican federal expansionism, and the Democrats have conceived a sudden and unhistorical love for federal power. Actually, if most of the new champions of states'-rights would be honest with themselves, the issue would not appear as states *v.* federal action, but would clarify as *any* action *v. laissez faire*. Most groups and individuals taking refuge in the sacred province of the states do not really care about the status of the states; they are opposed to governmental regulation or action of any kind. They raise the old cry of invasion of states'-rights chiefly to trade upon popular prejudice and traditional ideals, and, in doing so, fly in the face of inevitable evolution.

There is real danger that the Republicans will give too much attention to the presidential campaign and not enough to the congressional elections. A whole new House of Representatives and thirty-two Senators are to be elected. The seats to be filled include those now held by Robinson, Harrison, Glass, Couzens, Norris, Gore, McNary, Lewis, Borah, Capper, Dickinson, Bailey, and Costigan—a notable body of congressional leaders. A strong Republican group is especially needed in Congress at the present time. Even if Republican presidential defeat be conceded, a strong minority is needed in Congress to restrain such Roosevelt tendencies toward dictatorship and ill-advised legislation as have appeared or may appear. The safety of American institutions depends in large degree upon such opposition, especially in overturning the present Democratic top-heavy House and Senate.

Chapter V: The Use of Money in Elections[1]

by JAMES KERR POLLOCK
Professor of Political Science, University of Michigan

ON THE first day of April, 1936, the United States Senate adopted a resolution which had been before that body for several months. It provided "that a special committee consisting of five Senators, to be appointed by the Vice President, is hereby authorized and directed to investigate the campaign expenditures of the various presidential candidates, vice-presidential candidates, and candidates for the United States Senate, in both parties, the names of the persons, firms, or corporations subscribing, the amount contributed, the method of expenditure of said sums, and all facts in relation thereto, not only as to the subscriptions of money and expenditures thereof but as to the use of any other means or influence, including the promise or use of patronage, or use of any public funds, and all other facts in relation thereto which would not only be of public interest but which would aid the Senate in enacting any remedial legislation or in deciding any contests which might be instituted involving the right to a seat in the United States Senate."[2]

A similar resolution had passed the House of Representatives many months before, and both resolutions were quite similar to resolutions passed by preceding Congresses in election years.

---

[1] The most recent thorough treatment of the subject of campaign funds is that made by Miss Louise Overacker, *Money in Elections* (New York, 1932). See also the author's *Party Campaign Funds* (New York, 1926); Earl Sikes, *Corrupt Practices Acts* (Durham, N. C., 1928). For a treatment of the problem of money in English, French and German elections, see the author's *Money and Politics Abroad* (New York, 1932). The best single congressional document on the subject is the *Testimony on Remedial Legislation, Nye Committee Hearings, United States Senate, 1931.*

[2] S. Res. 225, 74th Congress, 2nd Session.

THE USE OF MONEY IN ELECTIONS

In fact, the practice is now well established of setting up investigating committees to look into all the facts relating to the expenditure of money in national elections. This has not been the case in the states.

But why should it have become a regular congressional practice to investigate campaign funds? Only occasionally and at irregular intervals are investigations made of lobbying, of banking, of business. But here is an investigation which is conducted almost every two years with perfect regularity, although not always with complete thoroughness. The answer is, that elections are the heartbeats of democratic government, and if they are manipulated through illegal expenditure of money, the stream of democratic policy is polluted at its source, and democracy is a sham and a delusion.

The members of the Congress must all be politicians. Their tenure of office is dependent upon popular favor. As practical men and women, they know the importance and value of campaign funds in determining the results of their election. Furthermore, they realize the touchiness of the voters when confronted with large political funds. Finally, they understand the possible connection between the expenditure of campaign funds and the determination of public policy. Hence the regular investigating committees in election years. Hence the increased and continuing publicity about campaign funds.

On the other hand, the necessity which Congress feels to pry into party and candidate expenditures is an indication of its distrust with existing legal restrictions. If political practices were carefully regulated by effective statutes, Congress would not necessarily feel impelled to create investigating committees. The British Parliament does not find it necessary to conduct such investigations. So the existence of the committees is an indication of the decrepit state of corrupt practices regulations, as well as evidence of congressional recognition of the fundamental importance of campaign fund publicity.

But why are political funds so important in the United States? Why are they so necessary to political campaigns? A hundred years ago political campaigns were relatively frugal affairs. The electorate, down to the turn of the present century, consisted of a relatively small fraction of the present percentage of voters. Candidates for office had but a relatively small number of voters to reach, and the appeal, if made at all, consisted largely of personal interviews. The congressional candidate could hitch up his horse to the old buggy and drive about his constituency without spending much money.

Today, with a potential voting population as listed in the census of 1930 of 67,000,000, and with an actual vote cast in 1932 of 36,000,000, the problem of appealing to the electorate becomes quite different. In the average congressional district about 300,000 persons must be reached. In running for governor in any of the larger states, candidates must deal with electorates which have millions of voters. A national campaign involves financial difficulties undreamed of by Jefferson and Jackson. This is not to say that these early statesmen were unmindful of the power of money in elections. It merely means that today the magnitude of the country, the enormous size and complexity of the electorate, and the availability of modern campaign techniques, has changed the whole face of elections. They have become very expensive affairs, and the possession of a campaign fund is in most cases a condition precedent to undertaking political activity.

In other words, aside from any of the abuses which have crept into the financial side of political campaigns, money must be collected in order to provide the necessary means of reaching the voters. A voter will not as a rule vote for a candidate who is unknown to him. But to make the candidate known requires the spending of money for literature, for advertising, for meetings, and—very important today—for radio. All of these items involve considerable financial outlays. Occasionally, of course, one finds a candidate like Senator Norris in Nebraska or Senator Couzens in Michigan who does not find it necessary to spend money during the campaign. But with most candidates the first thought has to be, "How shall I finance the campaign?" Hence we can lay it down as the law and the gospel that campaign funds are necessary under modern political conditions, and must be talked about not in terms of their elimination, but rather in terms of their proper regulation.

A little reflection will make it clear why American political campaigns are perforce particularly expensive to the country. In the first place, our political system, being federal, requires the election of many officials at various times. In the second place, insistence on local self-government has necessitated the election of numerous local officials. In the third place, terms of office have been short, thus requiring more frequent elections. Fourthly, Americans have gone to the greatest extreme in requiring all kinds of offices to be filled by election. Judges, administrative officers, boards and commissions, as well as executives and legislators, must be chosen in most jurisdictions by popular election. Consequently there is more electoral business to be done in the United States than in any other country in the world. And as in the case of any business, the larger the business the larger must be the outlay of funds. If elections were less frequent, if fewer officers were elected and if campaigns were shorter, much less money would have to be expended on elections. Even under these short-ballot conditions, however, money would still be necessary to present the claims of the candidates to the voters. One cannot conceive of elections without campaign funds.

We begin, therefore, by admitting the necessity of campaign funds in a democratic country like the United States. But to say that political funds are necessary is not to say that they are always properly handled. Hence, the next task is to throw light on the actual financial practices of candidates and parties in raising and expending money.

Sources of Political Funds

First, in dealing with the sources of political funds, we find a different situation today from that in the nineteenth century. When political expenses were small, political leaders did not have much difficulty in collecting the money necessary to finance a campaign. They usually called upon the office holders and the candidates, and almost always this source sufficed. But as political expenditures increased, mounting to large figures in the 'eighties and 'nineties, new sources of party revenue had to be found. It was not long before a new source of unexpected volume was uncovered. This source was the business men and corporations that might be helped or injured by legislative or administrative action. Mark Hanna soon perfected the system—until politicians themselves were astonished at the amount of money they were able to collect. However, with the enactment of the federal law of 1907 and of many state laws prohibiting contributions by corporations, the political parties were forced to turn to other sources of revenue. They continued quite widely to assess candidates and office holders, but this did not yield enough money for their purposes, especially in the national field, and it soon became the practice to conduct large public money drives. When parties had reached the stage where their funds came largely from voluntary contributions and not from blackmail, the modern period began and the mediaeval period ended—at least supposedly. In any event, the sources of party revenue today are not the same as they were in the nineteenth century.

At the present time the political party secures its money from three main sources: its friends, its office holders, and its candidates. The contributions received from its friends are voluntary, while the money received from candidates and office holders, although sometimes of a voluntary nature, comes as a rule from political assessments.

This practice of levying political assessment is probably the oldest form of party income. There are many historical references to the assessment of public officials, and as good a candidate as James A. Garfield in 1880 wrote to his national chairman, asking how much money the clerks in the departments at Washington were contributing.[3]

[3] *Appleton's*, vol. xii, p. 554.

Political assessments are gathered from candidates and office holders whether they are or aspire to be national, state or local officials. The practice is based on the principle that the candidates and the office holders are indebted to the party for their election or appointment. It is a very unfortunate but also a very natural feature of the spoils system; and since, under prevailing political practices, spoils appointees are or will be the greatest beneficiaries of the party's work, the argument is that they should show their appreciation and interest by contributing to party funds. Unless the party is kept in power they will lose their jobs; hence, in addition to voting, it is incumbent upon them also to contribute. To establish this practice definitely, parties have laid down the rule that an office holder is expected to pay a certain percentage of his salary every year or every campaign year to the party treasurer. In the case of candidates, they are expected to pay according to the positions they aspire to, and according to their means. No fixed percentage is ordinarily established for them, but both office holders and candidates know that they are expected to contribute, and they also know what their contributions are to be. The percentage naturally varies from state to state and from city to city. Sometimes office holders pay two per cent of each year's salary, and again they may pay three, four or five per cent. If the election is especially important and close they are sometimes called upon to pay the fixed percentage out of each month's salary for the duration of the campaign.

In national politics, however, the method of levying political assessments has almost entirely disappeared. The criminal code prohibits the solicitation of funds for political purposes from civil-service appointees, or by any person receiving a salary from the United States treasury. The civil-service laws of the United States dealing with political assessments have been reasonably successful in eliminating the evil from the national government. But the absence of civil-service laws in many states and cities opens the door wide to the business of political assessments, and the recent exemption from civil service of so many employees in the so-called emergency agencies in Washington has created a situation quite unprecedented and dangerous.

Of course, political appointees in Washington still continue to contribute to the local organizations which obtained their positions for them. Whether these contributions are voluntary, or assessments, is a question. Undoubtedly some of them are assessed, but this is not easy to prove. One way of covering up an assessment is to have the party account show a large contribution from a certain respected member of the party who is probably quite able to make such a contribution, and then have that contribution serve as a cloak for all assessments made upon federal office holders, from his state, in Washington. Of course, it is difficult to trace such a practice down to a point where a public disclosure can be made, but those who are intimately acquainted with political practices can detect such subterfuges, and now and then evidences come to the surface to indicate that the practice still survives.

The Brookhart committee, in its investigation into federal appointments in the South, found considerable evidence of coercive practices in the collection of campaign funds. Federal officeholders in particular were required to sign notes payable in installments over a period of two years, and these notes were then placed in banks for collection and collected like any commercial obligation, the returns going to the party organization.[4] "Such a system of raising party funds," said the committee, "is coercive. It throws the federal officeholder into the hands of the banks, . . . and in effect puts him in the seemingly apparent position, to say the least, of paying off a mortgage on his federal position." Another senatorial committee reported in 1927 that "in some sections of the country the practice of the sale of political influence for appointment to federal positions has been carried to such an extent as to bring about a condition

[4] *Senate Report No. 46,* 71st Congress, 2nd Session.

that is not only disgraceful but that interferes in no small degree with efficiency in public office."[5]

Representatives and Senators running for office are often called upon to pay assessments to their local party committees. The national committees, however, do not receive aid of this sort, but rely almost exclusively upon contributions from friends of the party and of the candidates. Thus, when one speaks generally of assessments as being a source of party revenue, one must remember that in the case of the national committees they are of no importance. (This is not to overlook, however, the very lucrative dinner held under the auspices of the Democratic national committee on Jackson's birthday in the city of Washington in 1936, when the very efficient Postmaster General was able to secure the attendance of several hundred Democratic office holders at the rate of $50 per plate, the proceeds of the dinner going to wipe out the deficit of the Democratic national Committee.)[6]

So far as state and local committees are concerned, political assessments undoubtedly form an important part of the money raised by them for political purposes. The briefest kind of investigation in almost any state, county or city will verify the truth of this statement. In many areas assessments amount to large sums and constitute the chief source of party income.[7]

In two states[8] the laws even provide that political assessments may be levied on candidates in amounts not exceeding the aggregate salary of the holder of each office. Other states, such as North Dakota, permit the assessment of elected officeholders, but prohibit it with appointed officials. Many states do not make any provisions at all; but regardless of the legal provisions throughout the United States, it is a general practice for both parties—and for that matter even for the Socialist party, since

[5] *Senate Report No. 1379,* 69th Congress, 2nd Session.
[6] See the Washington *Star,* December 26, 1935, for a comment on this method of procuring funds.
[7] See the author's *Party Campaign Funds,* pp. 119-125; also L. Overacker, *Money in Elections,* pp. 101-104.
[8] Oregon and Alabama.

assessments are an established feature of its system of party finance—to obtain considerable sums from their candidates and office holders. This is not the most productive source of party revenue, but without it the parties would at times be hard put to it to raise sufficient funds with which to conduct their campaigns.

The greatest portion of the money used in political campaigns is donated by the friends of the party. This term is quite comprehensive, for it includes the friends of the candidates, business men, former party office holders, and many other persons and groups of persons interested for one reason or another in the success of the party. National campaigns are financed almost entirely by contributions of individuals; and state and local campaigns, especially when large funds are required, rely considerably upon the donations of the party's friends.

There are always a certain number of persons who have political aspirations, and they show their interest in party affairs by making generous donations to the party treasurer. Then there are a few persons who genuinely believe that the good of the country depends upon the election of officials of a certain party, and they donate to the party fund for quite the same reasons for which they donate to a charity or a public benefit. Without these donations the party coffers would never be full. Also, there are persons who believe that their own business interests demand contributions in one way or another. Finally, there is a miscellaneous assortment of party followers who contribute small or large sums without having any particular reason for so doing.

It cannot be denied that many of the so-called "friends" of the party and of the candidates are really paying their tribute for the opportunity to break laws or make inordinate profits. The Seabury investigation in New York disclosed numerous instances of "shaking down" persons who were dealing or who expected to deal with various municipal authorities, for the purpose of getting political contributions.[9] The oil investigations

[9] William B. and John B. Northrop, *The Insolence of Office: The Story of the Seabury Investigations.*

THE USE OF MONEY IN ELECTIONS

disclosed anti-public motives in the contributions of Harry F. Sinclair and Edward Doheny.[10] The contributions to Frank L. Smith's campaign in Illinois in 1926, from the public utility magnates, totaled over $200,000.[11] The Federal Trade Commission recently revealed the fact that officials of public utility companies contributed $468,900 to the Republican national committee in the three presidential campaigns of 1924, 1928 and 1932, and $120,100 to the Democratic national committee during the same years.[12] The Nye Committee investigating the munitions industries has made public incomplete reports showing political contributions from officers and directors of the du Pont Company. These reports list contributions to both parties of $432,000 in the period from 1919 to 1934.[13] The investigations which have been conducted into the public activities of utility companies and other groups have developed significant material bearing on the use of money to influence public policy. An interesting analysis made by one of the leading students of campaign funds demonstrated the close connection between "Big Business" and such funds.[14] Clearly, the source of campaign contributions must be watched, and serious attention given to removing the anti-public influences which, unfortunately, are so important in determining our politics.

Without endeavoring further to ascertain the motives underlying party contributions, it is now important to indicate that in recent campaigns the evidence is overwhelming that most of the money with which the major parties wage their campaigns is contributed by the few rather than the many.[15] Despite a commendable tendency to increase the number of party contributors, the fact still remains that only a relatively small number of party members ever contribute to the campaign fund. In other

[10] *Senate Report No. 754*, 68th Congress, 1st Session (1924).
[11] Carroll H. Wooddy, *The Case of Frank L. Smith*.
[12] New York *Herald Tribune*, November 7, 1935.
[13] *Ibid.*, October 30, 1935.
[14] See L. Overacker in *American Political Science Review*, vol. xxvii, p. 776.
[15] L. Overacker, *Money in Elections*, chap. vi.

words, very wealthy individuals provide the major share of the funds required to finance campaigns. An analysis of the expenditures of national committees in recent years has shown that the amount raised in contributions of $100 or less has never exceeded $550,000 in either party.[16]

Probably the most serious complaints that have been raised against the contributions to party funds relate to their size. In the famous Republican pre-convention campaign of 1920, William Cooper Procter, together with two associates, guaranteed to underwrite a fund of $750,000, and Governor Smith has been constantly helped by large contributions from William F. Kenny. The large contributions to various party funds by the Mellons, by Thomas F. Ryan, by Harry F. Sinclair, by John J. Raskob, and by many others, are well known.

This is not to say that the small contributor is unimportant, but when it comes to conducting expensive campaigns, party treasurers have found that the money comes from relatively few individuals.

Thus it would seem that political parties should direct their efforts toward the prevention of large contributions. But as they do this, they cannot lose sight of the fact that the money must be forthcoming from some quarter, and there are only two alternatives to a continuation of large contributions: first, to get a large number of small contributions, or, second, to have the government finance the campaign.

In the past twenty-five years parties have endeavored at various times to broaden their subscriptions lists. A serious effort was made by the Democratic national committee in the period between 1916 and 1920, and Will H. Hays, the Republican national chairman in 1920, proceeded to organize the financial side of the campaign much on the basis of a Red Cross subscription campaign. In both these cases considerable sums were raised, but in neither case—and one can say, broadly, in no important instance—have the parties been able to get along without considerable donations in large figures from a relatively small num-

[16] *Ibid.*, p. 143.

ber of persons. There is no particular reason why this should be the case. The former Social Democratic party in Germany and the present Labour party in Great Britain have been able to carry on active political work by relying on small contributions from the rank and file. Perhaps in the near future it may be possible for some American political treasurer to prove to the satisfaction of his committee that it is not only as productive to raise money from the rank and file of the party voters, but that it is also politically much sounder. Commendable efforts in this direction are being made by both parties in 1936.

The Socialist party raises its money substantially in this way. Its system of dues stamps, together with collections at meetings and some solicited contributions, provide the necessary sinews of war.

Recently, with the approach of the campaign of 1936, the chairman of the Republican national finance committee announced that he would enlist the support of a million citizens by means of a certificate system, to the end that the Republican campaign could be financed by the rank and file and not by the wealthy few. The chairman of the Democratic national committee has developed a system of collecting contributions from thousands of persons by making them "nominators" of Franklin Roosevelt. It does not seem possible for the major parties to enroll five millions of their party members in such a manner as to secure from each of them a dollar or two with which to carry on election campaigns. At least until some such system is tried and proved wanting, honest citizens can hope for an improvement in the present practice of relying principally upon wealthy donors.

Another alternative to the method of widening party subscription lists is to ask the government to make contributions to defray the cost of campaigns. This suggestion is not a new one, and has often been voiced by prominent citizens. In 1909 Colorado enacted a law which provided that the state should appropriate a sum of money to each political party for the purpose of conducting political campaigns. Unfortunately this law was declared unconstitutional, and we have had no other experience with this proposition. But William Jennings Bryan, Governor Baldwin of Connecticut, Governor Carey of Wyoming, former Representative Lewis and President Theodore Roosevelt at different times advocated state assumption of campaign expenses. In his annual message of 1907 President Theodore Roosevelt said: "There is a very radical measure which would, I believe, work a substantial improvement in our system of conducting a campaign, although I am well aware that it will take some time for people so to familiarize themselves with such a proposal as to be willing to consider its adoption. The need for collecting large campaign funds would vanish if Congress provided an appropriation for the proper and legitimate expenses of each of the great national parties, an appropriation ample enough to meet the necessity for thorough organization and machinery, which requires a large expenditure of money. Then the stipulation should be made that no party receiving campaign funds from the treasury should accept more than a fixed amount from any individual subscriber or donor; and the necessary publicity for receipts and expenditures could without difficulty be provided."[17]

The treasurer of the Republican national committee recently proposed that each party should be allowed a certain amount of money for conducting its campaign throughout the country. This recent suggestion, although not new, may well be pondered. States already assume a considerable part of the cost of elections when they defray the ballot costs. This item was formerly handled by the candidates themselves. In both France and Great Britain the government at the present time permits the candidates to send political communications through the mails free of cost, and in France candidates are also provided with individual billboards for advertising purposes.[18]

In Democratic states much more attention must be paid to the

[17] *Messages and Papers of the Presidents*, vol. x, pp. 74-86.
[18] See James K. Pollock, *Money and Politics Abroad*, pp. 189 and 289-290.

genuine education of the electorate. At the present time entirely too much time and money are wasted by the parties and the candidates in quite useless and unsocial activities. Surely there is great need for the government, in some desirable way, to step into the campaign picture and at least assist the harried voter in getting the facts upon which to base his vote, even though the financing of the campaign is not entirely underwritten.

Size of Campaign Funds

If we are clear as to the sources of campaign funds and how they are raised, we should now give attention to the size of the funds collected by candidates, by parties and by groups.

First, as to the candidates. We find that expenditures vary from practically nothing, as in the case of a candidate like Senator Couzens, to $1,250,000, as in the notorious Pennsylvania senatorial primary of 1926. In the more populous states, candidates for governor and United States Senator are likely to spend several hundred thousand dollars. In the Middle Western agricultural states the expenditures of candidates are considerably less. Contests in the primary and under the convention system, for membership in the legislature and for county office, do not ordinarily call forth large expenditures. Nevertheless, money is as necessary here as elsewhere in the political arena, even though it does not receive as much attention.

Of course, it must be remembered that certain candidates, especially those who are incumbents, receive a considerable amount of free advertising which is not included in the above figures. The charitable benefactions of a wealthy candidate, the constant repetition of the name of a state officer in all the communications and public announcements, obviously contribute something toward making the candidate known. It is even true that members of the legislature whose names are connected with well-known statutes benefit considerably by this free advertising.

In some instances candidates' expenditures bulk large in nominating campaigns, but only in rare instances are they so large as to arouse comment. In fact, in most cases they are entirely overlooked. When some bitter primary campaign for United States Senator or governor comes along and national significance is attached to the fight, as in the Newberry, Vare, and Smith campaigns in 1918 and 1926, much attention is given by the public. The campaign for the Republican nomination for President in 1920 called forth the largest pre-convention expenditure the country had ever seen.[19] In 1936, however, less money was spent by the candidates before the conventions, also at the conventions—than in any recent presidential year. Ordinarily, however, the attention of the voter is directed mostly to party funds and not to expenditures by candidates. This is not the proper thing, for some serious abuses may arise from the expenditures of candidates, even though those expenditures may not be large. The great need for publicity in these matters, later to be emphasized, is very apparent in this field of candidate expenditures.

When the nominations are completed, campaigns are turned over, as a rule, to party committees. It is then that money-raising begins in earnest, and it is here that we find large expenditures for election purposes. National committees naturally top the list of party committees, and they organize large money-raising organizations, especially in presidential years. In 1928 both national committees expended between three and four million dollars for their own purposes. This represented the high-water mark of national committee expenditure in this country. In 1932 approximately a million dollars less was expended by each national committee.[20] In 1936, there is reason to believe, the level of 1928 will be reached, for there is great interest in the campaign and both sides are in a position to command large financial resources.

Congressional and senatorial committees are largely financed by the national committee. Their expenditures usually amount

---

[19] See the hearings and the report of the Kenyon Committee in 1920, *Sen. Rep. No. 823*, 66th Congress, 3rd Session.

[20] L. Overacker, *op. cit.*, pp. 73-75. Also *American Political Science Review*, vol. xxvii, pp. 769-784.

THE USE OF MONEY IN ELECTIONS 185

to between one and two hundred thousand dollars, in the case of the Republican committees. The Democratic practice is not to give these committees as much money, the national committee assuming most of the financial burden.[21]

State committees and county committees often spend sizable sums. In 1928 the Pennsylvania state campaign cost the Republicans $460,000, and the Democrats $170,000. In 1934 in the same state the election campaign of the successful Democratic candidate for governor, Earle, cost his committee $143,000, all but $2,000 of which the candidate contributed himself. The New York County Democratic committee filed an account in 1928 with the board of elections showing an expenditure of $245,000. The Philadelphia central Republican campaign committee spent $206,000 in 1934. Governor Lehman's independent committee expended $127,000 in his campaign for election in 1932 in the State of New York. Because of the difficulty of collecting complete figures, these instances can give only a partial picture. One tabulation made by the author a number of years ago in Ohio indicates the importance of regulating this important phase of party expenditure.[22]

The whole balance sheet, however, is not given when we have listed the expenditure of national, congressional and senatorial, state and county committees, for in the past twenty-five years, with the growth in importance and power of so-called "pressure groups," large sums of money are now being expended in campaigns by these interest groups. The yearly expenditure of the Anti-Saloon League of America and the various state leagues average $1,800,000 between 1920 and 1925.[23] And the Association Against the Prohibition Amendment expended upward of a half million dollars in the campaign of 1928.[24]

The recent revelations of expenditures by the American

[21] See James K. Pollock, *op. cit.*, p. 31. Also *American Political Science Review*, vol. xxiii, pp. 59-69.
[22] See James K. Pollock, *op. cit.*, pp. 32-39.
[23] Peter Odegard, *Pressure Politics*, p. 200.
[24] *Senate Report No. 2024*, 70th Congress, 2nd Session, p. 26.

Liberty League and by the Townsend Clubs have given us good illustrations of the enormous financial power wielded by groups which are separate and distinct from the political parties. At a time when many party organizations were languishing because of lack of funds, both the League and the Townsend organizations were literally swimming in money. In January, 1936, the League filed an account under the Federal Corrupt Practices Act showing receipts of $483,000.[25] No report was filed at this time by the Townsend organization, but the financial report made before the convention in the fall of 1935 showed that in twenty months of operation the plan had taken in $636,000. Since the total membership of this old-age pension group is still unknown, it is difficult to estimate exactly the amounts now being realized directly from the members. If one takes one million members as a base, the initial membership fee would total $250,000; the ten-cents-a-member contribution would reach $1,200,000 a year, and the sale of literature might run to $250,000 more. When the congressional committee finishes its investigation we should know more about the financial activities of this strong group. Consequently, it must not be forgotten that so-called non-party expenditures exert a considerable influence both in the determination of public policy and in the winning of elections.

One final item regarding political expenditures should be referred to. In many states provisions exist for the initiative and referendum, and in those states frequent use is made of these provisions. Many amendments to the Constitution and many statutes are proposed which arouse considerable interest and are of vital significance to the state. In these campaigns it has been found necessary to raise and expend large sums of money. First of all, if an initiative petition must be filed, it is a matter of many thousands of dollars to collect signatures, and when the proposal is actually before the people a very extensive campaign of education must be undertaken. A recent study in California has thrown light upon the way in which referendum and

[25] New York *Herald Tribune*, January 3, 1936.

THE USE OF MONEY IN ELECTIONS

initiative proposals call forth financial contributions from many supporters.[26]

It is now pertinent to raise the question as to whether or not the expenditure of such vast sums of money in political campaigns is justifiable. Too frequently the large size of campaign funds is referred to without any consideration being given to the question whether or not such large expenditures are reasonable or justified by the circumstances. Although there has been some fluctuation in the size of campaign funds, there is no evidence to show that campaign costs are increasing, when one considers the increasing size of the electorate and makes figures showing the cost per vote. Even when considered in relation to national income, political expenditures are not alarming. If anything, expenditures are standing still rather than rising; and as a keen student of the subject has put it, "It is safe to say that the amount spent in a presidential election is less than the cost of a first-class battleship, and much less than the annual expenditure of the American people for such luxuries as candy, chewing gum and cigarettes."[27]

Even in the most notorious cases, as for instance in the Pepper-Vare campaign in Pennsylvania in 1926, considerable justification can be found for large expenditures. In that case, however, as in most cases of large expenditures, one is able to find many objectionable practices, and one should therefore say that it is not primarily the size of the campaign fund which is the most important matter, but rather the method of collecting the fund and the method of its expenditure. A small fund can be expended in a most objectionable way. A very large fund could be expended in a very proper way. Nevertheless, so far as the public is concerned, the size of the fund has a good deal to do with determining its propriety. But, as has been pointed out above, the actual statistics of campaign expenditures, when taken in relation to both the number of votes cast, and the national income and the size of the electorate, show no increase.

[26] Unpublished Mss. to appear in the *American Political Science Review*.
[27] L. Overacker, *op. cit.*, pp. 75-76.

Measured in terms of the cost per vote cast, the combined expenditure of the two national committees in 1932 was lower than in any other recent campaign, being slightly less than thirteen cents.[28] Since the size of the fund is, therefore, not the most important item, greater attention should be given to the source of the fund and to its expenditure.

How Campaign Funds Are Expended

Campaign money, however execellently it has been collected, can be spent in a manner just as corrupting as if it originally had been obtained from questionable sources. American political expenditures have frequently been subjected to criticism because of the purposes for which the money has been spent, and many voters still believe that the direct bribery of voters is an important element in swinging campaigns. But nearly every politician will say today that although there is still a small purchasable vote, the direct bribery of voters has practically disappeared. Voters are no longer lined up in "blocks of five" and their votes purchased, even though we did find that in Pittsburgh, in the 1926 campaign, some ten thousand voters were employed as watchers. Today even the most unscrupulous political leaders do not depend upon the purchase of votes to win elections because they realize that the risk is too great and that elections are carried by winning the support of the great unorganized mass of citizens who do not belong to either party. Of course, politicians resort to all sorts of expedients to get people to vote, such as taking them to the polls in automobiles and doing their work for them while they vote. But without such hard-working politicians, it is doubtful whether enough persons would vote to make elections worth while. If it is true that clean campaigns require a proper expenditure of money, it is very important to check up on existing methods of political expenditure to determine which are desirable and which are undesirable.

Expenditures made in political campaigns may be classified

[28] L. Overacker, in *American Political Science Review*, vol. xxvii, p. 771.

in seven principal groups as follows: (1) publicity, including radio; (2) headquarters expense; (3) grants to lesser committees; (4) speakers, halls and entertainment; (5) field workers; (6) Election Day expenses; (7) miscellaneous. The character of these expenditures does not vary much between the two parties. What one party does the other party usually tries to do to the extent of its ability, and as a rule the managers use practically the same general methods of appealing to the voters.

The first item is publicity, for which purpose parties spend from twenty-five to fifty per cent of their campaign funds. Usually, whether the campaign is local, state or national, more money is expended for publicity than for any other purpose. The term "publicity" as used here has reference to the sums used not only for general advertising, but also for radio and for printing and distributing literature. Today there are three general kinds of publicity activity: first, advertising the candidates by means of newspapers, magazines, billboard posters, lithographs, buttons, banners and placards; second, by radio broadcasting; and third, by printing and distributing in pamphlet form the speeches of the candidates and special articles on labor, agriculture and other specialized subjects.

At the present time, probably the largest single item of expense is radio broadcasting. In 1932 the total political billing by the Columbia Broadcasting System was $368,000 of which $194,000 was Republican, $167,000 Democratic, and $6000 Socialist. The Republicans contracted for 29 broadcasts or 17½ hours over the WABC network, and the Democrats contracted for 23 broadcasts that consumed 18½ hours. In addition, the Columbia network contributed 56 hours of political broadcasting. The cost at that time of the WEAF hook-up of 58 stations was $12,250 an hour. Senator Dill in a broadcast estimated the approximate cost of the combined hook-ups in the last presidential campaign as approximately $1,250,000. "It is estimated," he said, "that the majority parties spent another five hundred thousand dollars or seven hundred and fifty thousand dollars for speeches over sectional networks, state-wide networks and independent station broadcasts not connected with the chain. Probably this would amount to two hundred and fifty thousand dollars more, making a total of around two million dollars spent by committees and candidates for the radio. The programs of public addresses by radio stations both on the chain and off the chain contributed in addition must have been worth at least a million dollars more. Adding these amounts spent for political speeches to the amounts contributed by radio stations, we have a grand total of approximately five million dollars' worth of broadcasting during the campaign." Political campaigns have come to be lucrative affairs for broadcasting companies.

In 1920 the budget of the Republican national committee provided for the expenditure of $1,346,000 for publicity purposes, and this item did not cover advertisements in foreign-language newspapers. In 1924 the same committee expended $741,000 for publicity purposes.[29] In 1920 the Republican national committee signed a contract for $159,000 for all of its billboard advertising in the United States.[30]

Another item which might appear insignificant in the advertising of candidates is the expenditure for buttons and lithographs. No campaign is complete without an array of lapel buttons and a considerable variety of pictures of the candidates. In 1920 Will H. Hays testified that about 15,000,000 pictures of the national candidates were issued by the Republican national committee, and the cost of this one item was $200,000. Although people often question the value of both buttons and lithographs, they have been retained by political leaders because it is felt that they constitute a very necessary item in the campaign.

Other publicity items are also expensive. Press bureaus and high-priced newspaper men are maintained by the party headquarters for the purpose of preparing news stories, editorials

[29] James K. Pollock, *Party Campaign Funds*, p. 147.

[30] In the Detroit area in 1934 about $10,000 worth of billboard advertising was used by the candidates for governor and United States Senator and sheriff in the general election. Unpublished report of W. L. Hindman, University of Michigan.

and cartoons for publication in newspapers throughout the country. Perhaps no other activity is so important as this. But high-class newspaper men cannot be hired for a song; they must be paid good salaries, and these salaries cut another big slice out of the party melon.

Political notices appearing in the newspapers and magazines of the country constitute an important part of the advertising work of party committees. The Democratic national committee received from one advertising firm alone a bill for $238,000 for work done in 1916, in placing advertising in several hundred newspapers throughout the country. Advertisements are placed by all political committees in foreign-language newspapers. Finally, the printing and distribution of campaign literature is an important part of the activities of any political committee. Besides the campaign textbooks, numerous pamphlets are printed in order to win the support of various classes of the population. All this printing is done on a large scale, and during a presidential campaign the whole country is flooded with these pamphlets.

Before we complain too much about the expenditures of the parties for publicity purposes, it may be well to reflect on expenditures by other agencies for similar purposes—merely by way of comparison. One reference to the publicity costs of Liberty Loan campaigns during the war is illuminating. The total sum expended for publicity in these campaigns, through the war-savings campaign of 1921, was $10,000,000. The cost of publicity for the Victory Loan campaign alone amounted to $3,590,000. This sum was expended from April through June, a period of about three months.[31] If such an enormous sum should be expended by a political party in so short a time for publicity alone, there would be loud complaints.

The second important item of expenditure in connection with political campaigns is the cost of maintaining headquarters. This amounts to from fifteen to twenty-five per cent of the total expenditure. Headquarters expenses include rent, furniture and

[31] *House Document No. 131,* 67th Congress, 2nd Session.

equipment, stationery and supplies, postage, clerk hire and telephone and telegraph tolls. In 1920 this item amounted to $800,000 for the Republican national committee. The sums expended for stationery, supplies and postage are large. The cost of preparing and sending out material is considerable; in the case of circulars it amounts to about ten cents per circular. Telephone and telegraph charges today mount up with surprising rapidity, but without this rapid means of communication national chairmen would be in a very difficult position. Expense cannot be spared when important business is pending.

Grants of money to lesser committees constitute the third item of expenditure. In the case of the Republican party this sum has usually amounted to about twenty per cent of the total. Three quarters of a million dollars was allocated to the state committees by the Republican national committee in 1932. The sending of these large sums into doubtful states has called forth some criticism, but it is difficult to see how, without such outside assistance, enough money can be raised in some states to conduct satisfactory campaigns. Some states are able to raise more money than is necessary for their own purposes, while other states find it impossible to do this. The difficulty in raising campaign funds is not altogether different from that of raising money by taxation. Some states contribute more than they spend.

Money expended for speakers, halls, bands and other means of entertainment constitutes a fourth item of party disbursement. It was thought at one time that radio broadcasting would result in reducing the number of "spellbinders" sent out over the country, but this has not been the result. In fact, the speakers' bureau of any commitee is quite as important a factor in the campaign as it used to be. From ten to fifteen per cent of the total campaign fund is devoted to these activities. In the Republican campaign of 1924, even though the radio was widely used, the speakers' bureau spent $366,000. The hiring of halls and the engaging of bands has its place in the transactions of committees, especially for large local rallies.

Another item of expenditure is the money paid to the workers in the field. In every campaign there are hundreds of party organizers, and always a considerable number of persons engaged in collecting money. Expenditures for the salaries of field workers amount to about five per cent of the total fund.

Election-day expenses constitute a very important item of expenditure in the larger cities and counties. The task of getting out the voters is a difficult one, and all the expenditure of money up to Election Day is useless if the voters are not brought to the polls. This round-up requires not only considerable money but also hard work. Runners, messengers and bell ringers must be employed. The aged and the infirm must be conveyed to the polls, and in some backward areas the "heelers" must be "heeled" and the watchers must be paid.

The seventh and last group of political expenditure is miscellaneous. Money must be set apart for special railroad accommodations for the leading candidates, for supplying the needs of the money-raising organizations, for bringing influential politicians to headquarters, and for numerous other minor purposes. These miscellaneous expenses amount to possibly five per cent of the total funds raised by party committees.

The use of money for all these various purposes is not always proper, nor is the amount expended always reasonable. The parties, like individuals, do not always know when to stop spending. It is to be expected, therefore, that a certain percentage of the money expended by political parties is simply wasted.

Experienced business men who have been attached to campaign committees have declared that from twenty-five to fifty per cent of the money spent in a national campaign is wasted. William Allen White wrote that "most politicians have easy consciences about the money entrusted to them by other politicians for political purposes" and that forty per cent of all money used in a campaign sticks to the fingers of each recipient.[32] Whether or not these figures are correct it is impossible to say, but it is certain that large sums are wasted. One of the most

[32] William Allen White, *Masks in a Pageant*, p. 163.

important causes of large expenditures is the length of political campaigns. If our campaigns could be shortened—that is to say, if the national conventions could be held in September rather than in June—much less money would be required for expenditure, and a considerably more efficient basis of expenditure would have to be set up. The campaign manager is quick to point out that political parties cannot always be as economical as they might be. Decisions must be made quickly. Orders must be placed, sometimes by telegraph. No time exists for bickering over the lowest price. Consequently, it seems inevitable that there should be some waste.

What has not yet been determined is the relative effectiveness of these various items of expenditure. We have very few scientific data on which to base an intelligent opinion as to whether more money should be expended for one item or for another. To date, rule-of-thumb methods have dictated political expenditures. But it will not be long until some careful manager is able to determine according to scientific and accurate standards just which items really produce the best results.

The Legal Regulation of Campaign Funds

Thus far we have considered the necessity for political funds, where they come from, how they are collected, and how they are expended. The emphasis at this point must be given to the manner in which all of these matters have been regulated by the various units of government.

Fifty years ago, following the enactment of the British Corrupt and Illegal Practices Act, the American states began to pass laws to prevent those election practices which were deemed contrary to public morals and decency. Bribery, treating, illegal registration and voting, and other unsavory and improper election practices, were included within the purview of these early so-called corrupt practices acts. Every state in the Union, except Mississippi and Illinois, now has some provision of law dealing more or less completely with these matters. These penal statutes, however, are to be distinguished from so-called publicity laws, which, with the first federal law in 1910, came to be looked upon as a necessary supplement to the corrupt practices acts. Today the federal government and all of the states, except Mississippi and Illinois, have legal provisions dealing with corrupt practices and publicity of campaign funds.

In eight states[33] the laws regulate only nominations and do not apply to elections, and in eleven states[34] they impose requirements upon candidates but do not apply to political parties. But in no fewer than thirty-four[35] states and the federal government, we find reasonably comprehensive legislation dealing with campaign funds. These state laws are extremely diverse, but there are certain fairly uniform requirements running through most of them. All of them contain provisions against bribery, and most of them contain provisions against contributions from corporations; and in other ways they indicate that their purposes are the same. They differ only in the ways in which they carry out those purposes. The provisions of these laws may be grouped into eight classes: (1) publicity concerning campaign receipts and disbursements; (2) limitations on the amount or size of expenditures and contributions; (3) enumeration of the purposes for which money can be expended; (4) restrictions as to the sources of campaign funds; (5) definitions of the persons and committees who may disburse money; (6) enforcement provisions; (7) penal provisions, and (8) miscellaneous.

First attention should be given to the publicity provisions of

[33] Arkansas, Florida, Idaho, South Carolina, Texas, Vermont, Virginia and Washington.

[34] Arkansas, Florida, Georgia, Idaho, Louisiana, North Dakota, South Carolina, Texas, Vermont, Virginia and Washington.

[35] Alabama, Arizona, California, Colorado, Connecticut, Delaware, Indiana, Iowa, Kansas, Kentucky, Maine, Maryland, Massachusetts, Michigan, Minnesota, Missouri, Montana, Nebraska, Nevada, New Hampshire, New Jersey, New Mexico, New York, North Carolina, Ohio, Oklahoma, Oregon, South Dakota, Pennsylvania, Tennessee, Utah, West Virginia, Wisconsin, Wyoming. Of these thirty-four, the following fourteen have probably the best laws: Indiana, Maine, Maryland, Massachusetts, Michigan, Minnesota, Montana, Nevada, Ohio, Oregon, Utah, West Virginia, Wisconsin and Wyoming.

these laws. The general requirements as to publicity stipulate that statements of receipts and disbursements shall be prepared, and shall be filed either before or after primaries and elections, or in some cases both before and after, in some public office where they will be open to inspection as public records. The forms on which the figures of receipts and disbursements are put are usually prescribed and prepared by the state, and in some cases distributed to candidates and committees. Twenty-two states require party accounts to be filed only after the election is over, while 11 states require both pre-election and post-election statements. Most statements of receipts and disbursements are required to be filed, in the case of the federal law, with the secretary of the Senate and the clerk of the House; in the case of state laws, with the secretary of state or with the county clerk or the county board of elections. After the statements are filed they are usually laid away in some dusty corner, probably not to be disturbed until they are destroyed. In every case, the statements are open to inspection by the public. As will be pointed out later, these expense accounts leave much to be desired, and do not serve the useful purpose which was intended.

The great majority of the states limit the amount of money that can be expended by candidates in primaries or elections or in both, while five states[36] limit also the expenditures of party committees. Two other states[37] limit the size of contributions that may be given in aid of campaigns. The principle of limitation of expenditures is widely accepted throughout the country, Pennsylvania and New York being conspicuous exceptions. The Nebraska provision prohibits the acceptance of a contribution of more than one thousand dollars.

Twenty-nine states enumerate the purposes for which money may be expended, and then prohibit the expenditure of money for any other purpose. It seems reasonable that the conveyance of voters to the polls and the unlimited hiring of workers should be included in these lists of what are legal expenditures. Un-

[36] Minnesota, Nevada, New Hampshire, Utah and Wisconsin.
[37] Massachusetts and Nebraska.

fortunately, however, such restrictions are not contained in every state law.

The fourth class of the provisions of the corrupt practices acts which deserve mention includes those which restrict the sources of campaign funds. Nearly every state prohibits the receipt of contributions from corporations, especially public-service corporations, and many states are careful to protect public officials by forbidding the solicitation of donations from appointive officers.

Again, corrupt practices acts are very careful to define what is meant by the term "political committee," and what rights such committees have. Legal provisions might well be directed to non-party committees as much as to party committees.

The enforcement provisions of state corrupt practices acts are probably their weakest point. It is partly because candidates know that action will not be taken against them that they give little attention to complying with the provisions of the law. In a few states[38] an attempt is made to concentrate responsibility for expenditure. In some states the accounts are to be inspected by the officer with whom the account is filed, and in Ohio and Pennsylvania and Delaware provisions exist for an investigation and audit of accounts after they are filed. But most states depend upon the ordinary criminal processes for the enforcement of their statutes.

The penal provisions of laws regulating campaign funds provide for the usual fines, imprisonment, forfeiture of office, disqualification to hold office, withholding of names from the ballot and for disfranchisement. Four states provided that a violation of the corrupt practices act by a successful candidate would operate to vacate the office and give it to the person receiving the next highest number of votes, but these provisions have been declared unconstitutional.

Numerous miscellaneous provisions are of some value. For instance, the requirement that all political advertisements must be plainly marked as such, and that newspaper support cannot

[38] Massachusetts, New Jersey and Utah.

be purchased, is intended to raise the level of newspaper practices. The prohibition against the receipt of anonymous contributions is quite general throughout the country, as is also the provision against promising appointments in return for political support. Many states prohibit betting, and several states direct provisions against the intimidation of employees by corporations.

Effectiveness of Campaign Fund Regulation

This detailed consideration of the various provisions of campaign fund laws would not be complete without indicating the effectiveness of this legislation. Little investigation is required to demonstrate that there is a very general disregard of most of the provisions, particularly of the state laws. Sometimes no publicity is secured, and in most cases little light is thrown on the financial dealings of candidates and parties. The enforcement is most haphazard and ineffective. Too much emphasis has been placed upon limiting the amount of the expenditures, without at the same time eliminating the various loopholes which are conveniently provided for getting around these limits. In fact, many of the limitations that are made are not limitations at all, for in the next sentence a statute frequently excludes from the limitations above mentioned many of the items requiring the greatest amount of money. For instance, the federal law, after limiting the size of the expenditures which may be made by a Senator or Representative, provides that "money expended by a candidate to meet and discharge any assessment, fee, or charge made or levied upon candidates by the laws of the state in which he resides, or expended for his necessary personal, traveling, or subsistence expenses, or for stationery, postage, writing, or printing (other than for use on billboards or in newspapers), for distributing letters, circulars, or posters, or for telegraph or telephone service, shall not be included in determining whether his expenditures have exceeded the sum fixed . . . as the limit of campaign expenses of a candidate."[39]

Opinions differ as to the real value of the laws in force.

[39] Section 309 (c).

Quite universal agreement has been indicated with regard to the inadequacy of the publicity provisions. The whole tendency of these and other provisions has been to raise the moral tone of elections, and it can hardly be denied that the various laws have been of considerable value in this respect. They have been largely instrumental in producing better political conditions today, and no amount of criticism should permit this fact to be covered up.

Nevertheless, one striking example should be given to demonstrate how ineffective even a good statute may be in the hands of easy-going officials and where the public takes no interest in the matter. This example occurred in Michigan in the campaign of 1932, when the Democratic candidate, William Comstock, was successful in getting the nomination of his party and in winning the election. The law of Michigan requires every candidate to file an expense account after every primary and election. After the election of 1932 it was discovered that Governor Comstock had not filed an account. He said that he had not filed an account after the primary and after the election, and that two years before, when he had been a candidate, he had also failed to file an account. "Purposely," he said, "I did not file any statement of expenses in my campaign because I wanted to show the people of Michigan how easy it was to evade the present corrupt practices act. There was no way or any agency that could get at the fellow who deliberately sat back and said, 'I won't do it.'" The law is very clear on this point; a candidate's name is not to be certified and placed on the ballot until he has filed an account. This was not done. Furthermore, no candidate who is elected is supposed to take the oath until an account is filed. And yet a justice of the supreme court administered the oath to this candidate. Furthermore, the statute even provides that the salary shall not be paid until the account is filed; so that in every respect the statute was flagrantly violated, not merely by the candidate himself, whose purpose seems to have been laudable, but also by the public officials who are supposed to see to the enforcement of the act. There has never been a more striking example of the ineffectiveness of these publicity laws; and yet many similar violations occur without ever coming to public attention.

After more than a quarter of a century of experience with the regulation of campaign funds, we are still confronted with serious problems. Attention must be given to several of these because of their immediate pressing importance. Probably the most serious problem in connection with regulating campaign funds is the failure to fix definite responsibility for all political expenditures.[40] We have permitted indiscriminate expenditure, and because of that fact we have been unable to enforce even the rather ineffective statutes which we have enacted. At the present time anybody can spend money for political purposes. Under a really effective statute, like the one now in force in Great Britain, only the candidate or his agent could spend money, and everyone else would be forbidden to do so. Now we have not only official party committees but also many personnel committees, subsidiary committees and various non-party committees. Too much latitude has been given to outside political groups who intrude themselves into political campaigns. A striking illustration of this was the activity of the so-called anti-Smith Democrats in Virginia in 1928.[41]

If we are to continue to permit indiscriminate expenditure in campaigns, we must be prepared to take the consequences of a serious attack upon the whole democratic system. If it is good for parties and candidates to render an account, it is also good for everyone to make an accounting who happens to spend money, and furthermore, and most important, there can be no effective regulation of expenditures so long as agencies of expenditure are so widely diffused. Under the British act, only the candidate or his agent is authorized to spend money. This definitely fixes responsibility; and under such a provision one

[40] See *Hearings, Select Committee on Senatorial Campaign Expenditures,* United States Senate, 72nd Congress, 1930-31 (Nye Committee). See, particularly, Part I, *Testimony on Remedial Legislation.*

[41] See *Senate Report No. 24,* 72nd Congress, 1st Session, for an account by the Nye Committee of this interesting episode.

does not find the loose handling of money which is such a characteristic of American campaigns.[42] In the next place, consideration must be given to the provision of greater publicity and closer scrutiny of campaign accounts. The accounts themselves are not satisfactorily made up. They are very difficult to analyze, they are frequently filed away in obscure offices, and they rarely provide the voters with the information which they are intended to convey. If the laws are really intended to provide publicity, it is not a difficult matter to insist that the accounts not only shall be scrutinized but that they shall be called to public attention by means of a report prepared in a clear and understandable manner by the officer with whom they are filed. Unless a candidate is convinced that his account will be checked over and made public, it is natural for him to take the whole proceeding very lightly.

It is pertinent to point out that most of the publicity in connection with national elections has been obtained not under the provisions of the federal act, but because the Congress has at various times set up investigating committees. Without such investigations, the public would not be adequately informed. Furthermore, certain disbarment proceedings, particularly in the Senate, have done much to throw light upon the use of money in elections.

The suggestion necessarily follows from this discussion that adequate steps should be taken promptly to provide some regular agency whose business it is to investigate and make public the campaign expenditures. This has been particularly indicated in the federal sphere. Just as it has been necessary and beneficial to create a commission to regulate railroads, and another commission to prevent unfair competition, and more recently another commission to regulate securities, so it has come to be desirable to set up some kind of permanent agency to handle the matter of regulating political expenditures. As Professor Beard put it in his testimony before the Nye Committee: "I think you ought

[42] See James K. Pollock, *Money and Politics Abroad*, chaps. viii, ix, and x.

to have a permanent agency equipped with permanent personnel that would become familiar with state and federal laws and be able to act promptly in the light of long experience. If you appoint a special committee or entrust it to one of the busy committees on elections you may not get the kind of service that you would if you have a man working every year for fifteen years, say, in corrupt practices legislation." Such an agency was proposed in a bill introduced in the 70th Congress by Senator Cutting.[43] With such an agency created, Congress would probably find the job of investigation and enforcement performed with less cost than under the present practice of setting up periodic and peregrinating committees. The necessity for such a permanent agency becomes increasingly clear as elections come more and more to decide our whole economic existence, and not merely the control of a few offices.

Another phase of present importance is the spectacle of huge party deficits. Parties are not now required to keep within their incomes. They may become definitely indebted and even enter into campaigns owing hundreds of thousands of dollars to banks and individuals. The Democratic campaign of 1928 ended up with a deficit of $1,600,000; it was not until 1936 that this deficit was wiped out, and then only by a procedure which drew down upon the chairman of the Democratic national committee a considerable amount of criticism. Some of the most deplorable political practices have been associated with the wiping out of campaign deficits, and it would not be surprising to find malodorous dealings in connection with the liquidation of any party deficit.

The constitutional questions arising in connection with an effective regulation of campaign funds present serious difficulties. To date, it has been felt that the federal Constitution prevented any attempt to regulate expenditures made in behalf of candidates for the presidential and vice-presidential nominations, and in the Newberry case the Supreme Court declared unconstitutional that part of the federal act which up to that time

[43] S. 4422, 70th Congress, 1st Session.

had regulated nominations. At the present time the federal law is, therefore, merely half a law; but in the recent case of Burroughs and Cannon v. United States, decided in 1933, the Supreme Court seems to have taken a rather strong position with reference to protecting the federal authority against the dangers of unlimited campaign expenditures.[44]

In this case the Supreme Court said: "The President is vested with the executive power of the nation. The importance of his election and the vital character of its relationship to and effect upon the welfare and safety of the whole people cannot be too strongly stated. To say that Congress is without power to pass appropriate legislation to safeguard such an election from the improper use of money to influence the result, is to deny to the nation in a vital particular the power of self-protection. Congress undoubtedly possesses that power as it possesses every other power essential to preserve the departments and institutions of the general government from impairment or destruction, whether threatened by force or by corruption." These are strong words, but perhaps the word "election" is used to mean only the general election, as Justice McReynolds so magniloquently asseverated in the Newberry case. Nevertheless, the court states clearly that "the power of Congress to protect the election of President and Vice-President from corruption being clear, the choice of means to that end presents a question primarily addressed to the judgment of Congress."

Constitutional doubts can be settled only in actual cases, and until Congress attempts to regulate the whole field of elections, including nominations, we can only speculate. The necessity for such complete regulation is clearer than ever at the present time. With a bitter presidential campaign in progress, the duty of Congress seems clear.

The present Congress has before it a thoroughgoing statute known as the Nye Bill, which was originally introduced in December of 1931.[45] The bill was the result of the work of the

[44] See 290 U. S. 534.
[45] S. 123, 74th Congress, 1st Session.

Nye Committee in 1930 and 1931, and represents the most complete and adequate treatment of the problem we have yet seen. This bill deals with every one of the difficulties above referred to, and would, if enacted, put the whole question of campaign fund regulation on a basis entirely different from the present.

The public aspects of the problem of campaign funds have necessarily occupied most of our attention. The party aspects are, however—at least, to the parties—equally important. Will the public contribute adequately to party funds? Will radio continue to cost the parties upward of twenty-five per cent of their total budgets? Will the parties be forced to rely principally on large contributions, or will millions of the rank and file come forth with small contributions? These are very real and vastly important problems for party committees; and since parties are indispensable to democratic government, they are also public problems. In any case, it is to be hoped that reliance on large contributors will be lessened, if not removed, in 1936. Would not an entirely new approach meet with satisfactory public response—for instance, securing a dollar from each of five million party members? Until such a democratic plan is tried, we cannot say that it is impracticable. It worked for the Social Democratic party in Germany; it works for the Labour party in Great Britain. The Townsend Clubs have collected millions in small donations. Why could it not work with American parties?

We have now passed, in this matter of campaign fund regulation, the first reading, which consists of much investigation and report. We have also passed the second reading—talk and discussion. We are now ready for the third reading and final passage of something to regulate effectively this vital and important matter—not to produce a lot of meddlesome regulations, but really to cope with this problem of financing political parties. We would then be doing justice to what is everywhere one of the greatest unsolved problems of democratic government.

Chapter VI: Pressure Groups and Propaganda

by HARWOOD L. CHILDS
Associate Professor of Political Science, Princeton University

THE "American Political Scene" is what it is, to a very large extent, because of the activity of pressure groups. Consider the picture. First of all, we perceive some 130,000,000 persons, distinct personalities, an aggregation of individuals varying in age, sex, occupation, race, intelligence, ideals and other attributes too numerous to mention. Closer examination reveals a certain amount of polarization, the operation of forces which tend to give unity and common patterns to the activities of fractional parts of this aggregate. In other words, we perceive that most individuals are acting in groups; a family listening to the radio, a church congregation waiting for the end of the sermon, a convention of party delegates balloting for candidates, a gathering of clubwomen conversing over teacups, a meeting of labor leaders resolving to strike. As the scene changes, the distribution of individuals among the groups changes. Some groups become more active, others quiescent. Most individuals appear to be acting in rather small groups, but at times some seen or unseen stimulus, some magnet, draws them together into larger patterns. It may be an election, a call to arms, a fireside talk from the White House. The expansion and contraction of group patterns, the redistribution of individuals throughout the complex matrix —this is the social process.[1] For a time it proceeds smoothly, then something happens. It is often difficult to discover what.

[1] "The whole social life in all its phases can be stated in such groups of active men, indeed, must be stated in that way if a useful analysis is to be had." A. F. Bentley, *The Process of Government* (Chicago, 1908).

It may be an act of God, some uncommon activity on the part of a particular group, or something that no naked eye can discern. Group patterns seem to fuse at the same time that larger patterns thus formed stand out more distinctly. The orderly process of social change is transformed into one characterized by tenseness, aggressiveness and conflict. This strange animation may be confined to a given section and to certain groups, or it may spread over the entire picture. Sooner or later the process assumes a slower and smoother tempo; the revolution is over; new group patterns emerge, and the interplay of group forces becomes less distinct. In a very real sense the key to an understanding of the "American Political Scene" is to be found in the activity of these groups.[2]

Although any group may be considered a pressure group, those of greatest political significance are the more or less permanently organized groups, having or representing certain common attributes or interests, which, to an appreciable extent, seek to mold public policy directly or indirectly.[3] In this sense political parties, legislative, executive, and judicial agencies of government, states themselves, international organizations such as the League of Nations, organized groups of racketeers, political machines, as well as such entities as chambers of commerce, trade associations, farmers' organizations, trade unions, church denominations, professional associations, and racial groups are

[2] A. Gordon Dewey, "On Methods in the Study of Politics," *Political Science Quarterly*, vol. xxxviii, pp. 636-651 (December, 1923), and vol. xxxix, pp. 218-223 (June, 1924).

[3] The concept "pressure group" was considered at a conference held at the University of Chicago on May 2-3, 1931, at the invitation of a special committee of the Social Science Research Council on Pressure Groups and Propaganda. The proceedings were issued in mimeographed form. Some writers distinguish pressure group and interest group. "A pressure group is defined by its techniques, an interest group by its objectives." R. M. MacIver, "Social Pressures," *Encyclopedia of the Social Sciences*, vol. xii, p. 347. As interest groups are also pressure groups, the use of the one or the other term is a matter of personal preference. As Professor Bentley points out (*op. cit.*, p. 211), "There is no group without its interest."

pressure groups.[4] It has been customary for students of politics to segregate, for detailed, virtually exclusive consideration, the state itself, official agencies of government, and political parties. This procedure has many advantages, provided it does not lead to a distorted and circumscribed conception of the extent and character of pressure group activity. In view of the fact that almost any social grouping may upon occasion exert influence which is politically significant, it is preferable to broaden the concept for general purposes, redefining or narrowing its scope in particular cases.

At any time, the number of pressure groups politically significant in the "American Political Scene" is large. To grasp the extent and the character of pressure group activity, it is necessary to comprehend the totality of political, professional, economic, religious, fraternal, racial and special-purpose groupings. Unfortunately, there exists no inclusive directory of pressure groups in the United States, but from numerous specialized directories may be obtained figures concerning the number of commercial and industrial organizations in the United States, professional associations, organizations in the field of public administration, religious denominations, labor and agrarian groupings, age and sex groups, welfare organizations, fraternal groups, racial groups, and special-purpose organizations. Out of this total complex of pressure groupings, possibly 500 are politically significant nationally, although any definite figure is likely to be misleading.[5]

The search for a generally satisfactory classification of pressure groups is difficult. The basis of classification may be any one of a large number of group attributes such as size of membership, objectives, pressure resources, or degrees of cohesion and permanence. The problem of classification is always a search for a basis most useful in the case at hand. One common basis

[4] For a penetrating analysis of pressure groups in relation to the struggle for political power, see C. E. Merriam, *Political Power* (New York, 1934).

[5] See E. P. Herring, *Group Representation Before Congress* (Baltimore, 1929), p. 19.

of differentiation is the name of the group. Another that is used frequently is the group objective. Both bases were employed with eminently satisfactory results by the authors of *Propaganda and Promotional Activities*.⁶ Were it possible to determine precisely the pressure resources of a group or its relative influence, classifications on these bases would be extremely useful. Only as group attributes become more precisely identifiable will it be possible to deal with the unit "group" more significantly.

The influence which any group exerts upon legislation, administrative activities, public opinion, or any political, social, or economic institution, depends upon its pressure resources, conditioned, however, by the corresponding influence exercised by other groups.⁷ Some groups encounter very little opposition, and with scanty resources produce marked changes in the political institutions of the country in which they function. Others with apparently tremendous resources are greatly handicapped by the environment in which they find themselves. In any case, all groups, whether they realize their objectives or not, play a part in making the existing political equilibrium what it is. The influence of a pressure group cannot always be determined simply by taking account of the number of officials it succeeds in electing, or by the number of laws favorable to it which are passed. The outcome of elections, changes in public opinion, trends in public policy, are resultants of the interplay of innumerable groups, and the particular group is merely one of a number of variable factors. Many of the claims of existing pressure groups, as well as the charges of their opponents, do not take account of the total situation, leaving us with an impression of power that may not exist.

Precise measurements of group pressure are extremely difficult to make. For example, to determine the real influence ex-

---

⁶ H. D. Lasswell, R. D. Casey, and B. L. Smith, *Propaganda and Promotional Activities—An Annotated Bibliography* (Minneapolis, 1935).

⁷ See A. F. Bentley, *op. cit.*, chap. vii; and H. L. Childs, *Labor and Capital in National Politics* (Columbus, 1930), pp. 178-181.

erted by the Townsend movement, the American Legion or the American Bankers Association, it would not only be necessary to find units of measurement, but to keep all other influences the same during the course of the experiment. It is conceivable that someone will discover a reasonably accurate device for conducting a controlled experiment of this character; but until this is done a healthy amount of skepticism should greet claims that such and such an amount of influence is being or has been exerted.

Proceeding more or less empirically, we may observe certain group attributes which appear important in attempting to estimate the pressure resources of a group. One of these is leadership.[8] There now exist numerous biographical and autobiographical studies of group leaders.[9] From time to time interesting comparative studies of selected leaders have been made.[10] More recently attempts have been made to study quantitatively larger selections of leaders, to the end that more convincing generalizations may be made regarding the specific traits of leaders in particular situations.[11] It is comparatively easy to identify both the nominal and even the real leaders of a group, to trace their life histories, to enumerate specific qualities or

[8] For a discussion of leadership and its significance in the case of political parties, see C. E. Merriam and H. F. Gosnell, *The American Party System* (New York, 1929), pp. 33-50.

[9] For a selected list of such studies, see H. L. Childs, *A Reference Guide to the Study of Public Opinion* (Princeton, 1934), pp. 13-21.

[10] C. E. Merriam, *Four American Party Leaders* (New York, 1926). Also W. B. Munro, *Personality in Politics* (New York, 1933).

[11] P. A. Sorokin, "Leaders of Labor and Radical Movements in the United States and Foreign Countries," *American Journal of Sociology*, vol. xxxiii, pp. 382-411; Jerome Davis, "A Study of One Hundred and Sixty-three Outstanding Communist Leaders," American Sociological Society, *Publications*, vol. xxiv, pp. 42-55, 1929; Frank W. Taussig and C. S. Joslyn, *American Business Leaders* (New York, 1932); J. Bernard, "Political Leadership among the North American Indians," *American Journal of Sociology*, 1928-29, vol. xxxiv, pp. 296-315. William E. Berchtold, in "Men of the Third Chamber," *New Outlook*, 1934, vol. clxiii, pp. 39-46 ff., has brought together an interesting number of short biographical sketches of non-party pressure group leaders.

traits which they possess.[12] It is infinitely more difficult to compare and contrast group leaders, and determine the weight of the leadership factor as it relates to the pressure which a group exerts. There is a very real need for quantitative and comparative studies of group leaders as a basis for a clearer understanding of the pressure exerted by specific groups within the "American Political Scene."[13]

The pressure which a group is able to exert is also related to the size, character and distribution of its membership.[14] Other things being equal, the larger the membership of a group the more pressure it will be able to use. But size of membership is by no means all important. In fact, size alone may be a handicap, may result in internal dissension, or may render the group so cumbersome as to make it ineffective. Hence the importance which realistic leaders place upon the distinction between mere

---

[12] For a rather comprehensive list of titles relating to leaders in advertising, press agents, publicity men, public relations counselors, educators, clergymen, lawyers, agitators, prophets, politicians, writers and lobbyists, see *Propaganda and Promotional Activities*, pp. 264-279.

[13] For an illuminating analysis of leadership, see Richard Schmidt, "Leadership," *Encyclopedia of the Social Sciences*, vol. ix, pp. 282-286. Professor Schmidt distinguishes among agents of authority, agitators and demagogues, and real leaders. Real leaders may be either representative or symbolic, dynamic or creative. In *The Process of Government*, pp. 223-235. Professor Bentley evaluates the relation between group leadership and group pressure.

[14] "When we have a group fairly well defined in terms of its interests, we next find it necessary to consider the factors that enter into its relative power of dominating other groups and of carrying its tendencies to action through their full course with relatively little check or hindrance. ... First of all, the number of men who belong to the group attracts attention. Number alone may secure dominance. ... But numbers notoriously do not decide elections in the former slave states of the South." Bentley, *op. cit.*, p. 215. For an analysis of group membership see *The American Party System*, chap. i, pp. 1-32, and A. N. Holcombe, *The Political Parties of To-day* (New York, 1923); for non-party groups, see Childs, *op. cit.*, chap. iv, pp. 81-103; Stuart Rice, *Farmers and Workers in American Politics* (New York, 1924). Excellent analyses of the composition of non-party pressure groups in certain foreign countries are contained in the series of volumes, *Studies in the Making of Citizens*, summarized and evaluated by C. E. Merriam, in *The Making of Citizens* (Chicago, 1931).

followers and those entitled to membership in a group.[15] The character of the members, their intelligence, their devotion to the cause, their willingness to defer to leadership, are quite as important as mere numbers. Moreover, the geographical distribution of the membership may be of decisive importance under certain circumstances. In the United States, for example, where the determination of public policy is so definitely related to a representative system based upon geographical units, a proper distribution of members throughout these districts may greatly facilitate the execution of group programs.

A third factor of importance in making the pressure of a group effective is the amount of its financial and material resources. Many groups which lack both effective leadership and large membership are able to compensate for these shortcomings through the use of money.[16] Professional leadership of a sort may be purchased.[17] Facilities for transmitting propaganda, more expensive than heretofore at the same time that they are more efficient, can be bought.[18] The serious student of the "American Political Scene" who seeks to understand the interplay of group pressures which make public policies what they

[15] One of the best discussions of this problem is to be found in Hitler's *Mein Kampf*, 1932 edition, Part II, chap. xi.

[16] Although students of politics have given attention to party finance (see especially James K. Pollock, *Party Campaign Funds,* New York, 1926), similar studies of non-party pressure group finances are notably lacking. See, however, Childs, *op. cit.*, pp. 31-41; P. H. Odegard, *Pressure Politics: The Story of the Anti-Saloon League* (New York, 1928), chap. vii, pp. 181-218; Summary Report of the Federal Trade Commission to the Senate of the United States on Efforts by Associations and Agencies of Electric and Gas Utilities to Influence Public Opinion, Senate Document 92, Part 71A, 1934, pp. 26, 38, 48, and 92-111. Scattered information of value may be obtained from reports of state and federal lobbying investigations and the reports of legislative hearings. See also F. C. Whitman, "The National Association of Manufacturers of the United States of America," thesis, Princeton University, 1936, pp. 40-43.

[17] Many of the nominal leaders of pressure groups are simply the spokesmen for employed public relations counsel and specialized advisers.

[18] In 1928 the cost of a National Broadcasting Company hook-up of 49 stations was $12,000 an hour, and a Columbia chain of 19 stations cost $4000 an hour. H. J. Bruce, *American Parties and Politics* (New York, revised edition, 1932).

are, inevitably comes face to face with the all-important fact of wealth distribution. Many of the pressure resources, but not all, can be bought, and those groups with large financial resources available can still wage an effective fight even though they are small in numbers.[19] Propagandists, possessors of technical skill of all sorts, organizers, artists, publicists, as well as the agencies of communication themselves, tend to go to the highest bidder. No comprehensive study of the financial resources of groups in this country has been made. Budgets range all the way from billions, in the case of governments themselves, to millions in the case of parties and ecclesiastical bodies, down to hundreds of thousands and thousands in the case of business, labor, agricultural and special-purpose organizations.[20] The published budgets of pressure groups seldom indicate, however, the full amount of financial resources available. This makes it difficult to calculate precisely this element in the resources of a pressure group.

And finally, of great importance in the outcome of group conflicts is the degree of cohesion, particularly opinion cohesion, within the group.[21] Objective indices of such cohesion are

[19] "In fact, only a little over six per cent of the population of the United States filed income tax returns in 1921, and only a minority of these were subject to the surtax. While the surtax payers together with their dependents form a larger proportion of the population, and have much greater political influence than these figures would appear to indicate, it is evident that capitalists and socialists alike must depend chiefly upon propaganda for the advancement of their special interests." Holcombe, *op. cit.*, p. 365.

[20] The budgets of a few of the more important non-party pressure groups are as follows:
American Federation of Labor (1934-35), $1,598,181.67
American Farm Bureau Federation (1932-33), $109,950.00
Chamber of Commerce of the United States (1934-35), $2,129,492.05
American Bankers' Association (1932-33), $607,695.77
American Bar Association (1932-33), $200,729.66
National Association of Manufacturers (1933, first eleven months), $213,300.00.

[21] Professor Bentley classifies pressure resources as follows: (1) interest, (2) membership, (3) intensity, (4) technique of group activities (*op. cit.*, pp. 211-17). He seems to use the word "intensity" in the same sense as the word "cohesion" is used here. "Intensity is a word that will

especially hard to find, and yet no analysis of the pressure resources of a group may validly ignore the significance of this vital factor. Much of the energy and time of group leaders is devoted to the development of this aspect of group existence. Some of the devices and strategies employed to bring about this cohesion relate to the creation of an organizational structure that will be adapted to the varied interests included within the group membership, the elaboration of organizational units to provide positions of power and influence within the group, the cementing of allegiance on the part of members by giving them a financial stake in the future of the organization through the establishment of benefit, insurance and other types of funds, and to numerous and varied schemes for relating individual interests of the members to the interests of the group.[22] Fascist, Socialist and Communist parties have demonstrated a keener realization of the importance of cohesion than our parties in

---

serve as well as any other to denote the concentration of interest which gives a group effectiveness in its activity in the face of the opposition of other groups" (p. 216).

[22] On the technique of creating group cohesion, see Merriam, *op. cit.*, especially chap. vii, pp. 184-230. On the relation of organizational structure to group cohesion, see studies of Fascist, Communist and Socialist parties, such as F. L. Schuman, *The Nazi Dictatorship* (New York, 1935); Herman Finer, *Mussolini's Italy* (New York, 1935); and Samuel Harper, *Civic Training in Soviet Russia* (Chicago, 1929). On the elaboration of organizational units to provide positions of power, consult literature on political parties relating to use of patronage, such as D. H. Kurtzman, *Methods of Controlling Votes in Philadelphia* (Philadelphia, 1935). On the use of finances to cement allegiance see Childs, *op. cit.*, pp. 30-41; Merriam and Gosnell, *op. cit.*, chaps. iv and v, pp. 99-195. The functioning of the Communist, Fascist and Socialist parties illustrates the importance of relating individual interests to the group and methods that may be employed for doing so. See, for example, description of Socialist methods in Switzerland in R. C. Brooks, *Civic Training in Switzerland* (Chicago, 1930), chap. iv, pp. 78-106. No systematic treatment of practices employed by non-party pressure groups in this country has been made. Studies of individual organizations have furnished, however, a number of suggestive illustrations. Studies of this character, especially in the field of ecclesiastical, fraternal and trade union organizations, would be especially significant. The best analysis of the whole problem, in relation to the state, is C. E. Merriam, *The Making of Citizens* (Chicago, 1931).

this country. The totalitarian party is a fruit of their shrewdness. Such parties which absorb the individual and his interests, rather than permitting them to serve simply in a segmental capacity, point the way toward a revival of methods for bringing about group cohesion and thus enhancing the pressure of a group; such methods have been best exemplified in the history of the Catholic Church.[23]

Although it is useful to distinguish various types of pressure resources, it is important to remember that each type complements and supplements the others, and that in the final analysis they must be considered as a unit. A brief analysis, such as this, suggests the difficulties encountered in trying to determine precisely the pressure or influence which a group may exert or, in fact, does exert.[24] One of the charges most frequently made with reference to lobbying and pressure group activity in this country is that certain groups exert more influence than they should.[25] Such charges have only persuasive value, however, unless we know more precisely what the influence of a group was in a particular instance. Reasonably accurate determinations of the pressure resources of groups, and the invention of techniques for measuring the amount of pressure actually used, must precede conclusions, to say nothing of ethical evaluations of the ends being served by such pressures. It is not altogether improbable that in the near future it will be possible to deal with pressure groups in such a way that the intricate pattern of group forces can be reduced to lines showing

[23] Not only churches and dictatorial parties, but many other groups, have recognized the importance of identifying, for example, the family as such with the group. See F. L. Keyes, "A Survey of Pressure Group Activity, 1830-1850," thesis, Princeton University, 1936.

[24] On measurement of group attributes, see Bentley, *op. cit.*, pp. 200-202; Childs, *op. cit.*, pp. 178-181; and E. E. Schattschneider, *Politics, Pressures and the Tariff* (New York, 1935).

[25] "In fact, with or without the use of corrupt practice, the lobby has exercised an undue influence upon legislation, and the knowledge of this fact is the second of the principal causes for the decline of the state legislatures in public esteem." A. N. Holcombe, *State Government* (New York, 3rd edition, 1931), p. 313.

the direction and intensity of the pressure that particular groups are applying. The parallelogram of forces thus plotted may then be used to forecast significant changes in public opinion, in public policy, and in institutions.[26]

What changes, if any, are taking place in the struggle of pressure groups for ascendancy? Is the struggle which is now going on during the election year of 1936 different in any important respects from that which was taking place in the past?[27] The activity of pressure groups has naturally been affected by all those aspects of social change which have so markedly modified our behavior. The spread of literacy under the ægis of expanded educational facilities has broadened the base of competition for public support. Improvements in methods of communication, particularly in the fields of journalism, radio broadcasting and the motion picture, have modified techniques of publicity, argument and persuasion, and have enabled groups to apply their pressure over wider areas.[28] Not only that, but these improvements in instruments of mass impression have enhanced the importance of the time factor, have, in other words, speeded up the tempo of pressure group activity and therewith social change itself. The Industrial Revolution, the growth of large business enterprises, and the consequent tendency toward wealth concentration, have produced marked changes in the distribution of wealth and, consequently, transformations in pressure group resources.[29] The expansion of governmental activities, the assumption of greater responsibili-

[26] "There is no political process that is not a balancing of quantity against quantity. There is not a law that is passed that is not the expression of force and force in tension. There is not a court decision or an executive act that is not the result of the same process. Understanding any of these phenomena means measuring the elements that have gone into them." Bentley, *op. cit.*, p. 202.

[27] See Keyes, *op. cit.*

[28] See M. M. Willey, and S. A. Rice, *Communication Agencies and Social Life* (New York, 1933).

[29] See *Recent Economic Changes in the United States*, report of the Committee on Recent Economic Changes of the President's Conference on Unemployment, Washington, 1929; President's Research Committee on Social Trends, *Recent Social Trends in the United States* (2 vols., 1932).

ties on the part of official agencies of government for the welfare of citizens, have altered the relation of the state as a pressure group to other non-official groups.[30]

Although it is impossible to be precise in such matters, the total effect of these changes seems to have been to increase the number of groupings and the variety of objectives being furthered. The conflict has become more intense, centering around the struggle for control over instruments of communication, over the government and the resources at its disposal, and over the material resources requisite to victory.[31] Economic groups are becoming more decisive in their influence, as against religious, racial and professional groups.[32] Lobbying in the nineteenth-century sense of the term is giving way to struggles for control of the minds of the masses.[33] One may also discern a tendency toward broader syntheses of underlying groupings, and the emergence of totalitarian groups, more cohesive, more determined, less willing to abide by preexisting standards of fair play, less given to compromise and adaptation to the purposes of other groups.[34] Before considering in some detail the implications to be derived from these considerations, it is desirable for us to renew our historical perspective, to consider the

---

[30] C. H. Wooddy, *Growth of the Federal Government, 1915-1932* (New York, 1933).

[31] O. W. Riegel, *Mobilizing for Chaos* (New Haven, 1934); H. D. Lasswell, *World Politics and Personal Insecurity* (New York, 1935).

[32] J. T. Adams, *Our Business Civilization* (New York, 1929); A. A. Berle, and G. C. Means, *The Modern Corporation and Private Property* (New York, 1933); E. W. Crecraft, *Government and Business* (New York, 1928); B. S. Hendrick, *The Age of Big Business* (New Haven, 1919); C. A. Beard, *America Faces the Future* (New York, 1932); Stuart Chase, *The New Deal* (New York, 1932); A. N. Holcombe, *The New Party Politics* (New York, 1933); George Soule, *The Coming American Revolution* (New York, 1934); B. Stolberg, and W. J. Vinton, *The Economic Consequences of the New Deal* (New York, 1935); R. G. Tugwell, *The Industrial Discipline* (New York, 1933); H. A. Wallace, *New Frontiers* (New York, 1934); S. C. Wallace, *The New Deal in Action* (New York, 1934).

[33] See S. M. Rosen, *Political Process* (New York, 1935), chap. viii.

[34] As for example in Russia, Italy, Germany.

rôle which pressure groups have played in this country since 1789.

The framers of our national Constitution were quite aware of the problems incident to the conflict of interest groups.[35] Whether or not we agree with the thesis that certain economic groups dominated that remarkable convention held in Philadelphia during 1787, the document therein perfected certainly reflected a balance obtained among sectional, religious, political and economic groupings.[36] The first statutes enacted by members of the First Congress likewise exemplified this struggle, this underlying contest between fundamental interest groupings.[37] A cross section of the political process as it was functioning during the early part of the nineteenth century reveals literally swarms of pressure groups, many of which have since expanded into nation-wide organizations still in existence: the Bible Society of America (1816); the Children's Aid Society (1853); the National Association of Cotton Manufacturers (1854); the National Education Association of the United States (1857); the American Medical Association (1847); the American Peace Society (1828); and numerous chambers of commerce, labor organizations, church denominations, temperance and anti-slavery societies.[38] Then, as now, such groups sought to influence the course of public policy by bringing pressure to bear upon governmental officials, by seeking to mold public opinion, by applying with the facilities at their command those age-old strategies of argument, persuasion, organization and publicity.

Of special significance to the student of political change and constitutional development has been the influence of pressure groups in relation to such amendments to the federal Constitu-

[35] R. M. MacIver, "Interests," *Encyclopedia of the Social Sciences,* vol. viii, p. 185.

[36] See C. A. Beard, *An Economic Interpretation of the Constitution of the United States* (New York, 1923).

[37] "Efforts to direct the process of lawmaking by pressure from selfish interests were made in the first congress." E. P. Herring, "Lobby," *Encyclopedia of the Social Sciences,* vol. ix, p. 565.

[38] F. L. Keyes, *op. cit.;* and C. R. Fish, *The Rise of the Common Man, 1830-1850* (New York, 1927).

tion as those dealing with anti-slavery, taxation, popular control of government, prohibition and woman suffrage. Although by no means immediately responsible for amendments which freed the Negro, granted him the privileges of citizenship and gave him the legal right to vote, the American Anti-Slavery Society cannot be ignored in any consideration of the factors bringing about this result.[39] The story of the adoption of the income tax amendment and the constitutional provision for direct election of Senators cannot be adequately comprehended without an understanding of the activities of pressure groups. The story of pressure politics as it relates to the adoption and finally the repeal of the prohibition amendment is to a considerable extent the story of the activities of the Anti-Saloon League, the Association Against the Prohibition Amendment, and numerous other pressure groups associated with them.[40] Likewise, the story of woman suffrage requires for its satisfactory interpretation an understanding of the activities of the National American Woman's Suffrage Association and the Congressional Union, two pressure groups that, subsequent to the adoption of the Nineteenth Amendment, became the National Woman's Party and the National League of Women's Voters, respectively. The story of these pressure groups has been told elsewhere.[41] It is sufficient to observe that nearly all great social movements, nearly all great transformations in the political and social life of the nation, are the products of this intergroup activity, of pressure groups utilizing substantially the same methods in the past that they are using today.[42]

[39] See Paul Fitting, "The American Anti-Slavery Society—a Study in Pressure Groups and Propaganda," thesis, Princeton, 1935. See also G. H. Barnes, *The Anti-Slavery Impulse, 1830-1844* (New York, 1934).

[40] Peter Odegard, *Pressure Politics: The Story of the Anti-Saloon League* (New York, 1928); E. H. Cherrington, *The Evolution of Prohibition in the United States of America* (Westerville, Ohio, 1920).

[41] C. C. Catt, and N. R. Shuler, *Woman Suffrage and Politics* (New York, 1926).

[42] "Modern historians have seen in the clash of interests, as the conjuncture of conditions and events favored one side or another, one of the universal factors in social and political change." R. M. MacIver, "Interests," *Encyclopedia of the Social Sciences,* vol. viii, p. 144.

The influence of pressure groups upon legislation has always been effective—one might say, decisive. This phase of the political process has received more attention perhaps than any other.[43] Most of the outcries against pressure group activity are stimulated by evidences of lobbying. Acrimonious fervor has been aroused in recent years by the pressure exerted on behalf of bonus legislation by the American Legion;[44] by the far-flung protective efforts of the National Electric Light Association, the American Gas Association, and their public utility associates;[45] by the supposedly insidious power over the minds of legislators exerted by munition makers,[46] the Ku Klux Klan,[47] the Anti-Saloon League,[48] and numerous "subversive" movements; Nazi, Communist, anti-vice, Townsendism, and other crusades too numerous to mention.[49] Of greater and more fundamental influence in the political process, so far as pressure itself is concerned, are the activities of basic social, and particularly economic, groupings. Since 1913, when the Chamber of Commerce of the United States was formed, its pressure has been felt with reference to practically all congressional legislation affecting American business, notably the Federal Reserve Act, World War legislation, the Transportation Act of 1920 and its amendments, budgetary reform, taxation, the tariff, the New

[43] See especially E. B. Logan, "Lobbying," Supplement to vol. cxliv of the *Annals of the American Academy of Political and Social Science*, July, 1929; E. P. Herring, *op. cit.*; and *Lobbying: A Bibliographical List* (Library of Congress, Division of Bibliography, 1932 [photostat]).

[44] See references, *Propaganda and Promotional Activities*, pp. 194-197.

[45] Ernest Gruening, *The Public Pays: A Study of Power Propaganda* (New York, 1931); and references in *Propaganda and Promotional Activities*, pp. 155-156.

[46] George Seldes, *Iron, Blood, and Profits* (New York, 1934); and other references cited in *Propaganda and Promotional Activities*, pp. 185-190.

[47] J. M. Mecklin, *The Ku Klux Klan: A Study of the American Mind* (New York, 1924).

[48] Peter Odegard, *op. cit.*; and references cited in *Propaganda and Promotional Activities*, pp. 211-213.

[49] *Propaganda and Promotional Activities*, pp. 197-206. Also R. H. Everitt, "Nazism and Fascism in the United States," thesis, Princeton, 1935; and F. E. Lumley, *The Propaganda Menace* (New York, 1933).

Deal legislation.[50] There are few aspects of the recovery program of the Roosevelt Administration that have escaped the scrutiny and criticism of the Chamber. The pressure of business opinion has been constant and increasingly insistent.[51] Likewise, the American Federation of Labor plays today, as it has been playing for decades, an important rôle in the molding and making of legislation in the United States.[52] And back of the legislation which has been proposed and that which has passed into law are the numerous agricultural organizations, of which the American Farm Bureau Federation is an extremely important member.[53] In addition, there are such organizations as the National Association of Manufacturers, the American Bankers' Association, the Association of Railway Executives, as well as numerous trade associations which by means of general publicity, letters to Congressmen, attendance at legislative hearings, conferences with legislative and party leaders, and in other ways, seek to influence the course of legislation.

In a very real sense economic legislation today—which, after all, constitutes a large part of our public statutes—is a reflection of the underlying struggle that is going on among three great sections of our population, business, labor and agriculture.[54] Within each of these great groupings there is a decided tendency toward cooperation under the leadership of the Chamber of Commerce of the United States, the American Federation of Labor and the American Farm Bureau Federation. This is not to imply that these three great organizations comprise within their membership all the specific interests within each sector.

---

[50] H. L. Childs, *Labor and Capital in National Politics* (Columbus, 1930); and C. E. Bonnett, "The Evolution of Business Groupings," *Annals,* May, 1935, pp. 1-8.

[51] R. J. Swenson, *op. cit.,* pp. 136-143.

[52] David A. McCabe, *op. cit.,* 144-151. See also H. L. Childs, *op. cit.*

[53] B. H. Hibbard, "Legislative Pressure Groups Among Farmers," *Annals,* May, 1935, pp. 17-24; C. V. Gregory, "The American Farm Bureau Federation and the AAA," *ibid.,* pp. 152-157; and list of references in *Propaganda and Promotional Activities,* pp. 109-112.

[54] See A. N. Holcombe, *Government in a Planned Democracy* (New York, 1935); also his *The New Party Politics* (New York, 1933).

But no understanding of the "American Political Scene" as it is now functioning can ignore the influence which these organizations exert upon the course of legislation. A candidate for public office, the author of a bill, a party leader who has the support of all three organizations, has an enviable prospect before him. Political experience shows, however, that it is often difficult to pursue a course that represents a common denominator between two of them, much less all three. These three groups constitute the basic economic cleavages in the country, and out of their struggles emerges and will emerge whatever there is of unity in the economic pattern of public policy.

No more enlightening portrayal of this interplay of group forces as it affects legislation is available than the recent study of Dr. Schattschneider, *Politics, Pressures, and the Tariff*.[55] This examination of the tariff history of the United States indicates how much a given type of legislation is molded by the interplay of pressure groups within the business sector, the activity of which stands out in vivid contrast to the lethargy of the generality of the business population. This study also illustrates how pressure groups beget pressure groups, and how accommodation among them is found, not in compromise, but in a progressive satisfaction of their demands by accepting each interest's desires for a higher tariff. Unaware of their own real interests in many cases, they have succeeded in deceiving themselves, and more particularly the public generally, as to the long-time advantages to be derived from a high tariff policy. This experience shows the unfortunate results ensuing from persistent one-sided pressure from one sector of the population.

The impact of group pressure upon the execution of public policy is as real as it is upon the formulation of public policy. The personnel of administrative departments and agencies, their number, the kind of services rendered, the amount of money spent, and the vigor with which laws are enforced, have all been

[55] E. E. Schattschneider, *Politics, Pressures, and the Tariff* (New York, 1935).

affected by group pressures,[56] The Chamber of Commerce of the United States, for example, was active in the movement for the adoption of a national budget system, has devoted a considerable amount of attention to the federal civil service, the postal service, and above all to the Department of Commerce. This pressure is reflected in the day-to-day functioning of the Federal Trade Commission, the Federal Reserve Board and the Tariff Commission.[57] From its inception the American Federation of Labor has always been solicitous for the Department of Labor, the Bureau of Mines, and legislation or administrative rulings affecting the salaries and the conditions of work, including hours of labor, of federal employees.[58] The American Farm Bureau Federation and other important agricultural organizations direct their pressure toward the Department of Agriculture and whatever bureaus or agencies affect their interests.[59]

Perhaps no better evidence of the influence of group pressures is afforded than the part played by them in relation to the execution of New Deal policies.[60] Under the NIRA, economic pressure groups were called upon for the first time to assume a definite responsibility in the sphere of public administration.[61] In each of the major branches of industry pressure groups were called upon to take the lead in formulating codes for their particular branch and assisting in administering these codes.[62]

[56] See E. P. Herring, *Public Administration and the Public Interest* (New York, 1936).

[57] H. L. Childs, *op. cit.*, pp. 216-234.

[58] *Idem.* See also E. P. Herring, *op. cit.*, chap xvi. "The American Farm Bureau Federation has taken an active interest in all legislation relating to agriculture, and has continued this interest in the administration of the laws finally enacted" (p. 267).

[59] See *Annals* for May, 1935, pp. 136-157.

[60] See L. S. Lyon, and others, *The National Recovery Administration, An Analysis and Appraisal* (Washington, 1935); S. C. Wallace, *The New Deal in Action* (New York, 1934); Rene V. Williamson, *The Politics of Planning in the Oil Industry Under the Code* (New York, 1936).

[61] *Idem.*

[62] *Idem.* See, for example, *Construction Industry Code Manual*, published by the Construction League of the United States, vol. i, no. 3, January, 1935, especially pp. 5-6.

Because of the amount of discretion left to the executive in the conduct of foreign relations, the influence of pressure groups in this important field is marked.[63] Those group pressures which appear to be most effective in determining the final result emanate from the State Department, Congress, and other official agencies of government, political parties, foreign groups and an almost endless number of domestic groups. Among these last are organizations fostering respect for American ideals and traditions; groups seeking to further the cause of world peace; economic organizations of exporters, importers, bankers, manufacturers, shipping interests—all seeking to further their interests at home and abroad. This situation necessarily renders difficult the position of the administrator in charge of foreign policies, and yet he cannot avoid the impact of these pressures. The interpretation of national interest finally arrived at is usually a reflection of the balance of group pressures at the time.[64]

From the foregoing it is evident that the direction of group pressure varies from time to time in accordance with the exigencies of the situation. Special attention has been given to the play of group pressures upon the legislative and administrative branches of the government and upon the process of constitutional change. But the direction of group pressure is by no means so circumscribed. Today it may be focused upon a public as inclusive as the world at large or the population of a nation. Tomorrow it may be concentrated upon smaller sectors, particular publics composed of leaders in various walks of life, business leaders, legislators, party officials. During the year of a presidential campaign each step in the election process experiences this pressure. Long before rival candidates enter the arena, pressure groups are active. They influence announcements of candidature, they follow closely the work of party agencies, they make their influence felt in party primaries, in

[63] See H. H. Sprout, "Pressure Groups and Foreign Policies," *Annals*, May, 1935, pp. 114-123; E. P. Herring, *op. cit.*, chap. v, pp. 69-88; C. A. Beard, *The Idea of National Interest* (New York, 1934.)

[64] See E. P. Herring, *op. cit.*, chap. v.

conventions, in the drawing up of platforms, in the election campaign itself. Mobilized for continuous activity, their pressure never ceases.[65] In a very real sense party platforms are the common denominators of pressure group platforms combined by party strategists in a way to appease if not to gratify those groups or combinations of groups temporarily reflecting a given balance of pressures.[66] That party platforms have tended to become vaguer and less distinguishable from each other, that they take on the characteristics of "empty bottles," is due in no small measure to this fact.[67] The place from which to watch the evolution of party platforms is not the balcony of convention halls, nor even the committee rooms of platform committees, but that spot which gives the onlooker and investigator an opportunity to observe the comings and goings of significant pressure groups.

Party leaders no less than professional propagandists are impressively conscious of the pattern of group leadership and organization within their constituencies. Candidates for office direct their campaign speeches in turn to each of the outstanding groups, appear before these organizations as occasion permits, and seek, without too noticeable a contradiction of addresses to other groups, to identify their personal candidacy with the aspirations of the particular group before which they are speaking.[68] This is quite as true in national as in local campaigns. Party organization, during the course of an intensive campaign, is shrewdly reconstructed or adapted to these pha-

[65] See H. L. Childs, *op. cit.*, pp. 190-196; Peter Odegard, *Pressure Politics: The Story of the Anti-Saloon League* (New York, 1928), chap. iii. *Summary Report of the Federal Trade Commission*, pp. 260-278.

[66] Peter Odegard, "Political Parties and Group Pressures," *Annals*, May, 1935, pp. 80-81.

[67] *Ibid.* See also A. N. Holcombe, *op. cit.*, especially chap. i; and C. E. Merriam and H. F. Gosnell, *op. cit.*, pp. 215-221.

[68] It is a familiar practice for party leaders to participate in pressure group conventions. An analysis of President Roosevelt's speaking tour in 1932 will indicate how speeches are prepared to appeal to specific groups of major importance. See in this connection R. V. Peel and T. C. Donnelly, *The 1928 Campaign; an Analysis* (New York, 1931); H. R. Bruce, *American Parties and Politics* (New York, 1932 edition), pp. 402-403.

lanxes of group interest. Special committees purposely constituted to relate group interests to party interests are set up—committees of women, of young people, of the aged; special committees to cater to the needs of racial, professional, economic and religious groupings.

The student of political processes needs to supplement his knowledge of parties, their platforms and activities, with a more detailed understanding of these groups which make the political scene what it is. A knowledge of the organization, membership, leadership, finances and objectives of non-party groups is quite as essential as a similar knowledge of parties as such. Pressure group conventions are the stuff out of which party conventions are made. The resolutions which are therein welded together from the interplay of interests represented by subgroups in turn become the material from which party managers construct their statements of public policy. A glance over the more important pressure group conventions of the past year not only reveals a multitude of resolutions on matters of public policy, but, interpreted in terms of the pressure resources behind each group, points the way to the governmental pattern of the future.[69] Students of government and party politics are no longer content with the statement that public opinion rules. They wish to know what makes public opinion what it is. Not the least among the multiplicity of factors responsible for a given state of public opinion are these groups and the pressure which they exert. Were it possible to plot pressure group objectives as a parallelogram of forces and compute the resultant, significant predictions might be made, not only as to what party platforms are likely to be, which parties will win, but also as to significant trends in public policy.

The principal methods employed by pressure groups for attaining their objectives may be considered under the two head-

[69] An examination of the resolutions adopted at some twenty pressure group conventions during the past year suggests the problems of public policy and the conflicts of interest before the parties in their forthcoming conventions.

ings: "propaganda" and "lobbying." In general, the methods are substantially the same whether the group is the state itself, a governmental agency, a political party, or any one of a number of unofficial groups. These terms are by no means mutually exclusive. Both refer to methods used to influence public opinion, the essential difference being the public upon which the pressure is exerted. "Lobbying" connotes attempts on the part of pressure groups to influence publics composed of legislative and executive officials.[70] "Propaganda," as herein used, refers to the conscious attempt to manage the minds of other and usually more numerous publics. Some writers would limit the term propaganda to pressure activity which is confined to the use of particular methods—such, for example, as the management of symbols.[71] Others distinguish intentional from unintentional propaganda, thus broadening the word itself to include practically all forms of human behavior which bring about changes in attitudes or opinions, whether intentional or unintentional.[72] Whether propaganda or lobbying is good or bad is an ethical question, depending in the last analysis upon the standards of value used to evaluate methods and objectives.[73]

[70] For attempts to define "lobbying," see E. B. Logan, *op. cit.*, chap. i, pp. 1-3. He defines the word as "activities of a person or body of persons who attempt to influence legislation in any way whatsoever" (p. 3).

[71] See H. D. Lasswell, "The Person: Subject and Object of Propaganda," *Annals*, May, 1935, p. 189: "Propaganda may be defined as a technique of social control, or as a species of social movement. As technique, it is the manipulation of collective attitudes by the use of significant symbols (words, pictures, tunes) rather than violence, bribery or boycott." And in "The Study and Practice of Propaganda," in *Propaganda and Promotional Activities*, p. 3, he says: "Not the purpose but the method distinguishes propaganda from the management of men by violence, boycott, bribery and similar means of social control. Propaganda relies on symbols to attain its end: the manipulation of collective attitudes."

[72] "Intentional propaganda is a systematic attempt by an interested individual (or individuals) to control the attitudes of groups of individuals through the use of suggestion and, consequently, to control their actions; unintentional propaganda is the control of the attitudes and, consequently, the actions of groups of individuals through the use of suggestion." L. W. Doob, *Propaganda* (New York, 1936), p. 89.

[73] Professor Lumley would narrow the meaning of the word "propa-

The emphasis which warring nations placed upon propaganda during the World War tended to discredit the word, especially during the ensuing decade of disillusionment, as the idealism prevailing during the war years gave way to resentment against the war and those who were responsible for it.[74] Propaganda, however, is a phenomenon of long standing, and is good or bad only in so far as the methods used and the objectives furthered are good or bad.

There is, of course, the possibility that pressure groups will resort to force, and peaceful efforts to manage the minds of others will give way to armed conflict. When force is used primarily as a means for changing the opinions of others, it is a nice question whether such a practice should or should not be classified as propaganda. Certainly, the display of force under certain circumstances may have a persuasive effect not unlike the use of other strategies. When, however, force is used, not for the purpose of controlling minds, but for pursuing objectives irrespective of the opinions of others, it falls outside the scope of propaganda as such. States as well as hooded clans recognize the opinion-forming power of terror, concentration camps, lynch law and other displays or uses of force. And the effect upon public opinion may be all out of proportion to the actual amount of force used.[75]

---

ganda" to include promotional activities which are veiled in one way or another. This conception implies that propaganda is always socially reprehensible. See F. E. Lumley, *op. cit.*, p. 44. In chap. xi of his study a number of definitions of propaganda are discussed. See, in this connection, R. J. R. G. Wreford, "Propaganda, Evil and Good," *Nineteenth Century*, 1923, vol. xciii, pp. 514-524; H. D. Lasswell, "Theory of Political Propaganda," *American Political Science Review*, August, 1927, vol. xxi, pp. 627-631; R. Dodge, "Psychology of Propaganda," *Religious Education*, October, 1920, vol. xv, pp. 241-252. E. L. Bernays, *Propaganda* (New York, 1928).

[74] See, especially, H. D. Lasswell, *Propaganda Technique in the World War* (New York, 1927); and *Propaganda and Promotional Activities*, pp. 71-83, for list of references.

[75] See *Propaganda and Promotional Activities*, pp. 43-49; also literature dealing with specific pressure groups such as the Communist and Fascist parties, the Ku Klux Klan, the Black Legion, Tammany, etc.

The basic strategies and techniques of propaganda are substantially the same today as they were during the Archidamian War.[76] Fundamentally the same methods are employed by the Republican and Democratic parties, the United States Chamber of Commerce and the American Federation of Labor as were employed by the ancients. Then, as now, there were both intentional and unintentional propagandists. Opinion leaders used every means available for making their propaganda perceived. Medicine men, priests and elders knew (probably by other names) principles of "revealed, delayed revealed, and concealed propaganda."[77] Such evidence as we have indicates that they were skilled in techniques of relating personal interests and attitudes to their own interests and objectives—or, in the words of professional propagandists, they knew how to identify private interests with public interests. They realized the importance of emotional as well as rational stimuli, of submission and suggestion, of prestige and selection, of the impression of universality and repetition. It is by no means clear that opinion leaders of today are more skilled in managing the minds of others than were leaders in the past. Techniques and practices have been analyzed and labeled, the art is perhaps less esoteric than heretofore, but the basic principles are quite the same.

The social significance of propaganda, however, has assumed a new meaning.[78] The opinion leader has at his disposal facili-

[76] See L. Pearson, "Propaganda in the Archidamian War," *Classical Philology*, January, 1936, vol. xxxi, pp. 33-52; and also, F. E. Lumley, *op. cit.*, for a historical survey of propaganda.

[77] See A. A. Goldenweiser, *Early Civilization* (New York, 1922); R. H. Lowie, *Primitive Society* (New York, 1925); Nathan Miller, *The Child in Primitive Society* (London, 1928); S. D. Porteus, *The Psychology of a Primitive People* (New York, 1931); Clark Wissler, *An Introduction to Social Anthropology* (New York, 1929); J. L. Maddox, *The Medicine Man* (New York, 1933). "The holders of power in any primitive system of government will seek to entrench themselves by the use of all kinds of social expedients, and will even invoke the influence of magic and religion to support them in their claim of privilege." Porteus, *op. cit.*, p. 255.

[78] For an analysis of the implications of propaganda tendencies, see Graham Wallas, *Human Nature in Politics* (New York, 1921 Edition, Part II, chap. i). See also H. D. Lasswell, *op. cit.*

PRESSURE GROUPS AND PROPAGANDA

ties for disseminating opinions such as the ancients never dreamed of. The raising of the standards of literacy have made obsolete the use of certain types of myths and stimulus-situations. The tools with which the modern propagandist must work are as different from those available to the Roman emperors as machine guns differ from crossbows. In quite the same way in which the Industrial Revolution brought with it division of labor and endless conveyors, so the coming of the machine age called for opinion leaders capable of utilizing effectively the printing press, the radio, the motion pictures and all the other tools now available to him for amplifying his message. Equipped with a good voice, a pleasing appearance, a general understanding of the limited store of information then available, and a rostrum, the opinion leader of two thousand years ago was quite a match for anyone. Today he would probably have as much influence as the Ethiopian had in his war against modernized tanks, airplanes and machine guns. In other words, the contest for opinion control is a business, and a gigantic one at that. The leader of the future will not be a jack-of-all-trades, but will of necessity be one who succeeds in enlisting the aid of a large number of technicians—the skilled rationalizer, the artist capable of conceiving and executing stimulus-situations with emotional appeal, the organizer, the fund-raiser, the agitator, the specialist in publicity.

There may have been a time when individuals possessed whatever qualities were requisite for successful leadership in matters of opinion. This is rarely the case today, as Hitler so keenly perceived.[79] The struggle among pressure groups as it is carried on evidences this fact. The day of personal leadership is rapidly passing, and in its place are struggles between aggregations of specialists—lawyers, fund-raisers, publicists, authors, journalists, photographers, radio announcers, advertisers, agitators—mobilized behind a given cause.

One of the basic strategies of propaganda is what may be

[79] *Mein Kampf*, p. 651.

called the strategy of argument.[80] No pressure group can rely entirely upon emotional appeals. By them the masses may be swayed, but not the intellectuals, the *prudentes*, the *élite*, whose support is so essential to any cause. These must be won over by the use of particular rationalizations and dialectics popular at the moment[81]—whether in the form of lawyer's briefs, preacher's exegeses, economist's statistics, or philosopher's systems. Parties, trade associations, labor organizations—all groups, in fact—earnestly search for rhetoricians, lawyers, philosophers, economists and historians to do this job.[82] There should be available at headquarters a volume or volumes to convince the most erudite. The American Liberty League creates its Committee of Lawyers for this task.[83] Political parties utilize the services of economists, historians and philosophers to rationalize their objectives. Trade associations, pressure groups of all sorts, create research departments to prepare and publish statistics. Some groups use several methods, to the end that the philosophically minded, the religiously minded, the legally minded, and the statistically minded may be duly impressed. Fortunate indeed is the political party, the state, the unofficial pressure group that has at its disposal such masterpieces of rationalization as Karl Marx's treatise on *Capital*; Locke's *Treatise on Government* or Thomas Paine's *Common Sense*. Fortunate indeed is the party or pressure group that can enlist in its support the argumentative prowess of the modern successor of John Marshall, Thomas Hobbes, John Wesley, or George Bancroft.

Pressure groups seek to supplement rationalizations of their objectives with stimulus situations which will implement mental

[80] See especially W. H. Mallock, "Scientific Methods of Propaganda," *Fortnightly Review*, February, 1922, vol. cxvii, pp. 300-308; also H. D. Lasswell, *op. cit.;* and C. E. Merriam, *op. cit.*, especially pp. 113-132.

[81] "Human institutions, in an environment which worships reason, fail in influence and prestige unless they appear to be firmly founded on reason and fundamental principle." T. W. Arnold, *The Symbols of Government* (New Haven, 1935), p. 9.

[82] And states. See Elisha Hanson, "Official Propaganda and the New Deal," *Annals*, May, 1935, p. 176.

[83] See New York *Times*, June 10, 1935, p. 20.

patterns of thought with emotional drives. Those democratic theories which conceived of public opinion as the outgrowth of rational processes of thinking have long since demonstrated their inadequacy. The findings of psychologists and others have emphasized the rôle played by emotions, interests and drives in the opinion-forming process.[84] Whether instincts—in the sense of specific tendencies to react to stimulii in a definite way—are innate or not, politicians, fund-raisers and advertisers are aware of certain types of response generally present in large masses of people. The pressure group and the propagandist seek to arouse these habitual responses and relate them to the opinions which they are propagandizing.[85] Campaign speeches, stunts, demonstrations, pictures, cartoons, parades—all are used for the purpose of relating to the objectives of the group such instincts as the desire for security, the "instinct" of fear, love, hate, the desire for gain, pleasure, humor.[86]

Irrespective of whether the stimulus-situation, the appeal, is directed toward the mind or the emotions or both, it must be perceived.[87] Hence the emphasis which is placed upon the strategy of publicity, the effort to utilize to the best advantage the available instruments of opinion dissemination.[88] Today, as never before, the tools for doing this are much more numerous and much more effective than ever before. The principal media are the press, including newspapers, periodicals, pamphlets and books; the radio, motion pictures and the theater, the educational system, art, fairs, expositions and the platform. All groups seek

[84] F. H. Lund, *Emotions of Men* (New York, 1930).
[85] L. W. Doob, *op. cit.*
[86] See C. E. Merriam and H. F. Gosnell, *op. cit.*, chap. x; H. R. Bruce, *op. cit.*, chap. xiv; R. D. Casey, "Party Campaign Propaganda," *Annals*, May, 1935, pp. 96-105; Peter Odegard, *op. cit.*; F. R. Kent, *The Great Game of Politics* (New York, 1928).
[87] L. W. Doob, *op. cit.*, chap. vii.
[88] Mr. Bernays has stated the strategy of publicity as follows: "The political campaign having defined its broad objects and its basic plans, having defined the group appeal which it must use, must carefully allocate to each of the media at hand the work which it can do with maximum efficiency (*Propaganda*, pp. 102-103).

to utilize as many of these perception-creating tools as possible. The success of their efforts depends to a large extent upon the character of the ownership which prevails over these instruments.[89] In many European countries the state itself has assumed monopolistic control over them. In this country control still resides in private hands, except in so far as the state imposes regulatory restrictions or limitations upon their use.[90]

The most important of these agencies of opinion dissemination today are the press, the radio and the motion pictures.[91] The use of the press as an instrument of opinion dissemination is conditioned by the fact that newspapers are controlled and owned by private publishers and operated primarily for profit. In comparatively few instances are newspapers operated mainly for propaganda purposes, and their use motivated by the desire to further the interests of a particular group, except it be the group of publishers themselves. Since they are operated for profit, their use is conditioned by the fact that approximately three-fourths of the revenue comes from advertisers,[92] a revenue which in turn is largely conditioned by the circulation of the paper. Hence the vigorous attempts to increase circulation by improving news services, introducing magazine material, avoiding definite editorial stands on controversial questions, using pictures and cartoons, adding sport, women, children, book review and financial sections.[93] Aware of this situation, pressure groups guide their publicity technique accordingly. They may use advertising as the most direct method of putting their case before a wide public. They create news by manufacturing events having a positive news value. They supply magazine material, cartoons, editorials, and such material as will of its own accord bring new subscribers to the paper. Persons skilled in the tech-

[89] See M. M. Willey and S. A. Rice, *op. cit.*
[90] See O. W. Riegel, *op. cit.*
[91] See *Propaganda and Promotional Activities*, for references, pp. 279-311, 316-326.
[92] See *Recent Social Trends*, chap. iii.
[93] *Ibid.;* and also W. G. Bleyer, *Main Currents in the History of American Journalism* (New York, 1927).

nique of obtaining newspaper publicity have developed, and these press agents are familiar personages on the propaganda staffs of pressure groups.[94]

The radio, which has more recently taken its place beside the newspaper press as a great instrument of mass impression, is likewise privately owned and operated in the United States, although through the licensing system the government exercises a considerable degree of indirect control over it.[95] As in the case of the press, the owners of broadcasting stations are not as a rule affiliated with any particular pressure group, but the stations are primarily business undertakings. Several considerations affect their use by competitive pressure groups. One is the possibility of government ownership,[96] a threat which makes radio owners cautious in allowing pressure groups to use their facilities. Programs too obnoxious to governmental officials or powerful groups throughout the country will be omitted, regardless of the revenue to be derived.[97] Government ownership is more dangerous than the threat of losing immediate profits. The government as a pressure group is usually in a much more fortunate position as far as getting radio publicity is concerned.[98]

[94] Stanley Walker, *City Editor* (New York, 1934).

[95] J. G. Kerwin, *The Control of Radio* (Chicago, 1934); L. F. Schmeckebier, *The Federal Radio Commission: Its History, Activities and Organization* (Washington, 1932).

[96] See "Study of Communications by an Interdepartmental Committee," letter from the President of the United States to the Chairman of the Committee on Interstate Commerce Transmitting a Memorandum from the Secretary of Commerce Relative to a Study of Communications by an Interdepartmental Committee, Senate Committee Print, 73d Congress, Second Session, 1934. Also J. G. Kerwin, *op. cit.*

[97] "We will not allow dramatization of political issues, if time is bought after the conventions. . . . Our reasons for not allowing dramatizations are as follows . . ." Quoted from letter of Edward Klauber, First Vice President of the Columbia Broadcasting System, to Thomas G. Sabin, Director, Radio Division, Republican National Committee, December 27, 1935.

[98] "The Columbia Broadcasting System will continue to distinguish between the office of President and the Government, on the one hand, and the political parties and their candidates on the other, without regard to whether a candidate is in office or not." Letter of William S. Paley,

With these considerations in mind, we see that the radio as well as the press may be used for propaganda purposes by purchasing time. This is an expensive procedure, and the use of the time so purchased is much more greatly circumscribed than is the use of space in the newspaper. The radio is an instrument of mass impression—much more so than the newspaper—and it is above all necessary for the user to adapt his propaganda to the types of programs which appeal to the mass mind. Music of various kinds is, by and large, the great common denominator, and the propagandist who can translate his opinions into music—or perhaps into humor—finds most ready access to this instrument.[99] Dictated by this same desire to make money and avoid government ownership is the devotion to sponsored programs of a certain proportion of the time available for radio broadcasting.[100] Much of this time is used for experimental purposes and for creating good will on the part of groups otherwise critical of present trends in broadcasting. The rise of the radio has been so rapid that many pressure groups have been slow to grasp its significance as a propaganda medium. The basic problem of publicity strategy so far as radio is concerned is to relate the interests of the group to the profit-interest of radio owners. Radio time may be purchased under the limita-

---

President of the Columbia Broadcasting System, to Henry P. Fletcher, Chairman, Republican National Committee, January 2, 1936.

[99] See Peter Odegard, *The American Public Mind* (New York, 1930), p. 227; also J. H. Morecroft, "How the Propagandists Work in Radio," *Radio Broadcast,* July, 1925.

[100] "In trying to conduct our operations on what we conceive to be a sound basis with the foregoing objectives in view, we sacrifice every year a good many hundreds of thousands of dollars of revenue, and do not sell time to any organization to do with exactly what it pleases." Letter of William S. Paley, President of the Columbia Broadcasting System, to Henry P. Fletcher, chairman, Republican National Committee, January 8, 1936. "As you know, we are required under the Communications Act of 1934 to operate as public convenience, interest or necessity requires. Naturally we wish not only to comply with the spirit and the letter of that Act, but to do all things possible within the scope of reasonable and sound business operations to perpetuate the American system of broadcasting" (*idem*).

tions already mentioned. A certain amount of free publicity may be obtained if the propagandist has a program to offer which creates good will for radio broadcasting or at least does not offend the mass mind and the powers which dominate public opinion and public policy.

The motion picture as an instrument of mass impression must be taken into account in any consideration of publicity strategy. As in the case of the radio, its sudden rise to a position of great importance in the opinion-forming process has been tardily perceived by many groups in this country. As it is privately owned and operated for profit, its use has been conditioned very largely by the balance sheet. Whereas three-fourths of the revenue of newspapers is derived from advertising, and whereas the sale of radio receiving equipment and time to advertisers are the principal sources of revenue in the case of radio broadcasting, the use of motion pictures is largely conditioned by the revenue to be derived from box-office receipts. Although the newspaper reader and the radio listener pay directly but a small portion of the cost of the items they read or hear, the cost of producing, distributing and displaying pictures is borne almost entirely by the theatergoer. It might have been otherwise. Advertisers are beginning to sense the possibilities of using the screen, certain pressure groups have begun to supply theaters with news reels,[101] and it is not at all unlikely that in the near future more attention will be devoted to the strategy of publicity as it applies to the motion picture. This is not to imply that this tendency is or is not desirable. We may only observe the tendency, which is a natural result of the intense competition of pressure groups for opinion control.

Propaganda technique and strategy comprise not only argument, persuasion and publicity, but also organization.[102] Various

[101] W. F. Laporte, "The Newsreel," thesis, Princeton, 1936.
[102] "Propaganda is feeble and ineffectual unless it fashions for itself an organization. An organization endows an idea with a degree of prestige which it can never obtain from the advocacy of scattered individuals." A. Lipsky, *Man the Puppet* (1925), p. 86. "The organization is the

organizational devices are employed for identifying individual attitudes with the cause, and for regimenting and cementing allegiance. Possibly too much attention has been given by students of propaganda to the seeming effectiveness of publicity as such. All that the strategy of publicity can do is to make the appeal, the stimulus-situation, perceived. Whether the appeal ultimately brings about a new integration in the minds of those propagandized depends upon the effectiveness of the strategy of argument and persuasion. And whether these changes in opinion and attitudes remain as the propagandist would have them remain is largely a question of organization.[103]

Party leaders and pressure group leaders generally realize the importance of creating an organizational structure adapted to the significant groups of interest represented within the membership—age, sex, occupational, race or class;[104] one that will provide for centralized and responsible leadership; one that will bind the membership together by a hierarchial network of subleaders definitely responsible for supervision and control over a limited group of subordinates. This multiplication of offices not only serves to keep individual opinions in line, but also gives added firmness to the ties which bind the office holders to the movement. Opinion allegiance may be further enhanced by giving to the individual member as well as to the corps of leaders financial stakes in the success of the organization, by setting up benefit funds, insurance funds and the like.[105] Of particular importance is the attempt to identify as many as possible of the interests of the members with that of the group by including in the organization an opportunity for the in-

---

largest single factor in the winning of elections." R. V. Peel, and T. C. Donnelly, *op. cit.*, p. 36.

[103] On the importance and strategy of organization, see A. Hitler, *op. cit.*, part ii; C. E. Merriam, and H. F. Gosnell, *op. cit.*, chap. iii; also C. E. Merriam, *op. cit.*, chap. ix; and H. L. Childs, *op. cit.*, pp. 41-60.

[104] In addition to references cited in Note 103, see studies of Communist, Socialist and Fascist parties; also histories of Catholic and other church organizations.

[105] See S. Neumann, *Die Deutschen Parteien* (Berlin, 1932).

dividual to develop his play, cultural, occupational and other activities.[106] Much of the cohesiveness of Socialist, Communist, Fascist and other totalitarian parties in Europe is due to the fact that the individual member finds within his own group an outlet for most of his interests. The effectiveness of party machines in some of our large cities, and the hold which many fraternal, trade union and religious associations have upon the opinions of their members, are directly related to this aspect of organizational strategy.[107] Propaganda in the sense of conscious attempts to manage the minds of others is an activity much more inclusive than that signified by the word "publicity."

The employment of these several strategies of propaganda by political parties is more or less characteristic of the practice followed by all pressure groups. The strategy of argument is illustrated over and over again in the numerous books, pamphlets, magazine articles, newspaper editorials, campaign textbooks and speeches which flood the country during an election year. Evaluated from the point of view of convincingness, much of this material is of poor quality, whether it is measured by legal standards of brief-making, standards of statistical presentation, the canons of logic or fundamental philosophical systems. It is a sad commentary on America that it has not as yet produced as impressive rationalizations of its fundamental political philosophies as have some foreign countries.

The strategy of persuasion is frequently illustrated in the repeated attempts by parties and pressure groups to stimulate the emotions. The use of emotional symbols to arouse hatred, fear, greed, love—such as slogans, pictorial stereotypes, dramatizations, flags and parades—is still, apparently, an essential part of the propaganda-strategy today. Every conceivable de-

---

[106] R. C. Brooks, *op. cit.*, chap. iii; A. Weber, *Der Kampf Zwischen Kapital und Arbeit* (Tubingen, 1921 Edition).
[107] See R. V. Peel, *The Political Clubs of New York City* (New York, 1935); J. T. Salter, *Boss Rule; Portraits in City Politics* (New York, 1935); C. E. Merriam, *op. cit.*; L. L. Lorwin, and J. A. Flexner, *The American Federation of Labor; History, Politics and Prospects* (Washington, 1933).

vice is employed to make the appeal perceived.[108] Individuals with prestige value and news value are made the channels through which opinions are disseminated. Overt acts and manufactured events are constantly being arranged as means for getting appeals into the newspapers. Radio time is purchased, news reels are prepared, every conceivable agency is used to make the group's stimulus-situation stand out. And underneath the more obvious efforts to mold public opinion, the organizer is at work erecting a human structure which binds the new adherent to the cause into an ever more rigid state of opinion-regimentation.

The state has never been indifferent to the struggles of pressure groups. The total body of citizens, and the officials who act for them, cannot ignore these conflicts of interest which go on within the state-group itself. As a rule, the state has permitted a maximum of pressure group freedom to compete for opinion control, so long as physical force was not employed and so long as the methods used did not violate accepted standards of taste and decency. The assumption has been that agencies of government were to be more or less reflectors, through their activities and policies, of the existing equilibrium of pressures. In the field of foreign policy as well as in that of domestic policy, the theory seems to have been that it was not for governmental officials to decide what the public interest was, but rather to discover what it was from a weighing of the relative pressures exerted by various groups as measured by legislative votes or popular elections.

Except in war time and during emergencies, comparatively few restrictions have been placed by the government in this country upon pressure group competition for control over public opinion. Laws of libel and slander, restrictions upon advertising and the use of the mails, and limitations upon the use of the radio, constitute the principal regulations of this character. The more important restrictions are those arising not because of positive action on the part of official agencies of government, but by reason of the existing distribution of propaganda re-

[108] See H. R. Bruce, *op. cit.* and references cited, chap. xvii.

sources. There is possibly no country in the world where propagandists compete with greater freedom from official control than in this country. This is not to say, however, that certain groups are not handicapped by lack of financial resources, effective leadership, and the tools with which to make their propaganda effective. Mainly in the field of parties has the state shown concern over standards of fair play. Election laws and corrupt-practice acts have sought to define more clearly the rules of the game in this sphere.

When, however, non-official and non-party pressure groups focus their pressure directly upon public officials, particularly legislators and administrators, it does give rise to official concern. This concern has led to numerous state and federal investigations of lobbying, the passage of laws regulating such methods of bringing pressure,[109] and, still more recently, to the prospect of national legislation upon the subject.[110] Such legislation, however, has not altered fundamentally the character of pressure group activity. Publicity is emphasized, and in some instances may have deterred practices generally regarded as reprehensible, but many students of the subject conclude that the real effect of such legislation is slight.[111]

If publicizing the propaganda and lobbying activities of pressure groups will not satisfactorily solve the problem, what can be done? Professor Bentley appears to support the thesis that little can be done to alter fundamentally the nature of pressure group activity, or, at least, its influence upon government, public opinion and other social institutions. He says: "In government we have to do with powerful group pressures which may at times adjust themselves through differentiated reasoning processes, but which adjust themselves likewise through many other

[109] See E. B. Logan, *op. cit.*; J. K. Pollock, "Regulation of Lobbying," *American Political Science Review,* May, 1927, vol. xxi, pp. 335-341.

[110] See "Investigation of Lobbying Activities," Hearings before a Special Committee to Investigate Lobbying Activities, United States Senate, 74th Congress, First Session, pursuant to S. Res. 165, Parts 1-4 (July 12, 1935 to March 6, 1936).

[111] See E. B. Logan, *op cit.*; and J. K. Pollock, *op. cit.*

processes, and which, through whatever processes they are working, form the very flesh and blood of all that is happening. It is these group pressures, indeed, that not only make but also maintain in value the very standards of justice, truth, or whatnot that reason may claim to use as its guides."[112]

Others argue that organized pressure groups should be formally incorporated into the governmental framework of the state via economic councils or a system of occupational representation. A number of European states have, during the post-war period, experimented with institutional devices of this character—not, however, without bringing to light serious shortcomings in this method.[113] The "corporate state" is a more thoroughgoing attempt to legalize, systematize—and possibly crystallize—state-group relationships. The NIRA in this country was in a sense an attempt to give official recognition by legislative fiat to significant pressure groupings and regularize their relations with the traditional agencies of government.

Professor Herring, whose researches in the field of pressure groups give particular weight to his conclusions, has recently considered the problem at some length.[114] Treating as unsuited to American conditions those devices employed in European states for regularizing state-group relationships, he calls for a more definite assumption by administrative leaders of responsibility for opinion-leadership, for public planning, and for interpretating and formulating standards of public policy. He writes: "There is need for promoting a purpose of the state over and above the purposes of the medley of interests that compose it. . . . As an agency for formulating a program and standing responsible for its consummation, the political party has proved inadequate. . . . The need of attempting to formulate an official program in the public interest by a responsible administrative

[112] A. F. Bentley, *op. cit.*, p. 447.
[113] E. Lindner, *Review of the Economic Councils in the Different Countries of the World* (Geneva, 1933), and other references in *Propaganda and Promotional Activities*, pp. 377-381.
[114] E. P. Herring, *op. cit.*, chap. xxiii.

PRESSURE GROUPS AND PROPAGANDA

agency arises from the experienced strength of minority groups in pressing their case by propaganda and organized agitation and from the now-recognized inability of the public to formulate opinion. . . . A strong executive at the head of a powerful administrative service may constitute an implicit danger, but such a situation is necessitated today by the more immediate and compelling conditions which call for unity and leadership."

As Professor Herring sees it, the process of formulating and carrying out public policy would proceed as follows: Upon the administrative branch would devolve the responsibility for getting the facts and clarifying the problems of public policy. In formulating particular policies, considerable use would be made of advisory committees representing the interest groups concerned. On the basis of such facts and advice, the administration would take the responsibility for framing legislation, a responsibility which could be more effectively carried out by making possible a greater degree of coordination within the administrative branch. The legislative function would be narrowed to the point of approving or rejecting proposals so submitted.

The difficulty, however, is this: Suppose that those called upon to follow refuse to do so. Will the administrative leaders resign as is the case in England, or will they proceed to enforce obedience as in Russia, Italy and Germany? Before suggestions of this sort are advanced, careful consideration of the consequences must be taken into account. As soon as we ask the government to enter positively and actively the arena of pressure groups and undertake to lead opinion rather than to reflect it, the democratic thesis is challenged. It may be that the "Führer" principle has more to commend it than the democratic principle. But before introducing it we should be fully aware of the implications.

To maintain within a given state the democratic principle of freedom, the responsibility for leadership in matters of opinion must be assumed by private individuals, unofficial pressure groups and parties.[115] Out of this conflict of ideals and programs the legislative branch—and, upon occasion, the electorate generally—must decide which policies shall be made effective. To argue that the public or the legislative representatives of the public are incapable of intelligent decisions is to deny the validity of the democratic thesis. To call for vigorous administrative leadership is to introduce into the pressure group arena an element which will inevitably work to the disadvantage of other groups and jeopardize the democratic procedure.

If the encouragement of administrative leadership in matters of opinion endangers the preservation of democratic processes, must we, therefore, rely exclusively upon a *laissez-faire* policy? Professor Schattschneider's intensive study in *Politics, Pressures, and the Tariff* clearly indicates that "liberty does not produce equality" in the field of group pressures. "Unsupervised conduct in pressure politics means that the few will control the process at the expense of the many. Selectivity is the basis of pressure politics. If all interests and all groups were equally active, pressure politics would be futile. . . . Democratic governments have established a *laissez faire* of pressures only to discover that it is perilous." The real problem, therefore, is to "democratize pressure politics."[116]

It is within the competence of the state, democratically motivated, to prescribe the "rules of the game," and so far as possible to raise the standards of pressure-group competition, thereby giving to the concept of "survival of the fittest" a more rational rather than a non-rational emphasis. By so doing, the ruinous consequences of ruthless pressure group competition may be avoided without abandoning the concept of freedom and accepting the fateful consequences of dictatorial state pressure in matters of opinion.

[115] G. E. G. Catlin, "The Rôle of Propaganda in a Democracy," *Annals*, May, 1935, pp. 219-226.
[116] E. E. Schattschneider, *op. cit.*, pp. 283-293.

APPENDIX

THE PLATFORMS OF THE TWO MAJOR PARTIES

Republican

America is in peril. The welfare of American men and women and the future of our youth are at stake. We dedicate ourselves to the preservation of their political liberty, their individual opportunity and their character as free citizens, which today for the first time are threatened by government itself.

For three long years the New Deal administration has dishonored American traditions and flagrantly betrayed the pledges upon which the Democratic party sought and received public support.

The powers of Congress have been usurped by the President.

The integrity and authority of the Supreme Court have been flaunted.

The rights and liberties of American citizens have been violated.

Regulated monopoly has displaced free enterprise.

The New Deal administration constantly seeks to usurp the rights reserved to the State and to the people.

It has insisted on passage of laws contrary to the Constitution.

It has intimidated witnesses and interfered with the right of petition.

It has dishonored our country by repudiating its most sacred obligations.

It has been guilty of frightful waste and extravagance, using pub-

Democratic

We hold this truth to be self-evident—that the test of a representative government is its ability to promote the safety and happiness of the people.

We hold this truth to be self-evident—that twelve years of Republican leadership left our nation sorely stricken in body, mind and spirit; and that three years of Democratic leadership have put it back on the road to restored health and prosperity.

We hold this truth to be self-evident—that twelve years of Republican surrender to the dictatorship of a privileged few have been supplanted by a Democratic leadership which has returned the people themselves to the places of authority, and has revived in them new faith and restored the hope which they had almost lost.

We hold this truth to be self-evident—that this three-year recovery in all the basic values of life and the reestablishment of the American way of living has been brought about by humanizing the policies of the Federal Government as they affect the personal, financial, industrial and agricultural well-being of the American people.

OBLIGATIONS TO CITIZENS

We hold this truth to be self-evident—that government in a modern civilization has certain ines-

lic funds for partisan political purposes.

It has promoted investigations to harass and intimidate American citizens, at the same time denying investigations into its own improper expenditures.

It has created a vast multitude of new offices, filled them with its favorites, set up a centralized bureaucracy and sent out swarms of inspectors to harass our people.

It has bred fear and hesitation in commerce and industry, thus discouraging new enterprises, preventing employment and prolonging the depression.

It secretly has made tariff agreements with our foreign competitors, flooding our markets with foreign commodities.

It has coerced and intimidated voters by withholding relief to those opposing its tyrannical policies.

It has destroyed the morale of many of our people and made them dependent upon government.

Appeals to passion and class prejudice have replaced reason and tolerance.

To a free people, these actions are insufferable. This campaign cannot be waged on the traditional differences between the Republican and Democratic parties.

The responsibility of this election transcends all previous political divisions. We invite all Americans, irrespective of party, to join us in defense of American institutions.

CONSTITUTIONAL GOVERNMENT AND FREE ENTERPRISE

We pledge ourselves:

To maintain the American system of constitutional and local self-government, and to resist all attempts to impair the authority of capable obligations to its citizens, among which are:

Protection of the family and the home.

Establishment of a democracy of opportunity for all the people.

Aid to those overtaken by disaster.

These obligations, neglected through twelve years of the old leadership, have once more been recognized by American Government. Under the new leadership they will never be neglected.

For the protection of the family and home:

We have begun and shall continue the successful drive to rid our land of kidnappers and bandits. We shall continue to use the powers of government to end the activities of the malefactors of great wealth who defraud and exploit the people.

SAVINGS AND INVESTMENTS

We have safeguarded the thrift of our citizens by restraining those who would gamble with other people's savings, by requiring truth in the sale of securities; by putting the brakes upon the use of credit for speculation; by outlawing the manipulation of prices in stock and commodity markets; by curbing the overweening power and unholy practices of utility holding companies; by insuring fifty million bank accounts.

THE CONSTITUTION

The Republican platform proposes to meet many pressing national problems solely by action of the separate States. We know that drought, dust storms, floods, minimum wages, maximum hours, child

APPENDIX

the Supreme Court of the United States, the final protector of rights of our citizens against the arbitrary encroachments of the legislative and executive branches of government. There can be no individual liberty without an independent judiciary.

To preserve the American system of free enterprise, private competition, and equality of opportunity, and to seek its constant betterment in the interests of all.

MONOPOLIES

A private monopoly is indefensible and intolerable. It menaces and if continued will utterly destroy constitutional government and liberty of the citizen.

We favor the vigorous enforcement of the criminal laws, as well as the civil laws, against monopolies and trusts and their officials, and we demand the enactment of such additional legislation as is necessary to make it impossible for private monopoly to exist in the United States.

We will employ the full powers

labor and working conditions in industry, monopolistic and unfair business practices cannot be adequately handled exclusively by forty-eight separate State Legislatures, forty-eight separate State administrations and forty-eight separate State courts. Transactions and activities which inevitably overflow State boundaries call for both State and Federal treatment.

We have sought and will continue to seek to meet these problems through legislation within the Constitution.

If these problems cannot be effectively solved by legislation within the Constitution, we shall seek such clarifying amendment as will assure to the Legislatures of the several States and the Congress of the United States, each within its proper jurisdiction, the power to enact those laws which the State and Federal Legislatures, within their respective spheres, shall find necessary, in order adequately to regulate commerce, protect public health and safety and safeguard economic security. Thus we propose to maintain the letter and spirit of the Constitution.

MONOPOLY AND CONCENTRATION OF ECONOMIC POWER

Monopolies and the concentration of economic power, the creation of Republican rule and privilege, continue to be the matter of the producer, the exploiter of the consumer, and the enemy of the independent operators. This is a problem challenging the unceasing effort of untrammeled public officials in every branch of the government. We pledge vigorously and fearlessly to enforce the criminal and civil provisions of the existing Anti-trust Laws, and to the extent

AGRICULTURE

The farm problem is an economic and social, not a partisan problem, and we propose to treat it accordingly. Following the wreck of the restrictive and coercive AAA, the New Deal administration has taken to itself the principles of the Republican policy of soil conservation and land retirement. This action opens the way for a nonpolitical and permanent solution. Such a solution cannot be had under a New Deal administration which misuses the program to serve partisan ends, to promote scarcity and to limit by coercive methods the farmer's control over his own farm.

One paramount object is to protect and foster the family type of farm, traditional in American life, and to promote policies which will bring about an adjustment of agriculture, to meet the needs of domestic and foreign markets. As an emergency measure, during the agricultural depression, Federal benefit payments or grants in aid when administered within the means of the Federal Government are consistent with a balanced budget.

We propose.

To facilitate economical production and increased consumption on a basis of abundance instead of scarcity.

A national land-use program, including the acquisition of aban-

that their effectiveness has been weakened by new corporate devices or judicial construction, we propose by law to restore their efficacy in stamping out monopolistic practices and the concentration of economic power.

AGRICULTURE

We have taken the farmers off the road to ruin.

We have kept our pledge to agriculture to use all available means to raise farm income toward its pre-war purchasing power. The farmer is no longer suffering from 15-cent corn, 3-cent hogs, 2½-cent beef at the farm, 5-cent wool, 30-cent wheat, 5-cent cotton and 3-cent sugar.

By Federal legislation we have reduced the farmers' indebtedness and doubled his net income. Cooperating with the States and through the farmers' own committees, we are restoring the fertility of his land and checking the erosion of his soil. We are bringing electricity and good roads to his home.

We will continue to improve the soil conservation and domestic allotment program with payments to farmers.

We will continue a fair-minded administration of agriculture laws, quick to recognize and meet new problems and conditions. We recognize the gravity of the evils of farm tenancy, and we pledge the full cooperation of the government in the refinancing of farm indebtedness at the lowest possible rates of interest and a long term of years.

We favor the production of all the market will absorb, both at home and abroad, plus a reserve supply sufficient to insure fair prices to consumers; we favor judi-

doned and non-productive farm land by voluntary sale or lease and subject to the approval of the Legislative and Executive branches of the States concerned and the devotion of such land to appropriate public use, such as watershed protection and flood prevention, reforestation, recreation and conservation of wild life.

That an agricultural policy be pursued for the protection and restoration of the land resources, designed to bring about such a balance between soil-building and soil-depleting crops as will permanently insure productivity, with reasonable benefits to cooperating farmers on family-type farms, but so regulated as to eliminate the New Deal's destructive policy toward the dairy and livestock industries.

To extend experimental aid to farmers developing new crops suited to our soil and climate.

To promote the industrial use of farm products by applied science.

To protect the American farmer against the importation of all livestock, dairy and agricultural products, substitutes therefor, and derivatives therefrom, which will depress American farm prices.

To provide effective quarantine against imported livestock, dairy and other farm products from countries which do not impose health and sanitary regulations fully equal to those required of our own producers.

To provide for ample farm credit at rates as low as those enjoyed by other industries, including commodity and livestock loans, and preference in land loans to the farmer acquiring or refinancing a farm as a home.

To provide for decentralized, cious commodity loans on seasonal surpluses; and we favor assistance with Federal authority to enable farmers to adjust and balance production with demand, at a fair profit to the farmers.

We favor encouragement of sound, practical farm cooperatives.

By the purchase and retirement of ten million acres of sub-marginal land, and assistance to those attempting to eke out an existence upon it, we have made a good beginning toward proper land use and rural rehabilitation.

The farmer has been returned to the road to freedom and prosperity. We will keep him on that road.

nonpartisan control of the Farm Credit Administration and the election by National Farm Loan Associations of at least one-half of the board of directors of the Federal Land Banks, and thereby remove these institutions from politics.

To provide in the case of agriculture products of which there are exportable surpluses the payment of reasonable benefits upon the domestically consumed portion of such crops in order to make the tariff effective. These payments are to be limited to the production level of the family-type farm.

To encourage and further develop cooperative marketing.

To furnish government assistance in disposing of surpluses in foreign trade by bargaining for foreign markets selectively by countries both as to exports and imports. We strenuously oppose so-called reciprocal treaties which trade off the American farmer.

To give every reasonable assistance to producers in areas suffering from temporary disaster, so that they may regain and maintain a self-supporting status.

LABOR

The welfare of labor rests upon increased production and the prevention of exploitation. We pledge ourselves to:

Protect the rights of labor to organize and to bargain collectively through representatives of its own choosing without interference from any source.

Prevent governmental job holders from exercising autocratic powers over labor.

Support the adoption of State laws and interstate compacts to

LABOR

We have given the army of America's industrial workers something more substantial than the Republicans' dinner pail full of promises; we have increased the worker's pay and shortened his hours; we have undertaken to put an end to the sweated labor of his wife and children; we have written into the law of the land his right to collective bargaining and self-organization free from the interference of employers; we have provided Federal machinery for the

abolish sweatshops and child labor, and to protect women and children with respect to maximum hours, minimum wages and working conditions. We believe that this can be done within the Constitution as it now stands.

We are opposed to legislation which discriminates against women in Federal and State employment.

REGULATION OF BUSINESS

We recognize the existence of a field within which governmental regulation is desirable and salutary. The authority to regulate should be vested in an independent tribunal acting under clear and specific laws establishing definite standards.

Their determinations on law and facts should be subject to review by the courts. We favor Federal regulation, within the Constitution, of the marketing of securities to protect investors. We favor also Federal regulation of the interstate activities of public utilities.

GOVERNMENT FINANCE

The New Deal administration has been characterized by shameful waste and general financial irresponsibility. It has piled deficit upon deficit. It threatens national bankruptcy and the destruction through inflation of insurance policies and savings bank deposits.

We pledge ourselves to:

Stop the folly of uncontrolled spending.

Balance the budget—not by increasing taxes but by cutting expenditures, drastically and immediately.

Revise the Federal tax system

peaceful settlement of labor disputes.

We will continue to protect the worker and we will guard his rights, both as wage earner and consumer, in the production and consumption of all commodities, including coal and water power and other natural resource products.

The worker has been returned to the road to freedom and prosperity. We will keep him on that road.

BUSINESS

We have taken the American business man out of the red. We have saved his bank and given it a sounder foundation; we have extended credit; we have lowered interest rates; we have undertaken to free him from the ravages of cut-throat competition.

The American business man has been returned to the road to freedom and prosperity. We will keep him on that road.

GOVERNMENT FINANCE

The administration has stopped deflation, restored values and enabled business to go ahead with confidence.

When national income shrinks, government income is imperiled. In reviving national income, we have fortified government finance. We have raised the public credit to a position of unsurpassed security. The interest rate on government bonds has been reduced to the lowest point in twenty-eight years. The same government bonds which in 1932 sold under 83 are now selling over 104.

and coordinate it with State and local tax systems.

Use the taxing power for raising revenue and not for punitive or political purposes.

MONEY AND BANKING

We advocate a sound currency to be preserved at all hazard.

The first requisite to a sound and stable currency is a balanced budget.

We oppose further devaluation of the dollar.

We will restore to the Congress the authority lodged with it by the Constitution to coin money and regulate the value thereof by repealing all the laws delegating this authority to the Executive.

We will cooperate with other countries toward stabilization of currencies as soon as we can do so with due regard for our national interests and as soon as other nations have sufficient stability to justify such action.

CIVIL SERVICE

Under the New Deal, official authority has been given to inexperienced and incompetent persons. The civil service has been sacrificed to create a national political machine. As a result the Federal Government has never presented such a picture of confusion and inefficiency.

We pledge ourselves to the merit system, virtually destroyed by New Deal spoilsmen. It should be restored, improved and extended.

We will provide such conditions as offer an attractive permanent career in government service to young men and women of ability, irrespective of party affiliations.

We approve the objective of a permanently sound currency so stabilized as to prevent the former wide fluctuations in value which injured in turn producers, debtors and property owners on the one hand, and wage earners and creditors on the other, a currency which will permit full utilization of the country's resources. We assert that today we have the soundest currency in the world.

We are determined to reduce the expenses of government. We are being aided therein by the recession in unemployment. As the requirements of relief decline and national income advances, an increasing percentage of Federal expenditures can and will be met from current revenues, secured from taxes levied in accordance with ability to pay. Our retrenchment, tax and recovery programs thus reflect our firm determination to achieve a balanced budget and the reduction of the national debt at the earliest possible moment.

THE MERIT SYSTEM OF GOVERNMENT

For the protection of government itself and promotion of its efficiency we pledge the immediate extension of the merit system through the classified civil service—which was first established and fostered under Democratic auspices—to all non-policy-making positions in the Federal service.

We shall subject to the Civil Service Law all continuing positions which, because of the emergency, have been exempt from its operation.

APPENDIX

BILL OF RIGHTS

We pledge ourselves to preserve, protect and defend, against all intimidation and threat, freedom of religion, speech, press and radio; and the right of assembly and petition and immunity from unreasonable searches and seizures.

We offer the abiding security of a government of laws as against the autocratic perils of a government of men.

FOREIGN AFFAIRS

We pledge ourselves to promote and maintain peace by all honorable means not leading to foreign alliances or political commitments.

Obedient to the traditional foreign policy of America and to the repeatedly expressed will of the American people, we pledge that America shall not become a member of the League of Nations nor of the World Court, nor shall America take on any entangling alliances in foreign affairs.

We shall promote, as the best means of securing and maintaining peace by the pacific settlement of disputes, the great cause of international arbitration through the establishment of free, independent tribunals, which shall determine such disputes in accordance with law, equity and justice.

NATIONAL DEFENSE

We favor an army and navy, including air forces, adequate for our national defense.

We will cooperate with nations in the limitation of armaments and control of traffic in arms.

We shall use every effort to collect the war debt due us from

CIVIL LIBERTIES

We shall continue to guard the freedom of speech, press, radio, religion and assembly which our Constitution guarantees; with equal rights to all and special privileges to none.

FOREIGN POLICY

In our relationship with other nations, this government will continue to extend the policy of the good neighbor. We reaffirm our opposition to war as an instrument of national policy, and declare that disputes between nations should be settled by peaceful means. We shall continue to observe a true neutrality in the disputes of others; to be prepared resolutely to resist aggression against ourselves; to work for peace and to take the profits out of war; to guard against being drawn, by political commitments, into additional banking or private trading, into any war which may develop anywhere.

We shall continue to foster the increase in our foreign trade which has been achieved by this administration; to seek by mutual agreement the lowering of those tariff barriers, quotas and embargoes which have been raised against our exports of agricultural and industrial products; but continue as in the past to give adequate protection to our farmers and manufacturers against unfair competition or the dumping on our shores of commodities and goods produced

foreign countries, amounting to $12,000,000,000; one-third of our national debt. No effort has been made by the present administration even to reopen negotiations.

SECURITY

Real security will be possible only when our productive capacity is sufficient to furnish a decent standard of living for all American families and to provide a surplus for future needs and contingencies. For the attainment of that ultimate objective we look to the energy, self-reliance and character of our people, and to our system of free enterprise.

Society has an obligation to promote the security of the people by affording some measure of protection against involuntary unemployment and dependency in old age. The New Deal policies, while purporting to provide social security, have, in fact, endangered it.

We propose a system of old age security, based upon the following principles:

We approve a pay-as-you-go policy, which requires of each generation the support of the aged and the determination of what is just and adequate.

Every American citizen over 65 should receive the supplementary payment necessary to provide a minimum income sufficient to protect him or her from want.

Each State and Territory, upon complying with simple and general minimum standards, should receive from the Federal Government a graduated contribution in proportion to its own, up to a fixed maximum.

To make this program consistent with sound fiscal policy the Federal revenues for this purpose must be abroad by cheap labor or subsidized by foreign governments.

OLD AGE AND SOCIAL SECURITY

We have built foundations for the security of those who are faced with the hazards of unemployment and old age; for the orphaned, the crippled and the blind. On the foundation of the Social Security Act we are determined to erect a structure of economic security for all our people, making sure that this benefit shall keep step with the ever-increasing capacity of America to provide a high standard of living for all its citizens.

provided from the proceeds of a direct tax widely distributed. All will be benefited and all should contribute.

We propose to encourage adoption by the States and Territories of honest and practical measures for meeting the problems of unemployment insurance.

The unemployment insurance and old age annuity sections of the present Social Security Act are unworkable and deny benefits to about two-thirds of our adult population, including professional men and women and all those engaged in agriculture and domestic service and the self-employed, while imposing heavy tax burdens upon all. The so-called reserve fund estimated at $47,000,000,000 for old age insurance is no reserve at all, because the fund will contain nothing but the government's promise to pay, while the taxes collected in the guise of premiums will be wasted by the government in reckless and extravagant political schemes.

REEMPLOYMENT

The only permanent solution of the unemployment problem is the absorption of the unemployed by industry and agriculture. To that end we advocate:

Removal of restrictions on production.

Abandonment of all New Deal policies that raise production costs, increase the cost of living and thereby restrict buying, reduce volume and prevent reemployment.

Encouragement instead of hindrance to legitimate business.

Withdrawal of government from competition with private payrolls.

Elimination of unnecessary and hampering regulations.

UNEMPLOYMENT

We believe that unemployment is a national problem, and that it is an inescapable obligation of our government to meet it in a national way. Due to our stimulation of private business, more than 5,000,000 people have been reemployed, and we shall continue to maintain that the first objective of a program of economic security is maximum employment in private industry at adequate wages. Where business fails to supply such employment, we believe that work at prevailing wages should be provided in keeping with State and local governments on useful public projects, to the end that the national wealth may be increased, the skill and en-

Adoption of such other policies as will furnish a chance for individual enterprise, industrial expansion and the restoration of jobs.

RELIEF

The necessities of life must be provided for the needy and hope must be restored pending recovery. The administration of relief is a major failure of the New Deal. It has been faithless to those who most deserve our sympathy. To end confusion, partisanship, waste and incompetence we pledge:

The return of responsibility for relief administration to non-political local agencies familiar with community problems.

Federal grants-in-aid to the States and Territories while the need exists upon compliance with these conditions: (a) A fair proportion of the total relief burden to be provided from the revenues of States and local governments; (b) all engaged in relief administration to be selected on the basis of merit and fitness; (c) adequate provision to be made for the encouragement of those persons who are trying to become self-supporting.

Undertaking of Federal public works only on their merits and separate from the administration of relief.

A prompt determination of the facts concerning relief and unemployment.

TARIFF

Nearly 60 per cent of all imports into the United States are now free of duty. The other 40 per cent of imports compete directly with the product of our industry. We would ergy of the worker may be utilized, his morale maintained and the unemployed be assured the opportunity to earn the necessities of life.

AID TO THOSE OVERTAKEN BY DISASTER

We have aided and will continue to aid those who have been visited by widespread drought and floods and have adopted a nation-wide flood-control policy.

YOUTH

We have aided youth to stay in school; given them constructive occupation; opened the door to opportunity which twelve years of Republican neglect had closed.

Our youth have been returned to the road to freedom and prosperity. We will keep them on that road.

keep on the free list all products not grown or produced in the United States in commercial quantities.

As to all commodities that commercially compete with our farms, our forests, our mines, our fisheries, our oil wells, our labor and our industries, sufficient protection should be maintained at all times to defend the American farmer and the American wage earner from the destructive competition emanating from the subsidies of foreign governments and the imports from low-wage and depreciated-currency countries.

We will repeal the present Reciprocal Trade Agreement Law. It is futile and dangerous. Its effect on agriculture and industry has been destructive. Its continuation would work to the detriment of the wage earner and the farmer.

We will restore the principle of the flexible tariff in order to meet changing economic conditions here and abroad and broaden by careful definition the powers of the Tariff Commission in order to extend this policy along nonpartisan lines.

We will adjust tariffs with a view to promoting international trade, the stabilization of currencies and the attainment of a proper balance between agriculture and industry.

We condemn the secret negotiation of reciprocal trade treaties without public hearing or legislative approval.

HOUSING

We maintain that our people are entitled to decent, adequate housing at a price which they can afford. In the last three years the Federal Government, having saved more than 2,000,000 homes from foreclosure, has taken the first steps in our history to provide decent housing for people of meager incomes.

We believe every encouragement should be given to the building of new homes by private enterprise, and that the government should steadily extend its housing program toward the goal of adequate housing for those forced through economic necessities to live in unhealthy and slum conditions.

RURAL ELECTRIFICATION

This administration has fostered power rate yardsticks in the Tennessee Valley and in several other parts of the nation. As a result, electricity has been made available to the people at a lower rate. We will continue to promote plans for rural electrification and for cheap power by means of the yardstick method.

CONSUMER

We will act to secure to the consumer fair value, honest sales and a decreased spread between the price he pays and the price the producer receives.

VETERANS

We shall continue just treatment to our war veterans and their dependents.

We pledge continuation of the Republican policy of adequate compensation and care for veterans disabled in the service of our country and for their widows, orphans and dependents.

FURTHERMORE

We favor the construction by the Federal Government of headwater storage basins to prevent floods, subject to the approval of the legislative and executive branches of the government of the States whose lands are concerned.

We favor equal opportunity for our colored citizens. We pledge our protection of their economic status and personal safety. We will do our best to further their employment in the gainfully occupied life of America, particularly in private industry, agriculture, emergency agencies and the civil service.

We condemn the present New Deal policies which would regiment and ultimately eliminate the colored citizen from the country's productive life and make him solely a ward of the Federal Government.

To our Indian population we pledge every effort on the part of the National Government to ameliorate living conditions for them.

CONCLUSION

We assume the obligations and duties imposed upon government by modern conditions. We affirm our "inalterable conviction that, in the future as in the past, the fate of the nation will depend, not so much on the wisdom and power of government, as on the character and virtue, self-reliance, industry and thrift of the people and on their willingness to meet the responsibilities essential to the preservation of a free society."

Finally, as our party affirmed in its first platform in 1856: "Believing that the spirit of our institutions as well as the Constitution of our country guarantees liberty of conscience and equality of rights among our citizens we oppose all legislation tending to impair them," and "we invite the affiliation and cooperation of the men of all parties, however differing from us

THE ISSUE

The issue in this election is plain. The American people are called upon to choose between a Republican administration that has and would again regiment them in the service of privileged groups and a Democratic administration dedicated to the establishment of equal economic opportunity for all our people.

We have faith in the destiny of our nation. We are sufficiently endowed with natural resources and with productive capacity to provide for all a quality of life that meets the standards of real Americanism.

Dedicated to a government of liberal American principles, we are determined to oppose equally the despotism of communism and the menace of concealed fascism.

We hold this final truth to be self-evident—that the interests, the security and the happiness of the people of the United States of

in other respects, in support of the principles herein declared."

The acceptance of the nomination tendered by this convention carries with it, as a matter of private honor and public faith, an undertaking by each candidate to be true to the principles and program herein set forth.

America can be perpetuated only under Democratic government as conceived by the founders of our nation.

Index

Adams, Henry, 90
Adams, John Quincy, 111, 158
Agrarian and urban interests, 28, 37-41
Aldermen, American and English, 94
Amendments to United States Constitution, 217
American Bankers Association, 209, 220
American Farm Bureau Federation, 220, 222
American Federation of Labor, 156, 220, 222, 228
American Gas Association, 219
American Legion, 209, 219
American Liberty League, 113, 156, 185, 230
American Medical Association, 217
American Peace Society, 217
Anti-Saloon League of America, 185, 218, 219
Appointees, party, 76
Archidamian War, 228
Association Against the Prohibition Amendment, 185, 218
Association of Railway Executives, 220
"Average" states, 21

Baldwin, Simeon E., 182
Bancroft, George, 230
Barclay, Thomas, 58
Barkley, Alben W., 135
Barnum, William H., 56
Beard, Charles A., 201
Belmont, August, 56
Bentley, A. F., 239
Bible Society of America, 217
Blaine. James G., 26

Block, Paul, 155
Borah, William E., 133, 140, 164
"Bosses," 63, 68-69
Breckinridge, John C., 160
Bribery of voters, 188
Bridges, H. Styles, 149
Brisbane, Arthur, 155
Brookhart committee, 176
Brooks, R. C., 116
Brown, Frances S., 85
Bryan, William Jennings, 27, 104, 134, 146, 149, 161, 182
Bryce, James, 31
Buchanan, James, 4
Buck, Philo, 103 (note)
"Bull Moose." *See* Progressive party.
Burke, Edmund, 114 (note), 118
Burns, Delisle, 95
Burr, Aaron, 111
Burroughs and Cannon v. United States, 203
Business in Presidential years, 127

Calhoun, John C., 19, 42
Campaign committees, 63
Campaign managers, 132, 143
Campaign of 1936, issues, 168
Campaigns, Presidential, 127-169
Carey, Robert Davis, 182
Catholic Church, 214
Chamber of Commerce of the United States, 219, 220, 222, 228
Children's Aid Society, 217
Cincinnati experiment, 87
Cities. *See* Urban and agrarian interests.
City committees, 63
City organizations, 64
City party elections, 71

INDEX

Civil service, 77
Class-consciousness, 41-44
Clay, Henry, 19, 42
Cleveland, Grover, 4
Climate, political, 22-23
Cohalan, Daniel F., 167
Colby, Bainbridge, 167
Commission of Inquiry on Public Service Personnel, 79-80
Committees, campaign, 63; city, 63; congressional, 59-60; county, 62; national, 55-59, 129; overlapping memberships, 84; senatorial, 59-60; state, 60-62; ward, 63
Communist party, 213, 237
Comstock, William, 199
Congress, First, 217
Congressional campaign of 1936, 169
Congressional committees, 59-60
Congressional districts, urban and rural, 35
Congressional Union, 218
Constitution, amendments, 217
Constitutional Convention of 1787, 217
Control, of government, 4-5; over public opinion, 238
Convention system, abolition, 66
Conventions, national, 128-142; elections to, 67
Coolidge, Calvin, 26, 135, 140
Corrupt practices act, 194
Coughlin, Reverend Charles E., 153, 167
County committees, 62
County party elections, 71
Couzens, James, 172, 183
Cox, James M., 5
Curley, James M., 134
Curry, John F., 65
Cutting, Bronson, 202

Dane County, Wisconsin, 96
Davis, John W., 5, 141, 153
Deficits, party, 202
Delegates, apportionment, 130; election, 131

Democracy v. "Führer" principle, 241
Democratic party, dominance, 81-82; strength, 43; 1936 platform, 243; vote in urban and rural districts, 36-41
Deviations from average vote, 21-25
Dickens, Charles, 118
Dickinson, Lester J., 141
Dill, Clarence C., 189
Doheny, Edward L., 179
Dooley, Mr., 92
Douglas, Stephen A., 160
Dunne, Finley Peter (Mr. Dooley), 92
du Pont, Irenée, 157
du Pont Company, 179

Earle, George H., 185
Elections, British, 182; British and French, 128; French, 182; nonpartisan, 87; use of money, 170-203
Elective offices in the United States, number of, 116
Electoral and popular votes, 6
Electoral votes, urban and rural, 34
Ely, Joseph B., 167
England, elections, 128, 182

Farley, James A., 58, 104, 143, 144, 150, 165, 166, 177
Farley, Thomas M., 96
Fascist parties, 213, 237
Federalists, 19
Financial resources of pressure groups, 212
Flint, John, 106
Force, use of, by pressure groups, 227
France, elections, 128
Fremont, John C., 26
"Führer" principle v. democracy, 241

Gandhi, Mahatma, 103
Garfield, James A., 174
Garner, John Nance, 166

INDEX

Garrison, William Lloyd, 125
Gladstone, William E., 105-106
Gosnell, Harold F., 43, 62
Government, control of, 4-5
Governmental opinion-leadership, 240
Governmental units in the United States, number of, 116
Great Britain, elections, 128, 182
Green, William, 156
Grove v. Townsend, 135 (note)

Hamilton, John D. M., 133, 143, 166
Hanna, Mark, 146, 161, 174
Harding, Warren G., 2, 75, 76, 141, 146, 148, 155
Harrison, William Henry, 159
Harvard men and politics, 95
Haskell, Henry, 133
Hays, Will H., 180, 190
Hearst, William Randolph, 155, 156, 165
Herring, E. P., 240, 241
Hitler, Adolf, 229
Hoan, Daniel W., 107, 109
Hobbes, Thomas, 230
Hoover, Herbert, 2, 12, 21, 26, 140, 147, 151, 154, 155, 161, 162, 166
House, Edward M., 90
Howe, Louis McHenry, 163
Hughes, Charles E., 26

Idaho potatoes in Wisconsin, 110
Industrial Revolution, 215, 229
Inge, William R., 91
Initiative and referendum, cost of, 186
Instability of parties, 5
Interests, economic, in Presidential elections, 28; special, and the parties, 47
Intermediate sections, 12-16
Investigations of campaign expenditures, 170

Jackson, Andrew, 7, 9, 19, 29, 42, 94, 158, 172

Jackson's birthday dinner, 177
James, William, 92
Jefferson, Thomas, 7, 9, 19, 29, 30, 42, 172
Johnson, Andrew, 14
Johnson, Hiram W., 141
Jones, James K., 56

Kelly, Peter, 108
Kenny, William F., 180
Kent, Frank R., 56, 61, 68, 142
Knox, Frank, 133, 140, 142, 166
Ku Klux Klan, 219

La Follette, Philip Fox, 104, 117
La Follette, Robert Marion, Jr., 104, 117
La Follette, Robert Marion, Sr., 1, 5, 12, 109, 117
Landon, Alfred M., 99, 133, 138, 139, 140, 146, 149, 155, 157, 164, 165, 166
Leaders, group, 209; precinct, 62
League of Women Voters, 100
Lehman, Herbert H., 157, 185
Lemke, William, 167
Lemke-Union party, 153
Lewis, David J., 182
Liberty Loan campaigns, 191
Limitation of political expenditures, 196
Lincoln, Abraham, 14, 98, 149, 160
Lippmann, Walter, 91, 117
Literary Digest straw votes, 151
Literature, campaign, 148
Lobbying, 226
Locke, John, 220
Long, Huey P., 99, 168
Lowden, Frank O., 141
Lowell, A. L., 113

"Machines," party, 72-73
Madison, James, 30, 48, 50
Managers, campaign, 132, 143
Marshall, John, 168, 230
Marx, Karl, 230
McAdoo, William G., 141
McGroarty, John Steven, 101

INDEX

McKinley, William, 134, 146, 149, 161
McReynolds, James C., 203
Meekins, Isaac M., 141
Mellons, the, 180
Merriam, C. E., 116
Michels, Robert, 88
Michelson, Charles, 147
Michigan election law, 199
Middle class, 44
Middle States, 13
Miller, Nathan, 157
Minor parties, 2, 152; in 1932, 54
Money, in party and primary elections, 69-70; use in elections, 170-203
Motion pictures, use of, 235
Murphy, Charles F., 65

Nathan, George Jean, 91
National American Woman's Suffrage Association, 218
National Association of Cotton Manufacturers, 217
National Association of Manufacturers, 220
National committees, 55-59, 129
National Education Association of the United States, 217
National Electric Light Association, 219
National Industrial Recovery Act, 222, 240
National League of Women Voters, 218
National Union for Social Justice, 153, 168
National Woman's party, 218
Negroes, 7; in state conventions, decision against, 135
New Deal, 151, 157, 163, 220, 222
New England, 8-9
New York City, 10
Newberry, Truman H., 184, 202, 203
Newspapers, use of, 232
Nice, Harry, 141

Nomination expenses, 86
Nominations, 85
Nonpartisan elections, 87
Norris, George W., 172
Northeastern States, 8
Nye bill, 203
Nye committee, 179, 201, 204

O'Brien, John P., 104
O'Brien, Thomas Charles, 167
Officeholders, campaign contributions, 174; in campaign work, 74-80
Offices, elective, in the United States, number of, 116
Officials, selection of party, 68
Oliver, F. S., 93, 97
Opinion, formation of, by governmental agencies, 240
Ostrogorski, M., 86

Paine, Thomas, 220
Parker, Alton B., 3
Parties, characteristics, 1-51; instability, 5; minor ("splinter"), 152; minor, in 1932, 54; new and old, 46; regulation of, 66; relations between, 3
Partisanship, 48
Party, functions of, 113-114 (note)
Party appointees, 76
Party officials, selection, 68, 69-74
Party organization, 53-87
Patronage, political, 74-80
Pennsylvania, positions, state, 77-78; primary law, 66
Pennsylvania party election law, 69
Penrose, Boies, 119
Pepper-Vare campaign, 187
Philadelphia, 63; local party elections, 71; positions, city and county, 78-79
Philadelphia Democrats, 82
Pinchot, Gifford, 85
Platforms, 5-6, 138, 224; party, in states, 68; Republican and Democratic, 1936, 243
Platt, Thomas C., 62

INDEX

Policies, general, selection of, 24-25
Politicians, and politics, definition of, 89; and statesmen, 51-52; and voters, 89-125; demands on, 120-125; detraction of, 97-98
Popular and electoral votes, 6
Popular vote, division of, 2
Populists, 2, 12, 19
Postmasters, political, 75-77
Potatoes, Idaho, in Wisconsin, 110
Precinct leaders, 62
Precincts, voting, in the United States, number of, 116
Presidential campaign of 1936, issues, 168
Presidential campaigns, 127-169
Presidential candidates, availability, 25
Presidential preference primary, 132
Presidential vote in 1932, 54
Press, use of, 232
Pressure groups, 86, 185, 205-242; defined, 206; regulation of, 239
Primaries, direct, 66
Primary, presidential preference, 132
Primary law, Pennsylvania, 66
Procter, William Cooper, 180
Prodger, Charlie, 100
Progressive party, 1, 12, 14, 136
Propaganda, 205-242
Publicity, expenditure for, 189
Publicity bureaus, 58
Publicity campaign, 146; legal requirements, 196

Radio, cost of, 189, 211 (note); in Presidential campaigns, 147; use of, 233
Raskob, John J., 58, 162, 180
Reed, James A., 16
Regulation of parties, 66
Republican party, in 1936, 164; in the South, 83; 1936 platform, 243; vote in urban and rural districts, 36-41
Roberts, Roy A., 133

Robinson, Joseph T., 136
Rogers, Representative Will, 123
Roman Catholic Church, 214
Roosevelt, Franklin Delano, 2, 20, 21, 47, 57, 75, 77, 95, 96, 98, 101, 104, 109, 115, 135, 140, 141, 144, 146, 147, 149, 151, 154, 156, 157, 162, 163, 164, 166, 167, 181
Roosevelt, Sarah Delano, 95
Roosevelt, Theodore, 1, 26, 42, 80, 95, 98, 109, 134, 140, 146, 149, 153, 182
Roosevelt, Theodore, *Autobiography*, 108
Roosevelt First-Voters League, 150
Root, Elihu, 164
Rural and urban interests, 28
Ryan, Thomas F., 180

Seabury committee, 96, 178
Sectionalism, maps, table, 17-28
Senatorial committees, 59-60
Senators, rural and urban constituencies, 32, 34; state, demands on, 120-123
Shakespeare, William, 90
Shouse, Jouett, 58, 156
Sinclair, Harry F., 179, 180
Slogans, campaign, 149
Smith, Alfred E., 5, 8, 10, 44-45, 50, 139, 141, 146, 155, 156, 157, 161, 162, 167, 180, 200
Smith, Frank L., 179, 184
Smith, Reverend Gerald L. K., 168
Snell, Bertrand H., 135
Socialist party, 80, 181, 213, 237
South, the, 6
Southwestern border sections, 16
"Splinter" parties, 152
Spoils system, 73-80
State committees, 60-62
State laws on elections and campaigns, 195
Statesmen and politicians, 51-52
Stattschneider, E. E., 242
Steffens, Lincoln, 100
Steiwer, Frederick, 135, 141, 166
Straw votes, 151

INDEX

Supreme Court decision on Presidential elections, 203

Taft, Charles P., 87
Taft, Robert A., 141
Taft, William H., 140
Tammany Hall, 43, 50, 63, 155, 162
Tariff, history of, 221
Terrell, Angus, 106
Texas, decision against Negroes, 135
Thomas, Norman, 152
Thompson, William H., 117
Tocqueville, Alexis de, 30
Townsend, Dr. Francis E., 153, 167, 186, 204, 209
Tunis, John R., 95
Turner, Frederick J., 16, 51
Tyler, John, 159

Union party, 153, 167
United States Chamber of Commerce, 219, 220, 222, 228
Units, governmental, in the United States, number of, 116
Urban and agrarian interests, 28-41

Van Buren, Martin, 110, 159
Vandenberg, Arthur H., 133, 141
Vanity Fair, 91
Vare, William S., 63, 65, 184

Vare-Pepper campaign, 187
Vice-presidential nominees, 142
Victory Loan campaign, 191
Vote, popular, division of, 2; popular and electoral, 6; Presidential, in 1932, 54
Voter and politician, 89-125
Voters, bribery of, 188

Wadsworth, James W., 157
Walpole, Robert, 93
Warburg, James P., 148
Ward, Artemus, 90
Ward committees, 63
Washington, George, 19
Webster, Daniel, 19, 42
Wesley, John, 230
West, the, 10-12
Wheeler, Burton K., 12
Whigs, 19
White, William Allen, 83, 99, 193
Wilson, Woodrow, 3, 4, 9, 20, 27, 43, 49, 76, 148, 149
Wisconsin, Idaho potatoes in, 110
Wisconsin state senators, demands on, 120-123
Wood, Leonard, 141

Young Democratic Clubs, 150
Young Republican National Federation, 150

Rebound   MAR 2 5 '42